THE NEW AGING

THE NEW AGING

Politics and Change in America

FERNANDO M. TORRES-GIL

Foreword by Arthur S. Flemming

AUBURN HOUSE

NEW YORK • WESTPORT, CONNECTICUT • LONDON

362.60973
T693n

Library of Congress Cataloging-in-Publication Data

Torres-Gil, Fernando M.
  The new aging : politics and change in America / Fernando M.
Torres-Gil ; foreword by Arthur S. Flemming.
      p.   cm.
  Includes bibliographical references (p.   ) and index.
  ISBN 0-86569-035-9 (alk. paper).—ISBN 0-86569-036-7 (pbk. :
alk. paper)
    1. Aged—Services for—United States.   2. Aged—Government policy—
United States.   3. Aged—United States—Economic conditions.
I. Title.
HV1461.T66   1992
362.6'0973—dc20   91-18649

British Library Cataloguing in Publication Data is available.

Library of Congress Catalog Card Number: 91-18649
ISBN: 0-86569-035-9 (hb)
       0-86569-036-7 (pbk)

First published in 1992

Auburn House, 88 Post Road West, Westport, CT 06881
An imprint of Greenwood Publishing Group, Inc.

Printed in the United States of America

∞™

The paper used in this book complies with the
Permanent Paper Standard issued by the National
Information Standards Organization (Z39.48-1984).

10 9 8 7 6 5 4 3 2 1

To my wife, Elvira,
my mother, Maria de Jesus,
and my grandmother, Andrea Arredondo de Raya

CONTENTS

Foreword *by Arthur S. Flemming*   ix

Preface   xi

Acknowledgments   xv

Abbreviations   xix

INTRODUCTION   1

1. THE THREE FORCES OF AN AGING SOCIETY   9

2. AMERICA AT THE CROSSROADS   33

3. THE POLITICS OF THE NEW AGING   75

4. ECONOMICS OF THE NEW AGING   93

5. THE AGING OF THE BABY BOOMERS   127

6. PROGRAMS, BENEFITS, AND SERVICES: PREPARING FOR THE NEW AGING   141

7. AMERICA IN THE TWENTY-FIRST CENTURY   165

Bibliography   181

Index   191

FOREWORD

The field of aging is at an important crossroads. The choices our nation makes will determine whether our society is going to contribute constructively to the well-being, not only of older persons, but of all age groups.

Dr. Fernando Torres-Gil has drawn on his in-depth experiences as a scholar, a teacher, and a public servant to provide us with an excellent understanding of where we have come from in the field of aging, where we are, and the choices we must make in the future as we move through what he has identified as the period of the New Aging.

Dr. Torres-Gil not only identifies the choices that confront us and those that lie just ahead but he shares with us his own conclusions. Readers will not always reach the same conclusions, but they will feel indebted to the author for making it possible for them to consider choices in the light of the background provided by him and his willingness to present both the strengths and weaknesses of various options, including the ones he advocates.

Throughout the book major emphasis is placed on the fact that many of the issues we confront as we journey through the period of the New Aging are intergenerational and that we must work out intergenerational solutions. The author makes clear his belief that health care clearly falls within this category—an issue that can only be resolved by a national community ready and willing to pool both its public and private resources in order to make universal right of access a reality.

Older persons are challenged in the book to serve not only as advocates for the members of their generation but to be leaders in insisting on actions that will respond to the needs of their children, grandchildren, and great-grandchildren and that will provide the younger generation with genuine opportunities for achieving their highest potential. Parenthetically, the author believes that the life plans of today's young people should recognize that they may live to be a hundred.

Dr. Torres-Gil has stated that his goal was to write a book dealing with the New Aging that would be provocative, informative, and prescriptive. He has done just that, and we are indebted to him for doing so.

Arthur S. Flemming

PREFACE

The United States is in the throes of fundamentally transforming its manner of treating the elderly. Recognizing that programs, benefits, and services developed in the past will inadequately serve the elderly of the next century, we are shifting our attitudes and viewing older people differently than ever before. The 1990s must be a decade of change, of making the political and policy decisions necessary to ensure that we respond realistically to a population much older and more diverse than today's. The 1990s must lay the groundwork for the New Aging.

I realized the need to rethink our approach to serving older people while implementing some of the programs already in place. As special assistant to two cabinet secretaries in the Department of Health and Human Services, I learned firsthand the importance of Social Security, Medicare, the Older Americans Act, and Supplemental Security Income to elders and their families. As a delegate to the 1971 and 1981 White House Conferences on Aging, I witnessed the political empowerment of older people over the past century. Serving as staff director of the U.S. House Select Committee on Aging showed me how antiquated views of old age, held since the 1930s, profoundly influence our present laws, regulations, and economics. As a member of the Social Security SSI Modernization Task Force in the early 1990s, I saw how a program created with good intentions could become a bureaucratic hurdle for beneficiaries.

These experiences renewed my belief in the accomplishments of the New Deal, but convinced me that its programs and methods for benefit distribution will not work for aging baby boomers. A demographic revolution affecting this country and other countries worldwide is creating a new set of political, economic, and social realities that are already influencing and will ultimately revolutionize our view of the elderly's role in society and the manner in which we provide public- and private-sector benefits to them.

One-third of all Americans—77 million people, born between 1946 and 1964—are now entering middle age. By the year 2010, they will be the elders of the early twenty-first century. Changes implemented in the 1990s affecting today's elders will impact aging baby boomers as well. They will directly affect providers of services to the aged and the ways in which younger populations prepare for retirement. They will influence decisions, inspire political action, and incite difficult, even contentious, debate on how to prepare for an increasing number of older people and how to realistically address associated political and economic costs.

It is vital, therefore, to understand why changes must be made, and how they will alter previous views of and present public support for the elderly. By examining the politics and public policies affecting the United States' growing older population today, we can better comprehend how aging in the future will differ markedly from aging in the recent past.

It is also important to note that change occurs rapidly and unpredictably in, an aging society. What we know today might be different in a few months. Thus, it is crucial that citizens stay informed about policy and political trends because events can unfold with great speed. This treatise does not attempt to give detailed information on contemporary events, which might make it obsolete in a short time. What is provided is a framework within which the reader can understand the circumstances occurring relative to older people and their families.

In that regard, a new set of circumstances, profoundly altering our view of the elderly and society's response to them is shaping the New Aging, an era best defined by examining the following:

• claims upon government based on generation
• diversity within the aging population
• longevity and an increasing life span

Within the framework of these three factors, this book examines the choices, controversies, and decisions associated with aging. Generational claims, diversity, and longevity provide a context for better understanding the "slow-motion crisis" emblematic of the demographic revolution now underway. Generational claims can breed conflict among groups loyal to particular age cohorts or intergenerational coalitions. Diversity gives voice to new groups—minorities, the disabled, women, rural populations—with a stake in aging issues. Longevity can provide fresh opportunities or create endless problems.

These three factors are at the core of how we pay for services; how we allocate public and private resources; how we make political decisions affecting an aging society. Within their context, arguments about Social Security payroll taxes, health-care coverage, and long-term care can be better understood.

This book explores the New Aging and the dramatic changes it will bring. Its purpose is to illustrate why our current delivery of services and benefits to the elderly must change to meet the pressures of generational claims, diversity, and longevity, and why adapting will be difficult. In addition, it investigates the tensions and conflicts that will arise if we do nothing to restructure existing benefits, programs, agencies, and services for the elderly.

The book speaks as much to advocates for the elderly as to those who disagree with existing large-scale entitlements and their manner of financing. The issues raised are of concern to providers of services and family members, who must shoulder the responsibility of caring for elders, as well as federal and state decision makers. Concluding chapters lay out a series of incremental and structural reforms that will enable us to cope with the pressures of the New Aging. These are intended to stir both interest and dissent, because in a democracy, social consensus can only be achieved through debate. Finally, the book aims to challenge the public and professionals in the field of aging to respond compassionately—to see aging as not just another political hurdle, but a tower of fresh opportunities and new directions benefiting both young and old, now and into the next century.

ACKNOWLEDGMENTS

This book reflects a culmination of experiences, influences, and perspectives that have driven my professional, academic, and political interests. In it, I attempt to provide insight into population dynamics and the demographic pressures of an aging society and how these will affect public policies and the political system. To the extent this book is useful and informative, I credit many.

Countless individuals and organizations assisted me in completing the manuscript. For the original idea, I especially thank Jean Lesher, formerly an executive editor at the publishing firm that produced one of my earlier books. Jean worked with me to create a focus and framework for my ideas.

The views and concepts in this book were greatly influenced by valued colleagues. Andy Achenbaum (University of Michigan) spent many hours reviewing my first draft; I am indebted to him for his conceptual contributions and friendship. Scott Bass (University of Massachusetts, Boston), Neal Cutler (American College and formerly a colleague at USC), Bill Lammers (USC), David Thompson (of New Zealand), and Jeanne Giovannoni (UCLA) (who had the grace to read the manuscript during a vacation in Spain), gave unselfishly of their time and energy.

Others, including Malcolm Morrison, Eric Kingson, Paul Hewitt, Bernice Neugarten, Rick Moody, Alan Pifer, Lydia Bronte, Ken Dyctwald, Philip Longman, Meredith Minkler, Cynthia Taeuber, Jack Cornman, Bob Butler, Carroll Estes, Elizabeth Kutza, and Percil Stanford helped shape the book's perspectives. Vern Bengtson and Jim Birren contributed greatly to my understanding of aging's sociological and psychological dimensions.

Certain organizations were invaluable in providing the collegial support and encouragement to tackle political issues (although my views may differ from theirs): the Families USA Foundation, its founders Kate and Phil Villers, and executive director Ron Pollack; the American Society on Aging (ASA), its executive director Gloria Cavanaugh, and board of directors; the American Association of Retired Persons, and its executive director Horace Deets; the National Council on Aging, and its president, Dan Thurz; and the National Hispanic Council on Aging, its national director Marta Sotomayor, and East Los Angeles chapter president Gil Vargas. The commitment of these organizations to the social welfare of older persons and vulnerable populations remains a source of inspiration.

The views held and activities engaged in by my academic and professional colleagues and myself were certainly influenced by many prominent statesmen in our field: Maggie Kuhn, founder of the Gray Panthers and tireless fighter for social justice; Claude Pepper, gentlemen and advocate to the end; the late Tish Summers, role model for older women; Arthur S. Flemming, indefatigable and irreplaceable spokesperson and leader; the late Nelson Cruikshank, union leader and former Chairman of the Federal Council on Aging; Charles Schottland, a professor of mine and public servant of the highest order; and the late Wilbur Cohen and his contemporary, Robert Ball, who demonstrate the meaning of "policy entrepreneurs" par excellence. All these exemplify lifelong commitment to serving the public good. I can only hope to achieve a portion of their stature, wisdom, and integrity.

Several elected officials and political appointees have influenced my political ideas. Rep. Edward R. Roybal, chairman of the U.S. House Select Committee on Aging, the staff, as well as Jorge Lambrinos and Henry Lozano gave me the opportunity to gain direct legislative experience while serving as the staff director of that committee. Rep. Roybal epitomizes integrity and remains the elder statesman of Hispanic politics. Rep. Esteban Torres and Marty Martinez gave me a start in working with Congressional candidates. To them I owe much of my ongoing education in Congressional politics. Mayor Tom Bradley of Los Angeles let me serve at the local level as a member of the City Planning Commission, refocusing my interest on the local community. Councilman Richard Alatorre, Supervisor Gloria Molina, Assemblyman Richard Polanco, and State Senators Charles Calderon and Art Torres also allowed me to dabble in their political worlds. George Pla involved me in countless political "projects," little knowing how much I gained from the experience. My ability to serve the public good was immeasurably enhanced by the White House Fellows program, the support of my class of 1978–1979, and the opportunity to work with Joseph Califano and Patricia Harris, former secretaries of the Department of Health and Human Services.

I must also thank various professors who instilled in me the importance of seeking knowledge and questioning conventional wisdom. They included William McCraw and John Ballard (San Jose State University), who first introduced me to political science and public administration. Brandeis University and Heller faculty, staff, and students set me on a professional career course: Millie and Josh Guberman, the "Hahns," James Schulz, David Austin, Roland Warren, Jerry Eggert, Wyatt Jones, Norm Kurtz, Gunner and Rosemary Dybwad, Larry Fuchs, Howard Freeman, and Rosina Becerra. Robert Binstock taught me the importance of clarity and logic, and the late Arnold and Helen Gurin stood by me throughout my turbulent youth and career. I continue to live by the teachings of all of these.

My most recent work can be credited largely to the unstinting support of the faculty, staff, and students of USC's Andrus Gerontology Center, Leonard Davis School of Gerontology, and School of Public Administration. The faculty at the Davis School was always supportive. I especially thank Kate Wilbur, Ruth Weg, Jon Pynoos, Eileen Crimmins, Mark Hayward, Tuck Finch, Sally Coberly, Bev Lowe, Phoebe Liebig, Robert Myrtle, Victor Regnier, Gerald Larue, Loren Lipson, and Bryan Kemp. Several individuals gave me the organizational support necessary to complete this book: Ed Schneider, dean of the Gerontology Center; David Peterson, director of the Davis School; and Ross Clayton, dean of the School of Public Administration. Gerontology Center staff were no less important: Joyce Kinjo and Linda Broder for handling my countless phone calls, and Gail Doss, Gitta Morris, Wendy Free, Maria Henke, Yvonne Sonnega, Maria Bergara, Pauline Abbott, May Ng, Evelyn Forbes, and Helen Jones. The university administration created the environment for faculty like myself to serve as a bridge to the policy world: Provost Cornelius Pings, Vice President Bob Billar, Graduate Dean Barbara Solomon, and President James Zumberge.

Crucial assistance in the preparation and completion of this book was provided by those who worked for me: Carolinda Douglass, Linda Wray, Linda Boich, and Carl Renold. Jeff Hyde's effective supervision of my research projects allowed me the flexibility to work on this book project. Brian Lipshy was critical in overseeing the entire process and largely responsible for the graphs and charts. Geri Servi and Mimi Kmet assisted in the editing of the manuscript; I thank Geri, in particular, for her expertise.

The greatest reward in any academic career is the chance to influence and be educated by students. The students in both my undergraduate and graduate courses at USC have been a source of great joy and have contributed to the refinements of the ideas in this book. Special thanks to those in the following courses: Ethnicity and Aging (Gero 433), Programs,

Policies, and Politics Affecting the Elderly (Gero 240), and Social Policy and Aging (Gero 540 and 645), but to all my students, everywhere, my gratitude.

During the two years it took to develop this book, I sacrificed many precious hours and moments with friends and family. They remained, however, patient, enduring, and at times refreshingly unconcerned with my project's success or failure. They accepted me, regardless. Jorge Corralejo (and the entire Corralejo family), Jaime Cervantes, and Richard Rivera did without me at many Clipper, Raider, and Dodger games. Luis Viniegra and his family wondered what I really did with my time, but welcomed me whenever I showed up. My San Jose compadres, Tony and Yolanda Estremera, Jim and Lupe Gallardo, Andy and Maria Lucero, Delia Alvarez, and Consuelo Rodriguez were always there to loosen me up. Lupe Ramos and her family, Cynthia Gonzalez, Lilly Lee, Julie Regnier, Valentine Villa, Julia Velasquez, Lourdes Birba and my poker crowd (Pedro Birba, et al.) were always available when I needed relaxation. My senior-citizen friends consistently put things into perspective and reminded me that aging is about the good things in life. Special thanks to the seniors from the San Jose Eastside Senior Center, who inspired my research, the Andrus volunteers, the East Los Angeles chapter of the National Hispanic Council on Aging, and Milton Tepper, Leon and Celeste Kaplan, Ted Ellsworth, and Juana Soria. I thank my sister Belen and her two lovely daughters (our godchildren), Maya Maria, and Vida Angelica for being a source of great warmth and joy. My immediate family (Mark, Eddie, Ramona, and Randy, Jeanne and John, Mario, Vincent and Olivia, Eric, and my nieces and nephews) and my extended family, the Rayas and the Arredondos (especially Virgy, Maryanne, Ronnie, Judy, Anna) were always there to welcome me into the fold whenever I surfaced.

In addition, I want to thank the publishers of this book (and Donna Deutchman for suggesting them) for their cooperation and support, especially John Harney, editorial director of Auburn House, for believing in this book. Thanks also to Paul O'Connell of Lexington Books, who valued the manuscript as well.

No one, however, has been more important to this project and to all my professional and political activities than my wife, Elvira Castillo. I am immeasurably indebted to her for her love, support, and belief in what I do. She never wavered and patiently bore the sacrifices of this project. To her, and to the other two women in my life, my mother and grandmother, I dedicate this book.

ABBREVIATIONS

ADEA	Age Discrimination in Employment Act
AIDS	Acquired Immune Deficiency Syndrome
AARP	American Association of Retired Persons
ACYF	Administration for Children, Youth, and Families
AIME	Average Indexed Monthly Earnings
CDI	Catastrophic Drug Insurance
CHSP	Congregate Housing Services Program
CMHC	Community Mental Health Center
COLAs	Cost of Living Adjustments
CPI-U	Consumer Price Index for all Urban Consumers
CMP	Competitive Medical Plans
CPSC	Consumer Product Safety Commission
DI	Disability Insurance
EEOC	Equal Employment Opportunity Commission
ERISA	Employment Retirement Income Security Act
FCC	Federal Communications Commission
FDIC	Federal Deposit Insurance Corporation
FSLIC	Federal Savings and Loan Insurance Corporation
FTC	Federal Trade Commission
FDA	Food and Drug Administration
GNP	Gross National Product
HCFA	Health Care Financing Administration
HEC	Home Equity Conversion
HHS	(Department of) Health and Human Services
HI	Hospital Insurance
HUD	(Department of) Housing and Urban Development

IG	Inspector General
IRA	Individual Retirement Account
JTPA	Job Training Partnership Act
LIHEAP	Low Income Home Energy Assistance Program
MCCA	Medicare Catastrophic Coverage Act of 1988
NIA	National Institute on Aging
NCOA	National Council on Aging
OAA	Older Americans Act
OASDI	Old Age, Survivors, and Disability Insurance
OASI	Old Age and Survivors Insurance
OBRA	Omnibus Budget Reconciliation Act
OMB	Office of Management and Budget
PBGC	Pension Benefit and Guarantee Corporation
PIA	Primary Insurance Account
PRO	Peer Review Organizations
PURPA	Public Utility Regulation and Policy Act of 1978
QCs	Quarters of Coverage
RVS	Relative Value Scale
SCSEP	Senior Community Service Employment Program
SEC	Securities and Exchange Commission
SHMO	Social Health Maintenance Organizations
SIPC	Securities Investors Protection Corporation
SMI	Supplemental Medical Insurance
SSA	Social Security Administration
SSBG	Social Services Block Grant
SSI	Supplemental Security Income
TRA	Tax Reform Act
UI	Unemployment Insurance
UMTA	Urban Mass Transit Act
USDA	United States Department of Agriculture
VREHL	Voting Rights of the Elderly and Handicapped Law–1982
WAP	Weatherization Assistance Program

THE NEW AGING

INTRODUCTION

THE HISTORY OF AGING IN AMERICA

The history of aging in America can be divided into several periods: pre–1930 (Young Aging), 1930–1990 (Modern Aging), and post–1990 (New Aging).[1] Prior to 1930, the status of older people and their treatment in society continued to reflect centuries of traditional norms and views: family and community responsibility for older persons, intergenerational family relationships, power and authority of elders. The United States, however, also reflected a young nation's orientation toward its youth and its aversion toward the "old" nations of Europe. Westward expansion, the building of cities and industry, family mobility (with its emphasis on merit rather than seniority), and democracy combined with low life expectancy to give limited attention to the elderly.[2] This Young Aging period saw little need for government to develop old-age policies such as those emerging in Germany and other European countries.

During the Modern Aging period, the elderly's role and society's approach to addressing their needs changed dramatically. During this sixty-year period, American society allowed government to play a central role in the social, economic, and personal lives of its members. This role included providing for their grandparents through various programs, agencies, and benefits. The nation adopted age as one of several criterion for defining eligibility for services and determining who was deserving and needy. The age segregation of the Modern Aging included the establishment of senior-citizen interest groups and an "aging enterprise" comprised of providers and professionals to serve a growing elderly population.

The Modern Aging period represents our initial attempt as a nation and a people to respond to a demographic revolution, creating large-scale programs and services to provide an extensive and expensive system of services and benefits to senior citizens. These were the product of our view of old age and the elderly in society then. It is this system upon which the elderly and their families now depend.

The Modern Aging has ended. We are entering a period that is precursor to the aging of the twenty-first century. The New Aging period begins in the 1990s, when we will have no choice but to alter our view of the role of the elderly and the manner in which government and society provide for them. In the 1990s, we will have to begin restructuring the programs of the Modern Aging, and rethinking ways to address the needs and desires of the growing number of elderly. Changes in the 1990s and beyond must be implemented in conjunction with other changes in the social, economic, and political fabric of American society. The pressures attendant to an increasingly older America will demand it.

PRESSURES OF AN OLDER AMERICA

The pressures confronting American society vary. The aging of the population, an overall increase in the median age, and the rising number of older people serve as catalysts for a reevaluation of the present structure of services available to the elderly. Since 1900, the number of Americans 65 years and over increased from one in twenty-five, to one in eight by 1986 (U.S. Senate 1988). This increase will continue over the next thirty years. Can we afford to maintain age-segregated entitlements for the elderly when up to a quarter of the population will be 55 years or over by 2010? Can we continue to spend up to 26 percent of the federal budget on benefits and services to an older population?

The dramatic increase in people considered old is having a cumulative effect on society. Shifting government priorities from young to older populations, heightened media interest in the "gray lobby," business efforts to cultivate a growing consumer market, and efforts to prepare for the aging of the baby boomers highlight our concern and fascination with the aging population.

This interest, however, is fraught with disagreement and controversy over our response as a society, as a government, and as individuals. Some see the elderly as an important resource contributing intelligence, productivity, and social stability. Others blame them for a host of problems and costs that weaken America's ability to compete in the international economy. The outcome of debates regarding today's elderly will affect future cohorts of aging and the elderly, and the actions already taken by state and local governments as well as the private sector have immediate repercussions for retirees and their families.

Programs developed since the 1930s to provide for older people are under intense evaluation, and the myriad criticisms surrounding them reflect a lack of social consensus about older people. Social Security is criticized for levying a high payroll tax on a work force that might never enjoy the level of assistance of today's beneficiaries. Medicare and Medicaid are under severe fiscal pressure, and federal and state governments continue to reduce coverage while increasing out-of-pocket expenses for health-care recipients. Corporations are retracting the health insurance coverage of their retirees and shifting retirement and pension programs from defined benefits to defined contributions.

Our national soul-searching about caring for the elderly causes tensions in society because it occurs in the midst of a large federal budget deficit, a political mood counter to raising revenues, national and state governments attempting to downscale the role of the public sector, and an uneasiness about America's political and economic power. A "doom and gloom" climate—based on the assumption that doing more for one group means doing less for another—pervades our analysis and limits options for addressing population aging. It is not surprising, then, to see criticisms of the current system of benefits to the elderly couched in the language of "generational conflict" and a growing polarization between senior-citizen lobbying groups and groups representing other needy populations.

The pressures facing us as we prepare for more older people early in the next century are further complicated by the political power of old-age organizations understandably wishing to preserve existing benefits and programs. In a political system where sophistication, high voting rates, direct mail, money, and access to legislators and political appointees influence decisions, old-age organizations and grass-roots groups of elders have distinct advantages.

Although senior-citizen lobbies might not always emerge victorious and cannot be given full credit for passage of old-age legislation, they do have the ability to pressure Congress and state legislatures. The repeal of the Medicare Catastrophic Coverage Act in 1989 and the budget debates of the early 1990s wherein senior-citizen groups effectively fought major cutbacks in Social Security and Medicare proved it.

The gray lobby, however, is a diverse collection of subgroups, some more politically influential than others. The elderly poor, older women and minorities, those who live in rural areas, and frail older people are often underrepresented by the more articulate and affluent senior-citizen groups. The needs and leverage of subgroups of older people must, at times, vie with the demands of others, including persons with disabilities, children, the poor, and minority populations. The increasing diversity of interest-group politics will influence change in public policies for the elderly.

There is no shortage of proposals addressing the problems of an older

America. Senator Daniel Moynihan, D–N.Y., created a national controversy in 1990 by suggesting we reduce the Social Security payroll tax and return to pay-as-you-go financing. His argument that Social Security reserves were being used to reduce the federal deficit and that a younger work force was unfairly burdened by higher taxes struck a chord among both Democratic and Republican legislators. His proposal elevated discussion about how to serve the elderly to a broader debate encompassing who will pay—who will carry the burden—for continuing entitlement to an older population.

Many other proposals have focused less on what is best for society and more on a narrow view of the elderly as an undeserving group. Daniel Callahan, in his widely discussed book, *Setting Limits*, suggested that we reduce the high cost of health care by rationing treatment to the very sick and terminally ill elderly (Callahan 1987).

Oregon's attempt during the early 1990s to ration health care through a prioritized list of procedures in their Medicaid program was such an approach. This proposal argues that, in a time of limited budgets, "all medically necessary services" cannot be provided to all eligible beneficiaries. The Oregon plan attempts to broaden the use of funds by "drawing the line" on the priority list at which point treatments would be denied. Further, it excludes Medicare recipients from this formula, thus creating ethical, political, and generational dilemmas.

Former Governor Richard Lamm achieved notoriety for arguing that we do too much for the aged at the expense of our younger populations and rebuilding the nation's infrastructure. Organizations such as the Americans for Generational Equity (AGE) and the American Association of Boomers (AAB) were formed to counter the political influence of senior-citizen groups and rein in programs for the elderly. The National Taxpayers Union Foundation concluded that "shifts in the age-structure and generational mix of the electorate may open the 'window of opportunity' for old-age entitlement reforms to its widest point by the late 1990s" (Barnes 1991, 216).

The flaw in these ideas and proposals is that they revolve around a narrow set of concerns—containing costs, fear of generational conflict, reducing government activism on behalf of needy populations—and presume that the elderly are rich, selfish, and undeserving. They are also limited by ideological and economic premises: an unwillingness to help the poor, homeless, mentally ill, and other groups; a political mindset against raising revenues to improve our education and health-care systems and to rebuild highways, bridges, and public transportation; an inability to plan ahead (beyond the two-year Congressional cycle or annual budgets); and a failure to recognize the tremendous social, racial, and demographic changes affecting this country.

Other proposals offer a broader vision. Alice Rivlin and Joshua Wiener

(1988), for example, argue for a social insurance program to cover long-term care. An unlikely coalition of large corporations, small businesses, organized medicine, labor and civil-rights groups, and senior citizens is generating intense pressure for some form of national health-care coverage. Harry Moody (1990) views the elderly population not as a burden on society but an important labor force improving the nation's economy. He urges us to view them as a source of productivity rather than a drain on public resources. Still others, such as Stephen Crystal (1982), Hugh Heclo (1988), and Robert Binstock (1983) suggest that social policies for the aged focus more selectively on the needs of the disadvantaged elderly unaffected by general improvements in the social and economic status of older people.

PREPARING FOR THE NEW AGING

We face in the 1990s a proliferation of proposals addressing the demographic revolution. These, however narrow or broad, implicitly assume major changes in our present method of delivering benefits and services to the elderly and our view of old age. Gerontologists such as Bernice Neugarten and Binstock were already suggesting by the early 1980s that we alter the eligibility criteria for entitlement programs to the elderly (Neugarten 1979; Binstock 1983). In "The Aged as a Scapegoat" (1983), Binstock attributed the view of elderly as a selfish interest group to the "compassionate ageism" promoted through the establishment of age-segregated programs. Only by changing that structure of old-age entitlement could we reintegrate the needs of older people with other segments of society. *The Wall Street Journal* noted that the "elite media" are revamping the image of older people as feeble, vulnerable, and financially strapped. According to the same publication, debates mark "the beginning of an overhaul of how the nation looks at the elderly" ("Here's the Latest Criticism of Social Security: It Works" 1986).

Increasingly, others (including those who work directly with older people and their families) are feeling we should overhaul our manner of paying for and delivering services and benefits to senior citizens. Most proposals, however, remain couched in ideological terms to reduce cost, avoid paying taxes, and expand entitlements because of political pressures. Few political reforms attempt to restructure social policies for the elderly by systematically analyzing how we got where we are and how we can best meet the changing circumstances of the next several decades.

In the midst of this overhaul we must do several things to avoid penalizing the "truly disadvantaged," to ensure a modicum of public and private benefits to future cohorts of the elderly, and to prepare for the New Aging in a fiscally sound manner:

- understand the social and demographic trends affecting an aging society;
- reexamine the intent and principles underlying our present system of serving the needs of older persons; and,
- consider what influence generational claims, longevity, and diversity will have on the current configuration of benefits and programs.

Responding successfully to the pressures of aging involves all segments of society: elderly and nonelderly groups, young and old, the poor, middle-class and upper-income individuals, whites and minorities. The irony of aging is that, ultimately, it affects us all. What we do and say about older people today will reverberate as we age. Adjusting to an aging society is more than a pack of political and policy debates; it is a highly personal matter.

In many respects, the United States in the 1990s is at a crossroads similar to that faced in the 1920s. Although we appear to be succeeding economically and politically in comparison to other nations, severe social dislocations exist, as measured by the tragedy of homelessness, crime, drugs, inner-city turmoil, and a health and educational system in crisis. With uneasiness, the public senses that beneath the seemingly tranquil surface of social and economic prosperity lurk serious problems that could create national instability.

Aging and the increasing number of older people will bring those problems to the surface, forcing us to take on the question of responsibility for those less fortunate. We will be required to decide where government responsibility ends and individual initiative begins. We will have no choice but to take stock of the tremendous changes and pressures on the family and on providers of social and health services.

Most important, the 1990s, much like the 1930s, will provide an opportunity to respond to immediate social needs and prepare for inevitable social and demographic changes by revamping not only the current age-based system of benefits and services but all social welfare policies. The New Deal of the 1930s successfully met the crisis of its day, and its development of public policies, programs, and government responsibility was directly responsible for victory in World War II and the economic prosperity in the three decades following. Now, however, as its chief architects pass on, a new set of intellectual and political challenges confront us. The 1990s will require change in the New Deal legacy while retaining its values: activist government; concern for the entire community (not just the politically influential); understanding of the social interconnectedness of the haves and have-nots; and willingness to sacrifice today to reap benefits tomorrow.

As we revamp the policies of the New Deal era forged by public and private initiative, we must ask: Who will be the leaders of the New Aging?

What statesmen will provide vision, practical ability, and sense of community? The generation spawning Robert Ball and Wilbur Cohen (who passed away in 1987), architects of Social Security and Medicare, Maggie Kuhn and Tish Summers, who gave us a positive image of old age, and Representative Claude Pepper, who provided political leadership to a once-disenfranchised constituency, will be gone by the turn of the century. Who will replace them and furnish leadership in our struggle to redefine social policies for an aging population?

The premises underlying the views of this book, while based on the pragmatic liberalism of the 1930s and 1940s, operate on the implicit understanding that the approach to big government of that period will be ineffective in the 1990s. Recommendations offered in later chapters incorporate the values of liberalism and pragmatism, the efficiency and effectiveness of the private sector, conservative concepts of self-reliance and individualism, and the reality of having to shape a set of reforms meeting the challenges of the New Aging. The book is not a partisan or ideological set of solutions. Instead, it intends to recreate a set of social policies that take into account longevity and the differing generational interests of a society that is demographically, socially, and culturally diverse.

In short, we need to reformulate a social contract between individuals, society, and government. Such a contract would make the individual responsible for taking greater charge of personal and economic well-being, but entrust government, at all levels, with the duty to provide for broader social needs in education, health, and public safety. Further, it would adopt a new view of the life-cycle process, created by longevity and diversity, directing individuals to prepare for a much longer life span. Finally, such a pact would involve a redefinition of those eligible for benefits and services and the manner in which we pay for them.

What lies ahead might be unclear, but our recognition of the problem can, like a crystal ball, give us both insight into what must be done and the courage and resolve to do it. Let us challenge the future before it confronts us. Accepting—even welcoming—a new definition of old age inspired by competing generations, increasing longevity, and mounting diversity will enable us to chart the course ahead with wisdom and compassion.

NOTES

1. Andrew Achenbaum, Ph.D. (University of Michigan), conceptualized the terms to describe these three periods. The politics of aging however, can be viewed in different time frames. For example, J. B. Williamson et. al. (1982), examine the role of age through time by observing the aged in preindustrial societies and the effect of modernization on the status of the elderly. Particularly helpful is

their use of four periods—Incipiency (1920–1950) and The Beginning of Senior Citizen Activism, Coalescence (1950–1965) and The Creation of Social Policies for the Elderly, and Institutionalization (1965–1980), the fruition of old-age political power—to describe developments in the politics of aging during this century. The fourth period (1980–1992) I characterize as a "Realignment" in the politics of aging.

2. One notable exception was the rise of private pension plans in the 1800s. The American Express Company established the first company pension plan in 1875, providing benefits to disabled workers over age 60 with at least twenty years of service. Thereafter, railroad companies, such as the B & O, and other firms established similar pension programs (Schulz 1988).

BIBLIOGRAPHY

Barnes, James. "Age-Old Strife." *National Journal* 4 (Jan. 26, 1991): 216–19.

Binstock, Robert. "The Aged as a Scapegoat." *The Gerontologist*, 23, no. 2 (1983): 136–43.

Callahan, Daniel. *Setting Limits: Medical Goals in an Aging Society*. New York: Simon and Schuster, 1987.

Crystal, Stephen. *America's Old Age Crisis*. New York: Basic Books, 1982.

Heclo, Hugh. "Generational Politics." In *The Vulnerable,* edited by John Palmer, Timothy Smeeding, and Barbara Boyle Torrey. Washington, D.C.: The Urban Institute Press, 1988: 381–412.

"Here's the Latest Criticism of Social Security: It Works." *The Washington Post*, Jan. 20, 1986.

Moody, Harry R. "The Politics of Entitlement And the Politics of Productivity." In *Diversity in Aging*, ed. S. Bass, E. Kutza, and F. Torres-Gil. Glenview, Ill.: Scott, Foresman, 1990.

Neugarten, Bernice. "Policy for the 1980s: Age or Need Entitlement?" In National Journal Issues Book, *Aging: Agenda for The Eighties*. Washington D.C.: Government Research Corporation, 1979, pp. 48–52.

Orloff, Ann Shola, and Theda Skocpol. "Why Not Equal Protection? Explaining the Politics of Public Social Spending in Britain, 1900–1911, and the United States, 1800s–1920." *American Sociological Review* 49 (1984): 726–50.

Rivlin, Alice, and Joshua Wiener, with Raymond Hanley and Denise Spence. *Caring for the Disabled Elderly: Who Will Pay?* Washington. D.C.: The Brookings Institution, 1988.

Williamson, J. B., L. Evans, and L. A. Powell. *Politics of Aging*. Springfield, Ill. Charles C. Thomas, 1982.

1
THE THREE FORCES OF
AN AGING SOCIETY

Men are better when they are old; things when they are new.
Korean Proverb

What is the New Aging? Why must we reexamine the aging of society in a new light? The New Aging reflects a change in our definition of old age and a need to alter the system by which we have provided for the elderly over the past sixty years. Our attitude toward "old people" and our vision of ourselves as old will alter family and personal lifestyles, interpersonal relationships, and the social value of contributions made by the aged. An important element of the New Aging is incorporating these new attitudes into pension and retirement programs, federal and state entitlements, and employment policies.

During the Young Aging (pre–1930) and Modern Aging (1930–1990) periods, older people were viewed differently than they are today. Prior to 1930, they enjoyed respect and leadership. Later, the Modern Aging period saw stereotypes develop of older people as poor, frail, deserving, and disadvantaged.

The New Aging will witness change in the image of the elderly due, in large part, to generational claims, diversity, and longevity. This new image will directly affect both the political and policy decisions in financing benefits to the elderly and our preparedness for their future cohorts.

CHANGING DEFINITIONS OF AGE

Growing old and having elderly people among us is nothing new. Reaching old age is quintessential to the human condition. Authors in the Bible and writers such as Plato and Aeschylus long ago reflected on the "Threshold of Old Age" and the importance of elders to family and community.

In traditional societies, older people (usually male) were held in relatively high respect.[1] They exercised leadership and control. Until this century, an elderly person taking an afternoon walk could expect polite greetings from youngsters, and could expect to be cared for by family members when health deteriorated. By the 1920s, however, a youth cult had begun in the United States, in part spurred by increasing prosperity, introduction of retirement programs, a growing middle class, and rising high-school and college attendance (Rapson 1971). This shift toward a youth culture reached its apex in the 1960s and has persisted.

The traditional status of the elderly has declined for other reasons: their increasing life expectancy and relatively larger numbers in society; urbanization and the geographical dispersion of the family; and social and upward mobility among young people. As early as 1893, Durkheim recognized the role of modern society in the decline in status among the elderly, remarking that the "worship of age is steadily weakening with civilization" (Durkheim 1964, 294).

Older people no longer assume that their age will command respect and deference by strangers, or that their innate wisdom on public matters will earn them appointments to important political positions. On the other hand, as a group, they are more active and independent. They do not want to "burden their children" and, even when frail and alone, they seek "intimacy at a distance." If they are sick, impoverished, or lonely, they expect local charities, volunteer programs, and area agencies on aging to provide home-delivered meals, home health services, and volunteer visitors.

In addition to a change in attitude about being old, the New Aging involves changing the definition of age. Since 1935 in the United States, an "older person" has been someone who is 65 years or older. This particular age marker stems from the age limit set for receipt of full Social Security benefits; its precedent was Germany's age requirement for receiving Social Insurance in 1898. Most federal and state entitlement programs have used age 65 to mark eligibility for old-age assistance, including Supplemental Security Income (SSI), the Social Security retirement program, and Medicare.[2]

Today, however, age restrictions are rapidly changing. Raising the Social Security retirement age to 67 will reinforce the upward motion of what is considered "old age."[3] We now distinguish between the young-old (those 65 to 85 years), who are basically active and healthy; and the old-old (85 years and over), who are more likely to face chronic illnesses. Middle age used to refer to those in their 30s. It now applies to people 46 to 65.

Without meaning to, we have revised norms and expectations regarding the behavior of the elderly and have redefined the meaning of old. Much of this change is healthy, simply reflecting an adjustment to the realities of modern civilization. Yet, stereotypes of older people fluctuate as we struggle to determine where responsibility for them lies. How much should public institutions assume? How much should the family and the individual assume? During the period of the Modern Aging, the elderly were predominantly stereotyped as a deserving group of poor and needy individuals. This affected advocacy efforts on their behalf and resulted in the passage of Medicare, the Older Americans Act, subsidized housing, and transportation and energy assistance. During the 1980s, however, we began to view them as a selfish group, rich and hedonistic, demanding more and more public resources at the expense of younger groups. We can expect a similar change in our view of the aged during the New Aging.

The reality, of course, varies. Some elderly are well-off and live in expensive condos; many others are poor. Some are supported by extended families; others must rely on Social Security for their primary income. Older people as a group, however, live longer, are healthier, better educated, and more affluent than ever before. In addition, they have more political influence than other age groups. Individually, though, they no longer have the authority or the central family role accorded them in ancient gerontocracies. Self-reliance and individual responsibility have emerged as virtues among the aged. Middle-aged and older people are more likely to understand the value of saving for retirement, and to seek mid- and late-life education and training. Nevertheless, if they become dependent and vulnerable, they expect to rely on a vast array of publicly funded, government administered social services and benefits.

The hallmark of the Modern Aging was a growing reliance on public benefits and services (while relying primarily on the family), but changes now occurring in these will affect adjustment to aging. Within today's social policies for older Americans, we will see a further redefinition of aging. The programs senior citizens and their families enjoy today will differ greatly in coming years. We can expect, for example, to see the eligibility age rise even further and to see major changes in Social Security and Medicare. The demographic, racial, economic, and political pressures of the New Aging will require reform of existing social policies for the elderly, regardless of how their providers and advocates may feel.

The New Aging refers to our changing views of caring for the elderly and our behavior as we become elderly. Programs and benefits that were once successful in reducing poverty among the elderly and providing them with a measure of security and dignity must be revised to include those changing views. We must decide how we can do this, and whether re-forming social policies for an aging society will affect other groups, such as minorities and poor children. Who will win or lose? Will change pit groups against one another or restore the decency, equity, and compassion that marked social policy during the Modern Aging period?

The answers to these questions will affect not only middle-aged and younger populations today, but senior citizens. A retiree, 65 years of age, can now expect to live another twenty to thirty years. Thus, any changes will directly affect today's elderly as well as younger groups. Therefore, all population groups have a stake in understanding why and how social policies must change to meet the exigencies of the New Aging.

Many proposals and arguments regarding benefits and services for the elderly are being aired today. The aim of this book is to put these ideas in their proper perspective by shedding light on the forest rather than on a few trees. To gain such a perspective, we must examine three major trends that encompass the pressures of an aging society and the types of changes and reforms likely to occur as a result of them.

THE THREE FORCES OF AN AGING SOCIETY

Three distinct forces will shape the New Aging: generational claims, diversity, and longevity. Together, these create the context within which our views of older people and society's response to aging will emerge over the next thirty years.

Certainly, other factors also influence a society undergoing fundamental demographic and social change. Economics, international trends, socio-economic characteristics of population groups and individuals, ideological movements, the influence of mass media, political elections, religion, and popular attitudes and values contribute to our view of the aged. Each affects public policy decisions toward elderly populations.

The three forces selected, however, encompass many of these. They involve the interplay of many demographic, political, economic, and social issues on politics, policy, and attitudes. Further, generational claims, diversity, and longevity encapsulate the unique contributions and impact of the elderly and our changing view of old age.

GENERATIONAL CLAIMS

In American society, distinct age groups, or cohorts, share historical bonds—individuals born in the same era, for example, or who witnessed the same major event (i.e., World War II). These influence their attitudes toward society and government. As a group moves through its life cycle, members become increasingly cognizant of aging, their impressive size as a group, and the public and private resources required to serve them.

Gradually, they view their claim to such resources as an age-based cohort almost exclusively comprised of members of their generation.[4]

Distinct Generations in American History

Distinct generations in American society today are likely to develop claims on society's resources based, in large part, on their identification with others sharing their period of birth. The U.S. population includes groups in their 80s and 90s. Their lifetime is a historical mosaic of rapid technological and social change, shifting roles of government, increases in life expectancy, and decreases in mortality and morbidity.

Figure 1.1 illustrates people and events from 1900 to 1990. It shows critical periods affecting American society, from large-scale immigration during the early 1900s to the widespread use of computers in the 1980s. Throughout the period, major events occurred influencing successive age cohorts: World Wars I and II; the first talking motion picture in 1927; the dropping of the atomic bomb in 1945; the Watergate scandal of the early 1970s.

Throughout these periods, age groups share common historical experiences creating common interests and attitudes. Subsequent groups share a historical perspective on earlier events and views about the present, including politics, policy, and aging. All these age groups can develop an identity based on generation providing them a collective voice in society. New Dealer, baby boomer, and yuppie are code words, however general, for generational affiliations.[5]

Using 1990 as a base, we can examine distinct generations. Paul Hewitt and Neil Howe (1988) identify three as part of the aging society. The "swing generation," comprised of people born between 1900 and 1926, represents today's elderly population. The "silent generation" is a relatively smaller group (the result of a fall in birthrate during the Great Depression) of people born in the 1930s. The largest group born in this century is the "baby-boom generation," born after World War II, between 1946 and 1964. In the 1990s, the baby boomers will become America's middle-aged. In addition to these three generations are the "baby buster" (or "boomerang") and "baby boomlet" groups, smaller groups of people born after 1964, who will constitute the work force through the early part of the next century.[6]

Figure 1.1 outlines the generations representing today's U.S. population. The elderly are those born from the early 1900s through the 1930s. The swing generation, again using 1990 as a base, will be the largest group of elderly over the next twenty years. They would be between 64 and 90 years of age. Their ages of greatest socialization (usually considered the teens and early 20s) occurred during the 1930s and the 1940s, a time of extraordinary turmoil—economic depression and a world war.[7] This group

Figure 1.1. People and Events, 1900–1990

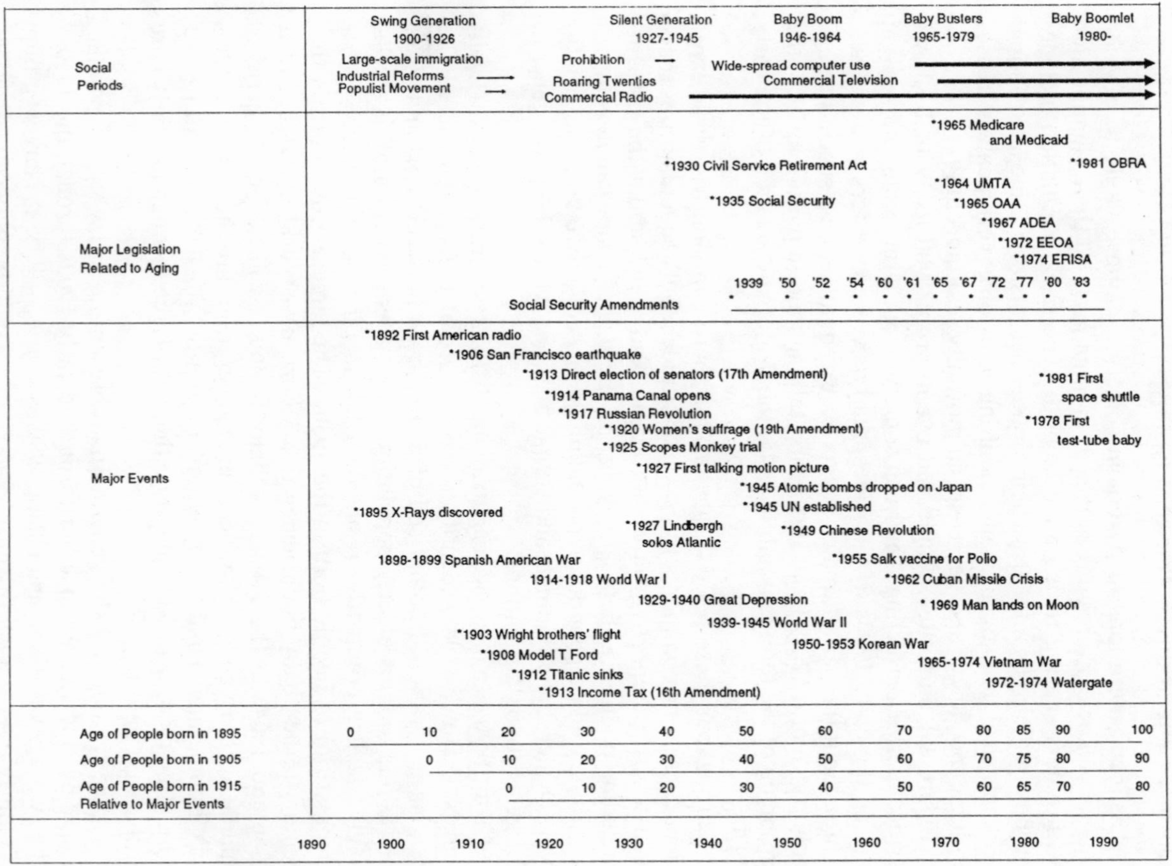

Social Periods

- Swing Generation 1900-1926
- Silent Generation 1927-1945
- Baby Boom 1946-1964
- Baby Busters 1965-1979
- Baby Boomlet 1980-

Large-scale immigration / Industrial Reforms / Populist Movement
Prohibition
Roaring Twenties
Commercial Radio
Wide-spread computer use
Commercial Television

Major Legislation Related to Aging

- 1930 Civil Service Retirement Act
- 1935 Social Security
- 1965 Medicare and Medicaid
- 1964 UMTA
- 1965 OAA
- 1967 ADEA
- 1972 EEOA
- 1974 ERISA
- 1981 OBRA

Social Security Amendments
1939 '50 '52 '54 '60 '61 '65 '67 '72 '77 '80 '83

Major Events

- 1892 First American radio
- 1895 X-Rays discovered
- 1898-1899 Spanish American War
- 1903 Wright brothers' flight
- 1906 San Francisco earthquake
- 1908 Model T Ford
- 1912 Titanic sinks
- 1913 Income Tax (16th Amendment)
- 1913 Direct election of senators (17th Amendment)
- 1914 Panama Canal opens
- 1914-1918 World War I
- 1917 Russian Revolution
- 1920 Women's suffrage (19th Amendment)
- 1925 Scopes Monkey trial
- 1927 Lindbergh solos Atlantic
- 1927 First talking motion picture
- 1929-1940 Great Depression
- 1939-1945 World War II
- 1945 Atomic bombs dropped on Japan
- 1945 UN established
- 1949 Chinese Revolution
- 1950-1953 Korean War
- 1955 Salk vaccine for Polio
- 1962 Cuban Missile Crisis
- 1965-1974 Vietnam War
- 1969 Man lands on Moon
- 1972-1974 Watergate
- 1978 First test-tube baby
- 1981 First space shuttle

Age of People born in 1895: 0 10 20 30 40 50 60 70 80 85 90 100
Age of People born in 1905: 0 10 20 30 40 50 60 70 75 80 90
Age of People born in 1915 Relative to Major Events: 0 10 20 30 40 50 60 65 70 80

1890 1900 1910 1920 1930 1940 1950 1960 1970 1980 1990

Illustration prepared by Brian Louis Lipshy.

exhibits unique values and attitudes about government and the political process. Its members came to accept and support activist government during the New Deal and are now the greatest advocates for federal entitlement programs such as Social Security and Medicare. This is not to say they are uniformly liberal or Democrat; a majority voted for Ronald Reagan and George Bush. This apparent contradiction reveals their traditional and conservative values of individualism, self-reliance, family, and patriotism, coupled with a belief that, in times of crisis, government has a responsibility to respond. The best-known advocates for senior citizens are members of this generation: Robert Ball and the late Wilbur Cohen, staunch defenders of Medicare and Social Security; Maggie Kuhn, leader of the Gray Panthers; and Arthur Flemming, civil-rights activist. Congressman Claude Pepper, D–Fla., who died in 1989, was a longtime crusader for the interests of senior citizens.

Members of the silent generation, born in the 1930s and early 1940s but socialized throughout the 1940s and 1950s, have benefited from the achievements of their parents, enjoying an extraordinarily affluent period from the 1950s through the 1980s. Now primarily in their 50s and early 60s, they belong to a group that Bernice Neugarten once called the "young-old." This is the group changing the definition of being old from poor and needy, to well-off and productive. They are creating a leisure and recreation industry, enjoying multiple pensions, retirement programs, and health benefits garnered from a strong postwar labor union movement. They are also reaping the fruits of dramatic increases in home equity values.

However, this generation lacks the political presence of the swing generation. Hewitt and Howe suggest the silent generation is vulnerable to the criticism by younger groups that their prosperity has been achieved at the expense of others, particularly because members of the silent generation are less respected than members of the swing generation, whose victories are perceived as having been hard won.[8]

Both generations—the old-old of the swing group and the young-old of the silent group—will be affected by any change in existing benefits and programs. They are vulnerable to the insecurity and anxiety provoked by reductions in Medicare reimbursements and increases in out-of-pocket expenditures, bankruptcies of pension and retirement plans, inflation's erosion of fixed incomes, and increasing costs in health care. It is these groups that become resentful when portrayed as somehow responsible for generational conflicts. For them, any changes to their entitlement programs must be based on the social vision and contract that was the original basis of those programs (i.e., need, universality, equity) rather than narrow purposes that create competition among disadvantaged groups (i.e., cost containment, deficit reduction, shifting resources to the young), or they will resist. Other age groups, especially the baby-boomer and baby-buster generations, will also be affected, although they can better control what might or might not occur throughout the remaining years of this century.

What does it mean to belong to a distinct generation in American society? How will change in social policies for senior citizens affect generations differently? Why will claims among generations be an important element in the New Aging?

The Importance of Generational Identification

Generational claims involve relationships among different age groups. Increasingly, policy makers and researchers are examining cohort and age-based competition and conflict. What happens, for example, when voters from the swing and silent generations (assuming they agree with each other) compete with baby-boomer voters? Do they agree on federal activism in government? Will all age cohorts support a national health-care system? Age cohorts can and do compete with each other, especially on the subject of taxes and paying for expanded benefits.

In the 1990s, the largest age groups will be the young-old, the old-old, and the middle-aged (baby boomers). Those in their 20s and 30s will be fewer. The question arises as to how middle-aged and young persons will view reforms of benefits to elderly populations. Will the middle-aged support raising the entitlement age for Social Security to age 70? Will younger age groups opt to shift their Social Security contributions to Individual Retirement Accounts?

In an aging society, the interaction of generations between and within themselves and with the political system will profoundly impact social, economic, political, and cultural institutions. Age consciousness and age identification will increase in the New Aging. The cumulative effect on society of increased longevity, a greater number of elderly, and cohort identification will create macrosocial consequences on financing benefits, distributing resources among competing age groups, and electoral politics (Riley & Riley 1986). Declining numbers of youths will create a labor shortage and a demand for increased immigration. Families must cope with caring for elders as well as children. The political system must accommodate a large voting block of older people, the politically disadvantaged position of minorities and immigrants, and the declining voter strength of younger groups.

In this century, the importance of generational identity has increased, perhaps influenced most by the homogenization of age by popular culture and mass communication (in other words, teenagers of the baby boomlet identify with each other, baby boomers relate to baby boomers). The young are increasingly segregated from the old, fostered in part by benefits restricted by age. A more egalitarian education system results in a large proportion of the population attending college at the same age and time (although in recent years more middle-aged and older people have been attending college with young people). Historical events such as the Vietnam War and the assassination of John F. Kennedy continue to bond particular age groups.

Increasing age consciousness will provide senior citizens with a greater sense of social identity. Longitudinal research indicates that, as members of a cohort age, they become more supportive of programs for older people. This trend reflects some self-interest, but also a willingness to accept becoming old in a new way. The inherent risk in the growth of generational identity is competition and conflict among age groups. The challenge of the New Aging will be to resurrect the concept of "mutual reciprocity" among generations and mitigate the potential that older and younger groups will lessen their support for each other.[9] The maturational hypothesis (Bengtson et al. 1985, 312) evidences that even younger groups (such as the Reagan-era cohort) with little interest in supporting publicly funded old-age programs may be more supportive as they age. Therefore, we can expect those becoming old early in the next century to reject suggestions by those who are younger to reduce benefits for the aged.

Naturally, belonging to an age cohort and identifying with a particular generation does not necessarily determine one's vote or political behavior toward another group. Taken alone, generational identity is an incomplete predictor of political view and participation. Other influences can carry greater weight, including level of education, racial and ethnic makeup, income and class status, and parents and families. Identifying with a generation, however, is an important ingredient in our view of ourselves, and will play a bigger role in coming years. Generational identification, based on age and history, creates politics suffused with the conflicting claims of one group over another. Understanding the experiences and expectations of age cohorts helps us understand competition and conflict among and within them and reveals areas for consensus and compromise. In addition, it facilitates the formation of alliances and coalitions among disparate groups.

DIVERSITY

We are a diverse society, no longer predominantly white, Anglo-Saxon, Protestant; largely middle-income and middle-class; mainly English-speaking and politically centrist. Today, we confront dramatic change in our socioeconomic, ethnic, linguistic, and political makeup.

Diversity is complex and multifaceted. It encompasses differences, heterogeneity, and distinctive subpopulations. It involves income, education, geographic location, race, gender, and physical attributes. Actually, the United States was never a homogeneous society. Waves of immigrants ensured that we were never all white and Anglo-Saxon. Our political and social structures, though, are heavily influenced by a certain set of characteristics. Our laws, social institutions, political values, and democratic traditions are inordinately tied to Great Britain and, to a lesser extent, Western Europe.

This predominant orientation of thought and mores is rapidly changing. Immigrants from the Third World and Pacific Basin are bringing Latin, Hispanic, and Asian influences. English predominates less. The role of women in the labor force and politics is expanding. New definitions of family multiply.

If the United States as a society is diversifying, why should elderly populations be any different? We have stereotypically viewed older persons as homogeneous: white, middle-class, and educated. Many laws and programs are predicated on notions of a population in which husbands worked and wives stayed at home to care for their children and grandparents. We know, of course, that the elderly population must reflect the diversity of the general population, but we tend to view people and their needs generally and, thus, lose sight of the extraordinary differences among them.

There is no absolute melting pot of cultures and ethnic groups at any age. The lifelong process of aging saddles the elderly with the same disparities setting them apart as when they were younger. Distinctions among racial and ethnic groups remain. Poor young people tend to become poor older people. The elderly population has always been heterogeneous, even if public laws and benefits in the past have treated them otherwise.

Elderly generations will further diversify in coming decades. More differences among and within groups will make responding to their needs complex and challenging. Fashioning a legislative response to fit distinct generations with unique ideas about caring for the elderly will be difficult. Today's swing generation, for example, was raised at a time when the family was expected to care for a frail older member. The baby boomers and baby busters look to nursing homes and home-health agencies to satisfy the needs of their parents and grandparents. The swing generation, while expecting government to assist when necessary, has always valued self-reliance and community spirit. Individualism and materialism are the ethos of younger groups today. How do we determine proper care for frail and dependent elderly when the attitudes of each generation differ?

Diversity goes beyond differences among generations. It involves many factors. How will they influence our willingness and ability to change the present system of services and benefits to older persons? How will diversity affect the provision of programs, benefits, and assistance in the New Aging? How will it affect the ability of providers and families to care for their elders and themselves? Why is it important to understand social and demographic change within the U.S. population?

Race/Ethnic Diversity

Perhaps no component of diversity is as topical as race and ethnic makeup. From 1890 to 1900, for example, 96.4 percent of immigrants entering the United States came from Europe.[10] From 1941 to 1980, this number dropped to 34.1 percent. Immigrants from Asia comprised 19.4 percent of the total number of immigrants; those from Latin America 34.5 percent (U.S. Department of Justice 1987). While nonwhites accounted for 24 percent of the U.S. population in 1990, this population is expected to grow to over 30 percent by 2030 (Population Reference Bureau 1990). Estimates show that by 2080, the percentage of non-Hispanic whites will drop from 79.9 percent in 1980 to 49.9 percent ("Profile of Tomorrow's New U.S." 1986).

The elderly population will undergo similar racial and ethnic flux. Projections for the early 1990s show that, of the total elderly population, 28.3 million will be white; 2.6 million black; 1.1 million Hispanic; and 603,000 other (Spencer 1986). An estimated breakdown of the 69 million elderly expected by the year 2050 shows 10 million blacks, 8 million Hispanics, and 5 million of other races (for example, Asian/Pacific Islanders and Native Americans) (Taeuber 1990). At present, nonwhite populations have fewer people over 65 years than whites. In the early 90s, about 14 percent of whites will be over 65, compared to 8 percent of blacks, and 6 percent of Hispanics (Taeuber 1990). Expected increases in life expectancy and reductions in mortality rates will mean an increasing proportion of elders among racial and ethnic populations.

Simply put, the elderly of the next several decades will have fewer white members and be less English-speaking than ever before. In restructuring laws, benefits, and services to meet their needs in the New Aging, we must consider a growing assortment of languages, customs, and racial characteristics.

Social and Family Changes

Besides racial and ethnic changes, future generations of older people can expect important shifts in social and family structure and lifestyle. The more visible changes will affect individuals and families. As the population ages, elderly women will outnumber men. Even today, as compared to 1930 when their numbers were about equal, elderly women outnumber men three to two. This ratio increases with age. By age 85, women might outnumber men five to two (Taeuber 1990). Women outlive men on average by seven to eight years. Population aging then will be increasingly dominated by the issues and concerns of older women. Laws, generally written by men and, thus, reflecting a male point of view, will need to be reconsidered.

Family variations will cause disparity by gender. Three- and four-generation households will become commonplace as life expectancy increases. Frequently, parents will be caring not only for their children, but for their parents and grandparents as well. The ability and willingness to do this will be severely tested by the declining number of children per household and the greater number of couples electing to remain childless. Issues such as affordable child and elder care, shortages of quality nursing and home-care services, elders caring for elders, and more older women living alone will surface. Family patterns will change, creating greater strains in caring for children and elders. Just over one-third of first marriages remain intact for life. Fewer than one in eight families consists of a married couple with children in which the mother does not work outside the home. Over 6 million households with young children are headed by a single parent, and this number could increase to 7.5 million by 2000 under current trends (Population Reference Bureau 1990). The 1990 census showed, for example, that the average American household was smaller than ever, and 23 million people (one-quarter of the country's households) live alone. The average number of persons living in a household was 2.63, down from 3.11 in 1970. Since 1960, social trends have ranged from more elderly widows living independently to low birth rates among young people delaying marriage (Vobejda 1991).

Society must address such changes in support ratios between young and older people. Demographers divide the population into three groups for purposes of economic and social support: those under 20; those 65 years and over (the elderly); and those 75 years and over (the old-old). They then compare them to every hundred people aged 20 to 64 years (the work force). Young and older people are considered dependent on support provided by the primary labor force. From 1990 to 2050, the estimated total support ratio of young-old to working age population will increase for whites from 68.7 to 83.5, while decreasing somewhat for Hispanics (81.1 to 74.5) (Taeuber 1990). For whites then, fewer people will be working to support younger and older members and, to the extent public resources fall short, they will be forced to rely on other groups. Another way to view changing dependency ratios is as "aged dependency ratios." This ratio compares the number of older persons (over 65 years) to all persons of working age (18 to 64). Over the last few decades, the aged dependency ratio has consistently increased. In 1950, there were 13 elderly for every 100 people of working age. By 1990, the ratio had increased to 20 per 100, and by 2030, it could rise to 37 per 100 (Population Reference Bureau, 1989).

Income and Economic Factors

Income and economic factors will add to the diversity of future generations of older people. More directly, our patterns of work and retirement will change. Already we see people retiring at earlier ages, with the average age of retirement presently at 62. This age might increase if the earnings limitation test is eliminated and if older workers feel a need to stay in the work force to maintain benefits. Older men are less likely to be working today than they were thirty years ago. From 1950 to 1988, men 55 and older in the labor force dropped from two in three to two in five (Herz 1988). Conversely, women (especially older ones) are entering the labor force in record numbers. Labor force participation rates for women rose from 35 percent in 1960 to 57 percent in 1990 (Population Reference Bureau 1990). Women 55 and older in 1988 accounted for four in ten of all older workers (Herz 1988). Future generations of senior citizens will see greater numbers of older women working or wishing to work, and fewer older males. This, of course, is subject to economic fluctuations and changes in retirement patterns. The traditional pattern, however, of males working until 65 while their wives stayed at home, is essentially broken.

The dark side to changes in retirement patterns is unemployment, a serious problem for older workers. They are more vulnerable to plant layoffs, corporate bankruptcies, and slowdowns in the economy. Once laid off, they have greater difficulty in finding comparable employment at similar wages (notwithstanding protections accorded by age discrimination laws). Older workers are also more apt to work in declining industries (auto plants, textiles, manufacturing). Furthermore, even those with generous pension and retirement plans will find their fixed retirement income eroded by inflation (unless they provide for cost-of-living increases). Company failures might reduce or even eliminate some pension plans. Their holders must then turn to the Pension Benefit Guaranty Corporation (PBGC) to recoup lost pension benefits or to public income programs such as Social Security, Disability Insurance (DI), and Supplemental Security Income (SSI).

Coupled with changing work and retirement patterns are changes in income and assets. Older people, as a group, have enjoyed tremendous economic gain from the 1940s through the 1990s. Poverty levels have declined and the median income (for those 65 and over) more than doubled between 1957 and 1987, thanks largely to Social Security Cost of Living Adjustments (COLA's) (Welniak 1989). More older retirees are covered by private or public pensions and retirement plans. In addition, with most members of today's generation owning their own homes (64 percent of Americans), the rapid appreciation in home equity during the 1970s and 1980s has provided substantial assets. The success of this single generation has created the impression that most older Americans are well-off and will enjoy continued economic security. Popular magazines and news stories in the 1980s portrayed affluent retirees enjoying their recreational vehicles, Florida condos, and ocean cruises. This characterization of the elderly has spawned resentment among younger people.

Unfortunately, the picture painted by the media is distorted, and in the 1990s we will hear more about the near-poor elderly. Many live near the poverty level, buoyed only by Social Security. In 1988, Social Security represented the largest share of an older person's income (38 percent), with assets the second largest share (25 percent) (Population Reference Bureau 1990). Poverty and near poverty pervade among certain subgroups, including women, minority older people, people living alone and in rural areas, and the very old. For example, while women constitute 58.7 percent of the total elderly population, they account for 72.4 percent of the elderly poor. Older blacks are nearly three times as likely to be poor as elderly whites (Villers Foundation 1987). Median income from Social Security is much lower for non-white than for white elderly. In 1990, for white males aged 55 and over, median income from Social Security was $6,924. For black males, it was $5,152; for Hispanic males, $5,483. For females, the median figures were $4,779 for white females; $4,012 for black females; and $4,107 for Hispanic females (Social Security Administration 1990).

Standard patterns of life expectancy and inflation will jeopardize even those reasonably well-off. Throughout the 1970s, 1980s, and into the 1990s, older people, as a group, did reasonably well economically (especially when company pensions remained solvent). This could change as they reach their 80s and 90s, however. Economic recessions and inflation would reduce pension assets. With health-care costs escalating, this could drastically reduce the elderly's living standards. Thus, any policy reforms contemplated for the 1990s must assume that the economic status of this group will decline. Present and future generations of well-off elderly have a direct stake in preserving public means-tested entitlement programs (Supplemental Security Income, Medicaid): Eventually, they themselves may need them.

Geographic Distribution/Migration

A final element of diversity is the migration and continuing shift in geographic distribution of the elderly. Since the 1950s, many older people with the economic wherewithal have migrated to Sunbelt states of the Southeast and Southwest (for sunshine, quality of life, lower costs), although most older people prefer to remain where they are familiar. By the 1990s, this migration extended into the central states (notably Oklahoma and Arkansas), the Northwest (especially the Seattle region), and the mountains of Colorado and Montana, helping to rejuvenate many rural and small-town counties. Further, reverse migration became notable, with older retirees leaving homes in Florida and other Sunbelt states to return to their homelands in New England and the Midwest.

Particular regions and areas will have large concentrations of the old and the very old (those 85 years and over requiring the most health care and social services). Only 5 percent of the elderly change their residence in any year; most remain in the community where they spent most of their adult lives. The Northeast and Midwest, in particular, will have large concentrations of the very old among their senior populations (18 percent or more), while inner cities will have disproportionate numbers of poor elderly compared to suburban areas (Population Reference Bureau 1990).

During the 1980s, many states witnessed dramatic growth in their elderly population. Seven states now claim more than a million older people each: California, New York, Florida, Pennsylvania, Texas, Illinois, and Ohio.

Increasingly, this mobility will generate political and economic questions for state and local governments. Should they encourage in-migration of retirees with pension and economic assets to bolster local economies? What happens when those retirees become frail and dependent on public resources for expensive health and long-term care? How will local municipalities respond to the political clout of large numbers of retirees, especially when their opinion voiced at the ballot box conflicts with local politics? Should states allow the elderly to carry over the lower property rates afforded them elsewhere (such as in California)? Local and state governments will need to address these and other questions as the elderly population becomes more diversified through geographic distribution and migration. For example, what does diversity as a whole portend? What effect will it have on senior citizen programs? Why must we factor it into our calculations for the future?

Diversity in the New Aging

Diversity will directly affect access to services, equitable distribution of scarce resources, and financing of benefits. A more heterogeneous elderly population will press for change in the current structure of state and local services. For example, growing numbers of Hispanic and Asian/Pacific Islander elderly will require bilingual and multicultural attention, and high poverty rates among black elderly will make their major sources of income—DI, SSI, and Social Security—a high priority. Also, economic dislocation, along with erosion of pension benefits, will lead, simply, to a greater number of needy older people.

As more elderly become impoverished and public benefit resources shrink, pressure will increase to means-test and target entitlement programs to the poor. Moreover, changing family structures will further burden women who serve as caretakers. Demand will intensify for public long-term care services such as respite care, home-health services, and in-home supportive services. In addition, training of health and social service professionals will soon need to encompass ethnicity, gerontology, sociology, economics, and demography.

Growing diversity will affect not only the elderly, but the character of the United States itself. Changes in family structure, economic variance, ethnic and racial diversification, and geographic mobility already present in the general population carry over into elderly groups. Younger people, especially children, face increasing poverty that possibly will culminate in an old age of deprivation and dependence. As the widening gap between rich and poor polarizes social strata, and the size of the elderly population increases, the importance of diversity grows.

Diversity will make solving problems complex and politically sensitive. Divisiveness and factionalism, inherent risks in a heterogeneous population, will strain unity and social cohesiveness. A myriad of special-interest groups, representing an increasingly fragmented society, will demand policy reform and pressure political decision makers. In the 1990s, and throughout the period of the New Aging, U.S. society will become stratified by age, race, economic and social class, and language. We might see a unique ethnic and political development, where a largely white, retiree group is supported by a largely young, minority population. Those developments will put a strain on our historical ability to assimilate diverse groups.

Nonetheless, diversity brings with it inherent benefits and opportunities. It prevents stagnation and complacency, often found in homogeneous societies where little changes over generations (e.g., Japan). Immigration will be viewed as essential to maintaining a healthy economy in an aging society. Diversity will force us to confront the need for change, to look ahead, and to respond to disparate interests. It might save us from the interest-group politics of previous decades, where legislation and policies tried to meet the needs of any politically influential group through categorical programs. Universal coverage and social insurance approaches that do not distinguish by social, racial, or age characteristics, but by need, might gain favor. In all likelihood, diversity will require an activist governmental presence to sort out competing demands. Diversity might force us to decide: What are the basic needs of every member of the population? What is the bottom line in allocating scarce public resources? How can we insure that the government meets basic needs (such as health and long-term care and national standards for training older workers) without diluting them by incorporating provisions for less needy groups? What are the underlying values and principles upon which a society should rely in allocating scarce resources? How can we respond to the collective needs of a diversified population, and not just those of the most vocal interest groups?

These and other questions will require answers in the 1990s. Diversity will complicate generational claims, and both will be affected by a third, inevitable force: longevity.

LONGEVITY

Living longer affects us all. Over two-thirds of the increase in longevity the world over, from prehistoric time until the present, has occurred since 1900 (Riley and Riley 1986). Of major importance, it is "affecting the number of years of life that lie behind as well as ahead, both for individuals and their relatives and significant others" (Riley & Riley 1986, 55). Increased longevity adds years within which we will alter plans, expectations, and lifestyles. Since before the time of Ponce de Leon, we have sought the Fountain of Youth. In a small way, by increasing our longevity, we have found it. An increased life span will directly influence our restructuring and modification of senior-citizen benefits and programs and our approach to aging.

What is longevity and how has it come to be crucial to the New Aging of our society? Longevity is a function of several factors: aging, mortality, life expectancy, and morbidity. These encompass when we will die, how illness can reduce life expectancy, and to what degree we are active and healthy in our old age. Longevity in human terms refers to the "maximum period of time that members of a species live under optimum circumstances" (Hayflick 1987, 22). According to Leonard Hayflick, this can reach nearly 115 years. Actual longevity, however, is charted in life expectancy rates.

In 1986, life expectancy for the total population at birth had reached 75 years: 71.3 years for men; 78.3 years for women. Differences exist among subgroups. By 1990, life expectancy at birth had increased to 76 years: 72 years for men; 79 years for women. The life expectancy of blacks in 1986 was 65.2 years for men and 73.5 years for women, compared to 72 years for white men and 78.8 years for white women (U.S. Bureau of the Census 1989, 72). Life expectancy increased for every age group. For example, between 1961 and 1986, men 65 years and over saw their remaining years increase from 13 to 14.7. Women witnessed a similar increase: 15.8 to 18.6 years (U.S. Bureau of the Census 1989, 72). Nearly half of today's 20-year-olds can expect to reach age 80, compared to less than one in four in the 1930s (Population Reference Bureau 1990).

Women continue to live longer than men by an average of 7 to 8 years. From 1950 to 1980, life expectancy at birth for the total population increased by 5.5 years, while for women it increased by 6.3 years (U.S. Senate 1988, 24). The gap, however, seems to be decreasing. Around 7 years in 1985, it was 7.4 years in 1980 and 7.7 years in 1970 (U.S. Senate 1988, 24).

Mortality and morbidity partially explain improvements in longevity. Death rates have declined significantly in the older age groups, more so for older women than men. These declines have especially benefited the young-old—those from 65 to 84 years. The three largest causes of death in older people are heart disease, cancer, and stroke. Death rates from heart disease and stroke have declined since 1968, especially for women. Cancer deaths, however, have increased (U.S. Senate 1988).

With advances in medical technology and research we can expect mortality and morbidity rates to improve and continue to extend life expectancy. If death rates continue to decline at the 1970s rate, the Social Security Administration (SSA) projects life expectancy at birth in the year 2000 will be 80.4 years (Population Reference Bureau 1984). The Census Bureau predicts that by 2020 the average life expectancy will be 82.0 years for women and 74.2 years for men (Schneider and Guralnik, 1990).

In comparing these rates to those of earlier periods, we can see a dramatic change in human longevity. In 1900, life expectancy at birth was around 49 years for white women, 47 years for white men. For other races combined, it was 34 years for women and 33 years for men (Taeuber 1990). What are the implications of increased longevity? How will it affect political and policy decisions regarding the care of the elderly?

Shorter life expectancies compress the life span and influence its attendant notions of lifestyle and group experience. An average life span of only 47 years gives different meaning to middle and old age. One would be considered elderly while in the 40s and 50s, middle-aged in the 30s and even 20s. Less time is available in which to achieve, to make a difference. When the life span extends into the 80s, each of its stages expands, allowing for multiple careers and a variety of lifestyles. It is no coincidence that the demand for large-scale programs devoted exclusively to the elderly gained impetus with increasing life expectancy.

Retirement and leisure in old age are relatively recent phenomena—a staple of old age only since the early part of this century. Multiple careers and late-life education and training are functions of increased longevity. Longevity and a longer life span necessitate changes in our lifestyles, values, careers, and interpersonal relationships. People in their 40s and 50s are considered young compared to those in their 70s and 80s. We can look toward four quarters of a life cycle: the first 25 years in which to grow and learn, the second quarter to achieve, the third to enjoy the fruits of our labor, and the fourth to be "elders" (Pifer and Bronte 1986).

Life expectancy is approaching 100. In 1986, for example, there were over 25,000 centenarians, compared to 15,000 in 1980 (U.S. Department of Health and Human Services 1987). As our ideas of aging rapidly change, the demand for reform of programs originally developed for a population with a shorter life span intensify.

Increased longevity raises critical questions regarding our care of the frail elderly. Will young married couples be able to care for their elders? Can we develop a comprehensive, long-term care system offering the elderly the choice of remaining at home with their families, living on their own in the community, or, when it becomes necessary, entering an institution such as a hospital or nursing home?

Longevity will also alter our views on work and retirement. Can we afford to retire at 62 or earlier, when a decreasing labor force requires the productivity of older people? Will the retirement income of retirees living an additional twenty to thirty years be sufficient?

Living longer raises ethical and philosophical issues. What is our role in society throughout a longer life span? How do we teach young people to plan for and use a longer life span productively? Our ability to prolong life also means we can prolong death. Should we control the use of medical technology for the terminally ill? Is it fair to foster an increased life expectancy when we give little priority to improving the quality of life for the very old? Will we allow euthanasia? What are the rights and duties of a new generation of elders in society?

Life expectancies at both birth and age 65 will, in all likelihood, continue to increase. The 1990 census, however, indicates a leveling off or decline in life-expectancy rates for some population groups (e.g., black males). If this were to become a trend, it would, of course, raise other implications. We would need to know why. Are their rates of alcoholism and homicide higher, or is there a natural biological cap? A reduction in life expectancy might mean fewer older persons in the next century, or it may mean fewer older persons with chronic disabilities. Regardless, the number of older persons will increase, and the dramatic increases that have, since early in this century, already occurred mean longevity's effect on the population will have to be confronted. In the absence of catastrophic events, we must assume that by the time the baby-boomer cohort reaches old age, we will be living longer than today. Given that assumption, we must question the ability of today's system of programs and benefits to adequately support a growing older population with increased life span.

Longevity also means that more elders living longer will be politically active. How will this impact public policy decisions? Will it exacerbate generational claims? How does the growing diversity of the population interact with a longer life span?

Generational claims, diversity, and increased longevity are forces that will shape the New Aging well into the twenty-first century. In fact, they are already at work. State and local governments must decide whether to allocate limited funds to the homeless, to working families without health insurance, to older persons requiring long-term care, or to some other needy group. Indicative of diversity and generational claims are political struggles underway between upper-income elders opposing tax increases to pay for added Medicaid protection and low-income groups seeking expanded health-care coverage by requiring higher-income groups to pay more. A growing awareness by baby boomers that Social Security might be less generous to them than it was for their grandparents and parents is manifesting itself in the establishment of lobbies claiming to represent their interests in an aging society.

The potential effect of these three factors might appear threatening, but we must not let our apprehensions prevent us from acting. By using generational claims, diversity, and longevity as a gauge to measure the challenges ahead and our ability to meet them, we can face the future with confidence. Yesterday's system of programs and benefits, however well-intentioned, will not fully meet the needs of the populace of tomorrow. We must recognize the urgent need for change in our system of providing for older people—for *all* people—and through a dynamic, albeit fluid process, prepare for the aging of the next century.

NOTES

1. The historical role of older people has changed over time. Age alone has not always commanded respect and deference. In nomadic societies, youth and physical strength were esteemed, although the elderly commanded important spiritual and social authority (e.g., oral history, religious customs). Agrarian societies elevated the status of older people (especially men) because they were more likely to own material resources (such as land or livestock) and could take advantage of inheritance customs, where a father could pass on property to his elder sons. Institutionalization of property rights gave the elderly considerable control over the young, but also created intergenerational tensions and resentments (Williamson et. al. 1982).

Industrialization and migration to cities favored productivity over age, thus eroding the status of the elderly. Many elders were left behind in rural areas or faced poverty and alienation when unable to compete for industrial jobs.

In times of war, youth acquires higher status, while in modern societies, particularly democracies, which value education and merit, status is not granted automatically to older persons. It must be earned. However, gerontocracies are likely where religion or authority prevail.

2. Use of age 65 for eligibility purposes is becoming less relevant to many individuals. The trend is toward earlier retirement, with age 62 a more common year for leaving the work force. There are indications, however, that this trend might be reversing. In addition, federal programs use other ages for benefit receipt: age 60 for Older Americans Act services; age 55 for the Title V Senior Employment Programs; age 62 for partial Social Security benefits and senior-citizen housing programs.

3. The 1983 Social Security Amendments provided for the first change in normal retirement age since the program's inception. The age will gradually rise to 67 by the year 2027. Early retirement will still be permitted at age 62, but with a greater reduction in benefits than at present (U.S. General Accounting Office 1986).

4. The terms "cohort" and "generation" are used interchangeably but have different meanings, depending on context. Generation indicates "sameness with one group; distinctiveness from another" (Bengston et al. 1985, 306). It can be applied in two ways: to a population living at one point in time ("the elderly generation of the 1990s must give up some benefits"); or to a group born during a common period ("the baby-boom generation will create their own popular culture as they age").

Cohort is defined as "an aggregate of individuals born within the same time interval (usually five or ten years)" (Bengston et al. 1985, 306). Such a cluster of individuals would be influenced by the same historical events and socialized according to similar experiences.

Generation, as a descripter, is used when referring to a particular group with a popular identifier: baby boom, baby boomlet, swing generation, silent generation. Generation is useful when comparing several groups at one point in time (for example, "The Baby Busters will be affected by the political decisions of the baby boomers"). Age cohort and age generation are used in discussing the passage of a particular cohort through the life cycle (for example, "the baby-boom cohort is approaching middle age, while the age cohort born in the 1920s is retiring and expecting to retain Social Security cost-of-living increases").

5. The cohort is a useful conceptual tool for understanding political behavior and attitudes of groups born at a particular point in time. While many other factors (e.g., education, income, class) influence an individual's political views, cohort "influences have an impact upon, and do leave traces within, the contemporary attitudes and behaviors of men and women" (Bengston et al. 1985, 308). A more refined cohort measure is to distinguish between inter- and intra-cohort relationships. Inter- and intra-cohort dynamics argue that rather than conflicts among generations at a given point in time (such as, parent vs. child vs. grandchild), conflict is more likely among and within cohorts based on factors other than age (such as poor elderly and poor young vs. wealthy elderly). The inter- and intra-cohort analysis allows for greater variations and diversity in an aging population where socioeconomic circumstances might be more important than belonging to a specific age group.

6. While she was my student at the University of Southern California, Skip Hallaron coined the term "boomerang generation" to describe how actions and inactions by the baby boomers will reverberate on the group that follows.

7. Socialization is the process by which an individual's values, beliefs, attitudes, and behavior are influenced by environment: family, education, class, culture, religion. Political socialization refers to the development of ideas and positions about politics, ideology, philosophy, and authority. Political socialization is most pronounced during the teens and early 20s, and the events, actions, and activities occurring then usually stay with an individual throughout that person's lifetime.

8. Neil Howe and his colleague William Strauss expanded the generational analogy to include a cyclical view of American history (Strauss and Howe 1991). They identify four distinct generational characteristics that repeat themselves throughout American history (including the twentieth century): the "Idealist" generation (baby-boomers) attempted to force social change; the "Reactive" generation (the baby boomlet) is more pragmatic and conservative (the authors also

call these the "13ers" as their generation is the thirteenth in American history); the "Civic" generation (today's senior citizens) faced challenges during the Depression and World War II; and the "Adaptive" generation (the silent generation) is a conformist, yet sensitive group that has benefitted from the Civic generation's actions. Strauss and Howe argue that these four generations act as a check-and-balance to correct each of the others' excesses.

9. During the 1990 annual meeting of the Gerontological Society of America, Vern Bengston presented the theme of "reciprocity" as crucial to minimizing generational tensions (1990). He argues that we must introduce the concept of reciprocal relationships—generations owe each other—in order to avoid generational competition.

10. Successive waves of immigrants to the United States faced unique brands of racism, nativism, and discrimination. Early Dutch and German settlers were discriminated against by Anglo-Saxon "Yankees" during the mid–1800s. Central Europeans (Hungarians, Slavs, Jews, Russians) were scorned by the established ethnic groups of the latter 1800s. Italians and Irish immigrants faced segregation and nativism by Europeans already settled in eastern cities, while Puerto Ricans faced similar discrimination by non-Spanish-speaking groups.

BIBLIOGRAPHY

Bengston, Vern. "Generations and Aging: Continuities, Conflicts, and Reciprocities." Presidential Address to the 43rd Annual Meeting of the Gerontological Society of America, Nov. 17, 1990. Boston, Mass.

Bengston, Vern, Neal Cutler, David Mangen, and Victor Marshall. "Generations, Cohorts, and Relations Between Age Groups." In *Handbook of Aging and the Social Sciences,* edited by Robert Binstock and Ethel Shanas. New York: Van Nostrand Reinhold Company, 1985: 304–38.

Durkheim, E. (1893). *The Division of Labor in Society.* New York: The Free Press, 1964.

Hayflick, Leonard. "Origins of Longevity." In *Modern Biological Theories of Aging,* edited by Huber R. Warner, Richard L. Sprott, Robert N. Butler, and Edward L. Schneider. New York: Raven Press, 1987.

Herz, Diane. Bureau of Labor Statistics. "Employment Characteristics of Older Women, 1987." *Monthly Labor Review* (September 1988): 3.

Hewitt, Paul, and Neil Howe. "Generational Equity and the Future of Generational Politics." *Generations* 12, 3 (Spring 1988): 10–13.

Marshall, Victor. "Tendencies in Generational Research: From the Generation to the Cohort and Back to the Generation." In *Intergenerational Relationships,* edited by Vjenka Garms-Homolova, Erika Hoerning, and Doris Schaeffer. Lewiston, N.Y.: C. J. Hogrefe, Inc., 1984: 207–18.

Pifer, Alan, and Lydia Bronte. *Our Aging Society.* New York: W.W. Norton & Company, 1986.

Population Reference Bureau. "America in the 21st Century: A Demographic Overview." Washington, D.C.: Population Reference Bureau and the Population Resource Center, May 1989.

———. "America in the 21st Century: Social and Economic Support Systems."

Washington, D.C.: Population Reference Bureau and the Population Resource Center, December 1990.

——. "Death and Taxes: The Public Policy Impact of Living Longer." Washington, D.C.: Population Reference Bureau and the Population Resource Center, September 1984.

"Profile of Tomorrow's New U.S." *U.S. News and World Report*, Nov. 24, 1986, 32.

Rapson, Richard, ed. *The Cult of Youth in Middle-Class America*. Lexington, Mass.: D.C. Heath and Company, 1971.

Riley, Matilda White, and John W. Riley, Jr. "Longevity and Social Structure: The Potential of the Added Years." In *Our Aging Society*, edited by Alan Pifer and Lydia Bronte. New York: W.W. Norton & Company, 1986: 53–78.

Schneider, Edward, and Jack Guralnik. "The Aging of America: Impact on Health Care Costs." *Journal of the American Medical Association* 263, 17 (May 2, 1990): 2335–40.

Social Security Administration. U.S. Department of Health and Human Services. *Social Security Bulletin: Annual Statistical Supplement*. Washington, D.C.: U.S. Government Printing Office, 1990.

Spencer, Gregory. U.S. Bureau of the Census. "Projection of the Hispanic Population: 1983–2080." *Current Population Reports*, ser. P-25, no. 995. Washington, D.C.: Government Printing Office, November 1986.

Strauss, William, and Neil Howe. *Generations: The History of America's Future, 1584 to 2069*. New York: William Morrow, 1991.

Taeuber, Cynthia. "Diversity: The Dramatic Reality." In *Diversity in Aging: Challenges Facing Planners and Policymakers in the 1990s*, edited by S. Bass, E. Kutza, and F. Torres-Gil. Glenview, Ill.: Scott, Foresman & Company, 1990: 1–46.

U.S. Bureau of the Census. *Statistical Abstract of the United States: 1989*. 109th ed. Washington, D.C.: U.S. Government Printing Office, 1989.

U.S. Department of Health and Human Services. "America's Centenarians: Data from the 1980 Census." Washington, D.C.: U.S. Government Printing Office, 1987: 12.

U.S. Department of Justice. *1987 Statistical Yearbook of the Immigration and Naturalization Service*. Washington, D.C.: U.S. Government Printing Office, 1987: Table 2, p. 3.

U.S. General Accounting Office. "Retirement before Age 65: Trends, Costs, and National Issues." (GAO/HRD 86–86). Washington, D.C.: U.S. Government Printing Office, July 1986.

U.S. Senate. *Aging America: Trends and Projections*. Washington, D.C.: U.S. Government Printing Office, 1988.

Villers Foundation. *On the Other Side of Easy Street: Myths and Facts about the Economics of Old Age*. Washington, D.C.: The Villers Foundation, 1987.

Vobejda, Barbara. "Average Household Shrinks as More in U.S. Live Alone." *The Washington Post*, May 1, 1991.

Welniak, Edward. U.S. Bureau of the Census. "Money, Income for Households, Families, and Persons in the United States: 1987." *Current Population*

Reports, ser. P–60, no. 162. Washington, D.C.: U.S. Government Printing Office, 1989.
Williamson, J. B., L. Evans, and L. A. Powell. *Politics of Aging*. Springfield, Ill.: Charles C. Thomas, 1982.

2
AMERICA AT
THE CROSSROADS

With ruin upon ruin, rout on rout,
Confusion worse confounded.

John Milton, *Paradise Lost*

This chapter looks at the development of social policies for the elderly and the current state of old-age benefits and services. Such an exploration will reveal ways in which these programs and benefits must be changed to meet the requirements of the New Aging. Examining the characteristics of social policies helps us understand existing pressures to reform them and what effect such change will have on future cohorts of older people. This chapter will explore the underlying premises of the major social programs, the transformation, over time, of their original intent, and our contradictory expectations that make them complicated instruments of social engineering. As importantly, it will shed light on the competing philosophical and ideological views of a democratic and capitalist system influencing our response to the social and cultural concerns of older people and other dependent populations.

THE DEMOGRAPHIC IMPERATIVE

Before examining social policies for the elderly, we must understand the demographic revolution underway in the United States. Population aging fundamentally affects public policymaking and attitudes.[1] In the public arena, population aging has implications for the system of delivering and financing health and social services to the elderly and their families.

In the private sector, population aging affects recruiting and employment policies as well as the design of benefit and compensation packages. The metamorphosis of old-age benefits and programs over the next several decades will coincide with the aging of the U.S. population.

At the beginning of this century, fewer than one in ten Americans were 55 and over; one in twenty-five was age 65 and over. By 1986, one in five Americans was at least 55 years old; one in eight was at least 65 (U.S. Senate 1986). Since 1900, the percentage of Americans 65 and over has tripled (4.1 percent in 1900 to 12.1 percent in 1986), and their number increased by over nine times (from 3.1 to 29.2 million) (AARP 1987). By 1987, 12.2 percent of the U.S. population was 65 and over, up from 9.2 percent in 1960, while the median age increased from 29.4 years to 32.1 years during the same period (U.S. Bureau of the Census 1989). By 1990 the median age had increased to 33 years with projections that it would reach 36 years by 2000 and 40 years by 2010 (Social Security Administration 1990). The number of Americans 65 and older increased by 21 percent between 1980 and 1990, compared to an 8 percent increase for the remainder of the population during that same period (AARP 1990).

The 75-plus population is the fastest growing age group in the elderly population. The 65–74 age group is eight times larger than in 1900; the 75–84 group is twelve times larger; and the 85-plus group is twenty-two times larger (AARP 1987). The 85-and-over group is expected to quadruple in size between 1980 and 2030.

The real increase, however, is yet to come. The dramatic growth of the older population during the 1960s and 1970s will slow somewhat during the 1990s because of the relatively smaller number of babies born during the Great Depression of the 1930s. The most rapid increase in the New Aging will occur between the years 2010 and 2030, when the baby boomers reach age 65.

The projected growth of that population will raise the median age of the U.S. population from 33 today to 37 by the year 2000, and to age 42 by 2020 (U.S. Senate 1989). The proportion of people 65 years and over will grow from 13 percent in 2000 to 22 percent in 2030, representing approximately 66 million people 65 years and over (AARP 1990). The aging of the U.S. population will revitalize in 2010, with the maturation of the baby boomer. By then, over a quarter of the U.S. population will be at least 55 years old; one in seven will be at least 65 years old. By 2030, when the baby boom cohort (by then, the "senior boom") enters later life, fully one in three will be 55 years and older; one in five will be 65 and over (U.S. Senate 1986).

The demographic drama will not end there. As described in Chapter 1, the elderly population will have diversified. A greater proportion will be nonwhite (Hispanic, black, Asian-Pacific Islander, Native American). Young people will be fewer. The Census Bureau projects that by the year

2030, the number of Americans under 35—55 percent of the population in 1989—will drop to 41 percent. After the year 2030, if current trends continue, deaths will outstrip births every year ("Older, Slower-Growing America Predicted" Feb. 1, 1989). What does this mean? In simple terms, the U.S. will be a nation of older, more diverse and complex groups with a declining proportion of youth.

What do these facts mean for social policies to older people? How will population aging affect our values, attitudes, and reactions to political forces? How will these projections affect our views of providing public benefits and programs to older persons?

Increases in the absolute number of older people and expanding longevity mean, in crudest terms, more people requiring assistance and more without families. To the extent that we want to provide a basic level of health, income, and social services (as we attempt to now), government, the private sector, and families must increase the current level of benefits, services, and programs severalfold. How to do so and pay for such increase is the dilemma of the next twenty years.

Demographic change also leads to greater awareness of aging. When one-fifth or a quarter of the population reaches 55, a critical mass develops, where norms, values, and peer influence add to our awareness of aging. Advertisements and marketing campaigns targeting older people are proof that a senior lifestyle is developing.

With this greater awareness of aging and its attendant affiliations will come increased political consciousness aimed at preserving and enhancing benefits and privileges to the elderly. A larger, more potent constituency—based on numbers, voting power, and shared interests—will extraordinarily impact public and political decisions concerning receipt of and payment for services.

We can expect greater tension and competition over the escalating cost of assisting an older and larger age cohort. Generational politics might become the norm, combined with class, race, and ideology. Increasingly, we might, as taxpayers and voters, judge issues by our age and generational status. Chapter 3 explores the issues resulting from the politics of the New Aging.

What the economy can bear and how the federal budget is affected will be critical public and private policy concerns. Assuming the economy does not improve, choices and tradeoffs among equally legitimate needs will become more frequent. Pressures to means-test or target resources to the more needy might increase, as will efforts to preserve entitlement programs and avoid attaching a "welfare stigma" to them. Chapter 4 examines the economic implications of population aging.

On the other hand, handling demographic pressures need not be only doom and gloom. A more educated older population living longer can provide a larger, healthier, and productive base for filling labor shortages and boosting a high technology economy prizing adaptability and learning. An older constituency makes up a tremendous consumer and products market whose disposable income will greatly influence an expanding economy. Greater social stability and fewer crimes will be the hallmarks of a more mature population.

This rosier projection, however, presupposes we have redefined aging by minimizing stereotypes, ageism, and age discrimination. It assumes we have redefined the provision of old-age benefits to account for increased longevity and greater diversity within the population, and that we have instituted new methods for educating and training an older population in order to integrate them into a mainstream economy.

The demographic respite of the 1990s provides a golden opportunity to reexamine our views of older people and the manner in which we will provide for those who need public and private assistance. We can alter the premises underlying public policies—premises that assume dependency and stereotypic age characteristics—and modify benefits and services to fit a healthier, longer-living population with a more diverse set of needs.

The 1990s are an opportune time for reshaping social policies, but to do so will not be easy. We have already made a great personal and public investment in the existing system of public services and benefits. During the period of the Modern Aging, a vast array of legislation, regulations, benefits, and services evolved to assist older people and their families. Individuals and families have come to depend on a multiplicity of agencies, jobs, funding, and programs. Interest groups and constituencies have much at stake in preserving the current set of social policies. It is painfully clear, however, that given our demographic fate and the exigencies of the New Aging, business as usual is a poor approach. Before suggesting changes, we must first examine existing programs and their history.

THE EXISTING ARRAY OF SOCIAL POLICIES

What are the laws, programs, and services comprising our current public response to the needs of older people? Why are they often referred to as the "aging network?" How is this network structured, and what are its characteristics?

Our mesh of social policies for older people is many things to many people. To a frail, older person living alone, it often is a bewildering set of forms, tied-up phone lines, and harried bureaucrats. For those working in gerontology and social work, it is an expanding and exciting profession. For advocates, liberals, and believers in big government, it is a sacred welfare state. To the private sector and voluntary agencies, it often seems a quasi-socialistic intrusion on families and individuals. For many senior citizens and their families, it is an important source of income, social support, and benefits.

All these perceptions contain some element of truth. Existing social policies for older people include a vast array of fragmented, complicated, but important agencies, services, and benefits. They encompass legislation authorizing a variety of direct and indirect benefits and services, agencies to administer them, a constituency protecting them, and professionals to work with the elderly and their families.

The source of most legislation and resultant benefits is the federal government. State and local governments provide substantial additional services and are charged with their delivery. Insurance companies and contract agencies handle much of the paperwork associated with reimbursement. Nonprofit and for-profit organizations coordinate and deliver services to the aged.

This array of social policies can be viewed in many ways. One possibility is to regard them as policy areas focused on specific issues. There are several examples.

Income policy. There are laws and benefits intended to provide supplemental income in retirement or to compensate or replace money lost due to early retirement or disability, or to provide a minimal income for the very poor. The former include the Old-Age Survivors Insurance (OASI) program (part of the Social Security system) and private or public pensions. The latter include Disability Insurance (DI) and the Supplemental Security Income (SSI) program, both part of Social Security legislation. Income policy can also include tax benefits, often provided at the state and local level: property-tax relief, capital gains exclusion for sale of personal residence, retirement-income credit, and tax exemption of benefits from Social Security and railroad retirement systems.

Health policy. Medicare (HI) is the primary provider for costs associated with hospital care and certain medical services for the elderly. Medicaid, although designated a health-care coverage program for the very poor, serves as the major provider of nursing-home care for middle-income senior citizens. Non-institutional long-term care—respite, adult day health care, home health care, hospice, case management, and social/ health maintenance organizations (SHMOs)—is paid for by a hodgepodge of uncoordinated benefit programs such as Medicare, Medicaid, federal waivers to states to use Medicare and Medicaid, federal and state demonstration programs, and private, for-profit agencies.

Housing policy. Publicly subsidized housing and rent for senior citizens, and tax credits to mortgage firms and developers are the key aspects of housing policy. Primary programs include public housing, with specific units designed for the elderly; Section 202, a direct loan program for constructing senior-citizen housing; and Section 8, a rental subsidy program. In addition, the federal government is developing a congregate

housing services program (that is, providing both housing and social supports). In the private sector, life-care retirement communities, mobile-
home parks, boardinghouses, and condominiums for the elderly proliferate.

Social services policy. The Social Services Block Grant (Title XX of
the Social Security Act), although not specifically for older persons, is a
major source of in-home supportive services for families and their parents.
The Older Americans Act is the best-known of social service benefits,
providing a wide array of nutrition services, multiservice centers, information and referrals, ombudsman and legal assistance, transportation,
employment and training, and case-management programs.

Civil rights and legal policies. These include antidiscrimination laws
and enforcement agencies. Efforts to combat ageism and age discrimination resulted in establishment of the Age Discrimination in Employment Act of 1967 (ADEA) and, more recently, amendments forbidding
mandatory retirement in public and private sectors. The Equal Employment Opportunity Commission is charged with enforcement and the U.S.
Commission on Civil Rights and Federal Council on Aging play watchdog
roles.

Volunteer policy. Volunteer programs for older persons include the
Senior Companion Program, Foster Grandparent Program, Retired Senior
Volunteer Program (RSVP), and the Service Corps of Retired Executives
(SCORE). Programs are administered under the auspices of ACTION—
the federal agency behind the Peace Corps.

Actually, U.S. social policies for the elderly were never intentionally
divided along these policy areas, nor did they arise out of carefully con-
structed plans for the expansion of housing, health, social, civil-rights, or
volunteer policies. Sixty years of political evolution coincidentally (some
would say accidentally) produced these social policies. No two are equal
in terms of dollars or public support. The Social Security Act, the primary
public income policy, captures most public funds and attention. Medicare
and Medicaid, the heart of our health policy, remain the country's quasi-
national health-care system. Other policy areas, specifically housing, social services, and volunteer policies, are secondary in terms of funding
and size, yet by all measure they are equally important in the lives of
older people and their families.

Another way to view social policies for the elderly is by examining
their method of delivering and financing benefits and services to the aged
or their families.[2] Primary federal and state delivery approaches include:

Universal entitlement. These are benefits guaranteed to individuals
based on age and without regard to income. Programs providing services
to older people, regardless of their financial status, include OASI, Medicare, and the Older Americans Act. These tend to enjoy wide support
because they do not exclude people based on income or assets and are

not viewed as "welfare." Although some restrictions are being introduced (such as taxation of partial Social Security benefits), these benefits are viewed as an "earned right" and serve as important sources of support to the families of older people.

Targeted programs. Eligibility for these programs depends on income and assets, and the poor and very poor are usually targeted. The programs involve extensive paperwork and require eligibility workers. Supplemental Security Income (SSI), Disability Insurance (DI) (sometimes coupled with OASI—OASDI), Medicaid, and the Social Services Block Grant are primary means- or asset-tested programs. Disability Insurance, however, relies primarily on a determination of physical disability. Although targeting recipients based on income, assets or physical disability is an effective way to utilize limited funding, these programs enjoy less political support than entitlement programs.

Third-party reimbursements. These are benefits paid to another person or party providing a direct service to an older person or his or her family. Health and long-term care benefits often rely on third-party reimbursements. With Medicare, for example, insurance companies or other organizations under contract with the federal government process claims.

Direct services. Some programs and agencies provide a direct service instead of monetary payment or benefit. The Older Americans Act, SHMOs, and Social Services Block Grant programs provide services using trained professionals. Senior-citizen centers, home-delivered meals, legal assistance, physical therapy, geriatric social work, respite care, and information and referral services are part of an expanding industry of agencies and social service providers. Case management, coordinating a variety of social and supportive services to disabled and ill older people, is an important tool for serving the needy.

These approaches to the delivery and financing of benefits and services, like social policies, were not developed as part of a "master plan." Each is a product of its own legislation and the political decisions that led to its implementation. We have no public consensus on which approach to delivery is best. Advocacy groups for the elderly push for expansion of entitlement programs, while cost-conscious public officials and groups representing the poor argue for a targeted approach. Gerontologists and social workers claim social services composed of trained and licensed staff are essential to quality care; others prefer the utilization of social services funds to provide direct benefits through vouchers. Insurance companies, medical peer review organizations, and contract agencies fear million-dollar federal funding losses if third-party reimbursements are altered.

Increasingly, debates about provision of public and private services to the elderly focus on the method of paying for and delivering those services. In large part, disagreement exists because we view the fundamental pur-

40 The New Aging

poses behind the laws dictating manner of implementation differently. Do
we add long-term care to the Medicare program, thus creating an entitlement to all senior citizens regardless of income? Or, do we add long-term
care to the Medicaid program and, therefore, limit services to low-income
people only? Our answers to these questions are influenced by divergent
philosophical and ideological beliefs reflecting our uncertainty about
whether family, individual, private sector, or government should take
responsibility for the elderly.

Legislation and Benefits

Existing benefits to older people and their families can be further broken
down by legislative origin and specific service provided. Most policies
originate with a federal law authorizing certain services and benefits,
outlining eligibility criteria, establishing administrative structure, and ap-
propriating funds for such services. As shown in Figure 2.1, several major
legislative acts and programs provide the bulk of benefits and services.
Within these, especially the Social Security Act, are many more *titles*,
or sections of an act authorizing major programs and benefits, and *amendments*, revising, adding, deleting, or modifying provision of benefits.

The Social Security Act

The Social Security Act, first passed in 1935, is the cornerstone of
legislation for older people. It is also called the "third rail" of politics—
to touch it is to risk political suicide. The act sets up three trust funds:
Old-Age and Survivors Insurance (OASI), Hospital Insurance (HI), and
Disability Insurance (DI). It includes Medicare Part A and Part B, Medicaid (a federal-state partnership), Supplemental Security Income (SSI),
and the Social Services Block Grant (Title XX).

It encompasses the largest portion of the federal budget. Social Security
and Medicare paid $327 billion in benefits in 1989, most of it tax-free. In
1989, thirty-nine million people received monthly checks (40 million in
1990), and 130 million paid into the system expecting to receive benefits
later. Contrary to popular thought, only about half of that $327 billion
was paid in monthly benefits to retired workers (Detlefs and Myers 1988).
The rest went to disabled workers; families of workers who have retired,
become disabled, or died; and, to cover medical expenses under Medicare.
The specific sections of the Social Security Act are the underpinning for
old-age benefits.

Social Security Act benefits and programs remain the best known, most
expensive, and most diverse of social policies for the elderly. From its
beginning as the OASDI program, it has expanded to include a greater
variety of benefits and protections. To most people, however, Social

Figure 2.1. Benefits and Services

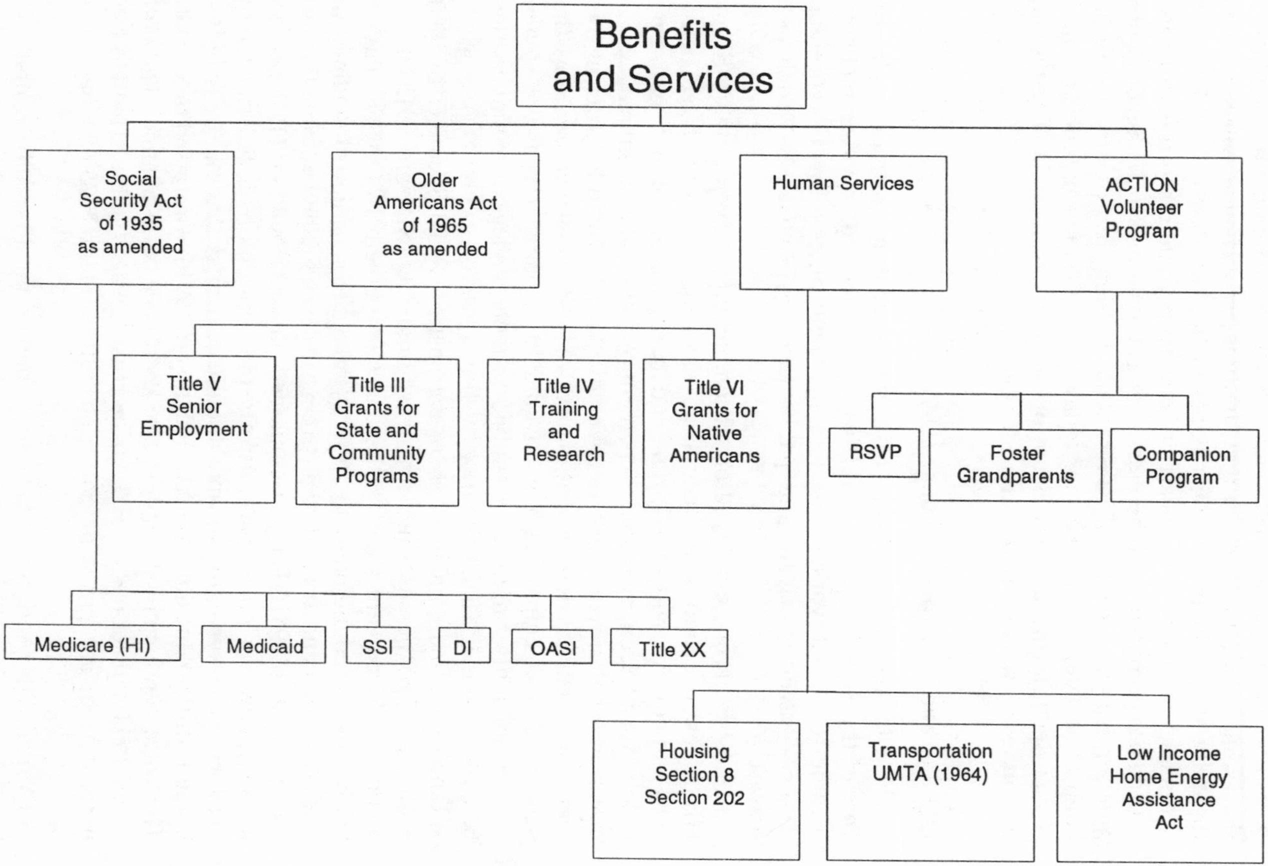

Illustration prepared by Brian Louis Lipshy.

Security is the monthly check to retirees. Its complexity masks comprehensive health and social benefits also provided. Social Security is the
basis for the "social contract," an implicit understanding by members of
the swing generation that, in their lifetime, government will not fundamentally alter benefits or their manner of funding.

Social Security is at the heart of controversy and discord surrounding
retirement preparation in the New Aging. Financing Social Security programs raises the specter of generational burden in providing for future
cohorts of older people. Yet, for today's beneficiaries and their families,
Social Security means a modicum of security and income. The thought
of tampering with it creates considerable anxiety.

Old-Age and Survivors Insurance (OASI)

The Old-Age and Survivors Insurance trust fund is traditionally the
core of the Social Security Act. It was established to provide a minimum
income to retired workers and to supplement other forms of retirement
income—savings, private and public pensions, and assets (such as a
house).

Almost everyone employed or self-employed is covered by OASI and
HI. A few exceptions are federal government employees hired before
1984 and covered only by HI; state and local government units opting not
to join Social Security (about 70 percent of state and local employees are
covered); and railroad workers covered by the Railroad Retirement System. The Omnibus Reconciliation Act of 1990, however, requires that
state and local employees not covered by a public retirement system
(except students employed by public schools, colleges, or universities)
be covered under Social Security by July 1, 1991.

Employees and employers share the cost of Social Security. In 1990,
each paid 7.65 percent into two trust funds: OASDI and HI. Of this
amount, 1.45 percent went to HI, and 6.06 percent to OASDI. Payroll
tax has increased dramatically. Shortly after the program's founding, the
rate was 1 percent. It reached 3 percent in 1960; 5.2 percent in 1971; and
6.65 percent in 1981. The self-employed pay a higher rate (15.3 percent
in 1991); however, this is partially offset by a credit on the federal income
tax form. The maximum taxable amount (earnings that can be taxed) is
limited. In 1990, the limit was $51,300, and in 1991 it was raised to $53,400.
The wage cap is annually indexed to keep pace with inflation. The Omnibus Reconciliation Act of 1990 increased wages subject to the 1.45
percent Medicare Part A payroll contribution rate to $125,000, beginning
in 1991.

To qualify for retirement benefits, a person must be fully insured and
have the required number of Quarters of Coverage (QCs) under Social
Security. Most workers need 40 QCs to qualify—about 10 years of work.

Retirement benefits are based on the Primary Insurance Account (PIA), a factor of Average Indexed Monthly Earnings (AIME), which, in turn, is based on one's lifetime earnings history. The PIA is the amount payable at normal retirement age (NRA—when full retirement benefits are paid): 65 for those born before 1938. Early retirement means a lower percentage of the PIA (80 percent for retirement at age 62). Beginning in 2003, normal retirement age will gradually increase, rising to 67 by 2027 and the age–62-early-retirement-benefit will gradually change from 80 percent to 70 percent of the NRA benefit level (Detlefs and Myers 1988).

Disability Insurance (DI)

Disability Insurance is not an age- or means-tested program.[3] If one works under Social Security and become severely disabled, one can receive a monthly benefit equal to the PIA at the time of the disability. Disability is defined as a severe impairment, mental or physical, whereby an individual can no longer perform substantial gainful work. The impairment must be expected to last at least twelve months or to result in early death. Benefits for disabled workers increase if they have spouses and dependent children.

DI is a benefit of last resort for disabled people without other sources of income. It is especially important for groups, such as black males, with relatively low life-expectancy rates (Gibson 1987). How strict or generous its definition of disability and eligibility should be is a source of argument. The definition itself is a severe one—"inability to engage in any substantial gainful activity"—making it difficult for DI recipients to engage in part-time work. The burden of proof is on the individual. The personal nature of DI was illustrated during the 1980s, when the Reagan administration was accused of insensitivity for denying large numbers of claims and terminating the benefits of many already receiving them. Ultimately the courts intervened to ensure that disabled beneficiaries were not unfairly penalized by policies focused on reducing DI expenditures rather than serving eligible beneficiaries. Nonetheless, the disability program remains problematic for the 4.3 million persons who depend on it. It can take an average of three months to process an initial claim. If the claim is denied, an appeal can take up to a year before benefits arrive. Nearly two-thirds of those rejected who take their case to an appeals judge win ("U.S. Payment of Disability Claims Faulted" 1991). In 1990, Congress improved certain features of the program by streamlining the attorney fee process, ensuring the availability of legal assistance, and permanently extending the provision permitting continuation of disability benefits pending appeal, thus allowing DI beneficiaries to protect their benefits without the legal process's interpretation (U.S. Senate Special Committee on Aging 1991).

Medicare (Title XVIII)

Medicare, signed into law by President Lyndon Johnson in 1965, is the U.S. version of national health care for the aged. It has an age requirement but does not means-test. It is the primary source of publicly funded health care for the elderly.

Medicare has two parts: Part A, Hospital Insurance (HI); and Part B, Supplementary Medical Insurance (SMI). In the late 1980s, a third part, Catastrophic Drug Insurance (CDI), was added but subsequently scaled back. HI protects senior citizens against hospitalization costs, certain related inpatient institutional care, and home health services. SMI deals mainly with doctors' fees.

Parts A and B have different financing mechanisms: HI is primarily paid for by taxes based on covered work before eligibility for benefits; SMI is defrayed by monthly premiums and general revenues from the federal government. Those eligible for Part A are also eligible for Part B (although Part B is voluntary). Part B recipients pay a monthly premium ($29.90 in 1991 and $31.80 in 1992). In addition, they must pay an annual deductible and a patient coinsurance charge. Medicare Part B pays 80 percent of expenses, subject to a maximum of the standard charges recognized by Medicare and considered medically necessary. The Medicare Catastrophic Coverage Act of 1988 would have paid all expenses after the patient had spent $1370 on medical care.

Medicare is acute-care oriented. It primarily covers hospital and skilled-nursing facility costs. It provides limited home health services and hospice benefits and covers mammography screening. It does not cover noninstitutional social services for the chronically ill: personal comfort items, dental services, eye exams and glasses, hearing aids, orthopedic shoes. Part B, the SMI program, covers medical costs: physician services, physical and occupational therapy, diagnostic and laboratory services, and some durable medical equipment.

Medicare is the single largest health-care program for older people in the United States and has greatly improved the availability of hospital care for older people. It is under great strain, however. Its costs and the imposition of cost-containment features (a prospective payment system and a relative value scale) have precipitated more stringent requirements and higher out-of-pocket costs for the elderly. Medicare may face bankruptcy after the year 2000 if medical and doctor bills continue to rise at the 1980s rate. By 1990, Medicare was spending $66.7 billion on Part A, and $43 billion for Part B, serving approximately 30 million persons over age 65 and 3 million disabled Americans of all ages. The cost of the program grew 37 percent faster than the economy during the five years prior to 1990 (Rosenblatt 1991). While Part A is financed by the payroll taxes of 138 million workers and their employers (through the hospital insurance fund), monthly insurance premiums finance only 25 percent of Part B, with the remainder funded by general tax revenues. Fiscal pressures on Medicare will grow. Today, four workers pay taxes for each person enrolled in Medicare. By the middle of the next century, however, this number may drop to two (Rosenblatt 1991).

The Health Care Financing Administration (HCFA), responsible for overseeing Medicare, is experimenting with Health Maintenance Organizations to see if services can be provided at lower costs and without complicated reimbursements. Pressure to include long-term care, not medically prescribed—respite and home care, homemaker/chore services—is intense. A prospective payment system, added to Part A in 1983, imposed cost containment for the first time. Under the Omnibus Budget Reconciliation Act of 1989, cost containment was extended to Part B and doctors will be paid differently than in the past. Reimbursement will be based on a "relative value scale," which assigns a value to service and skills, not treatment. This will reduce the wide disparity in fees that now discourages doctors from going into family practice and geriatric medicine and will reduce reimbursements for medical and surgical specialities and increase payments for general and family practitioners. Although Medicare remains the "national health-care system" for the elderly, its escalating costs and complicated reimbursement processes make using the program difficult both for providers and beneficiaries.

Medicaid (Title XIX)

Title XIX of the Social Security Act authorizes a Medical Assistance (Medicaid) program. If a program can be more complicated than OASI or HI, Medicaid fits the bill. When it was enacted in 1965, it was intended to provide medical care to the poor and medically indigent. Since then it has become the defacto long-term care program for middle-class elderly, paying for the bulk of publicly funded nursing-home care. In 1988, for example, federal and state Medicaid expenditures for nursing-home care amounted to an estimated $19.2 billion, representing approximately 45 percent of total national spending for nursing-home care and over 90 percent of public spending. Medicare, in contrast, accounted for only a small portion of nursing-home care ($800 million in 1988), representing less than two percent of national spending and less than 4 percent of public spending (U.S. Senate Special Committee on Aging 1991).

Medicaid, unlike Medicare, is a grant-in-aid to states. States have the option to participate and have choices on type of eligibility and services covered and fees charged. Not surprisingly, at least fifty different state Medicaid arrangements exist. States choose whether to cover only those enrolled in welfare programs (Aid to Families with Dependent Children [AFDC] and SSI) or to include the medically needy (those who might qualify for money payment programs but exceed asset/income limits for eligibility). In recent years, the federal government has required states to expand eligibility and coverage. For example, The Omnibus Reconciliation Act of 1990 requires that states cover Medicare cost-sharing premiums, deductibles, and coinsurance for beneficiaries 65 and older with incomes below 100 percent of the poverty line and assets below twice the SSI asset level, known as Qualified Medicare Beneficiaries (QMBs). By 1995, the requirement will cover QMBs with incomes below 120 percent of the poverty line.

Medicaid is a means-tested program. States determine income and asset levels required for eligibility. The federal government categorizes services states can offer, including inpatient hospital services, skilled nursing-home services, physicians' services, and some outpatient hospital services.

States find this program a costly burden, even with the federal government picking up 50 to 83 percent of the cost, depending on per capita income of the state. Many older people deplete their assets with medical expenses and turn to Medicaid for skilled nursing-home coverage; therefore, up to 68 percent of the program's funds are being used to pay for nursing-home care (Gelfand 1988). In turn, states have fewer funds for the nonelderly poor. The Reconciliation Act of 1990 provides states with important options. They can provide home- and community-based care to functionally disabled people 65 and over who are otherwise eligible for Medicaid (defined as individuals who are unable to perform two out of three activities of daily living—toileting, traveling, and eating), or have Alzheimer's disease and meet specific tests of functional disability. In addition, states may provide community-supported living-arrangement services for beneficiaries with mental retardation or a related condition. The federal government, however, does not provide additional funds and sets a funding cap on state funding of these options.

Medicaid is seen as a "welfare" program; thus, it does not share the political support enjoyed by OASI and HI. States chafe at the tendency for Congress and the federal government to impose added benefits and requirements without providing additional dollars. In recent years, states have trimmed services, imposed stricter eligibility criteria, and lowered payments to providers, making it harder for poor and older people to receive needed health care and discouraging medical practitioners from participating in the program.

Social Services Block Grant (Title XX)

Title XX of the Social Security Act (passed in 1974) authorizes states to provide social services enabling people to become self-supporting and self-sufficient, protecting children and adults unable to protect themselves, and preventing and reducing inappropriate institutionalization. In

1984, Title XX became a Social Services Block Grant (SSBG) permitting states to receive funds directly from the federal government and to use them with little federal regulation and reporting. Appropriations in FY 1990 and FY 1991 were $2.8 billion for each year (U.S. Senate Special Committee on Aging 1991).

The Social Services Block Grant has traditionally been seen as a program to help children and low-income families, but it also provides important social services to older people. These include: adult day care, foster care, homemaker services, nutrition programs, protective assistance, and services in long-term-care residences.

The importance of this program is demonstrated by the limited availability of state and federal funding for supportive social services to older people and their families. Unless a family can afford to pay private, for-profit agencies for home health, visiting nurses, and homemaker/chore services (essentials for someone caring for a homebound elder or younger person), the only sources for publicly funded services are the Older Americans Act and Social Services Block Grant. In many states, this program is the primary source of in-home supportive services for low-income people.

Supplemental Security Income (SSI) Program (Title XVI)

The Supplemental Security Income program provides benefits to low-income elderly and disabled or blind individuals who satisfy both income and asset eligibility requirements. Authorized in 1972 by Title XVI of the Social Security Act, the SSI program began in 1974 to provide a nationally uniform guaranteed minimum income for the aged, blind, and disabled (U.S. House of Representatives 1988).

To be eligible for SSI payments, monthly income must be under the federally guaranteed payment level (in 1988, $354 for individuals and $532 for couples). About 4.4 million low-income individuals receive SSI. Approximately, one-third were eligible on the basis of age, the rest due to disability or blindness (U.S. House of Representatives 1988).

Becoming eligible for SSI is difficult and can be a demeaning process. The paperwork is imposing and documentation requirements are strict. Recipients must provide personal information about who they live with and what others contribute to them. Those most likely to be eligible are unlikely to have the language, education, or physical ability to fulfill stringent requirements (such as bank statements, receipts, an address). Only about one-half of older people eligible to participate in the SSI program receive benefits, although the Social Security Administration launched several outreach programs in the early 1990s to increase awareness about the program.

SSI is an example of the need to better coordinate social services. SSI applicants must file for all other benefits to which they may be entitled and certain benefits, such as Medicaid and food stamps, may depend upon SSI eligibility. Besides the complexity and amount of paperwork involved, the problem for beneficiaries is that categorical eligibility varies among programs. Conflicting definitions and eligibility groups may confuse recipients and discourage them from seeking all services possible.

Despite its inadequacies in reaching the most vulnerable and needy, SSI is the program of last resort for the poorest in our country. In 1990, the commissioner of Social Security, Gwendolyn King, established the SSI Modernization Task Force (chaired by Dr. Arthur Flemming) to evaluate the strengths and weaknesses of the program. In part, due to those efforts, legislative efforts are underway to increase the program's low minimum payments, to liberalize eligibility requirements, and to reduce the complexity and red tape associated with that program.

Older Americans Act

The Older Americans Act is the primary source of human and social services for the elderly. Enacted in 1965, it has a budget of approximately $900 million dollars and the ambitious goal of "assuring the well-being of the elderly" while serving as the focal point for aging policy within the federal government. The act's administrative structure for accomplishing these goals at federal, state, and local levels includes the federal Administration on Aging (AoA), state units on aging, and locally based area agencies on aging.

One might wonder how $900 million dollars in the hands of one small agency (AoA) within the mammoth Department of Health and Human Services can meet such goals. Despite constraints, the act has created an "aging network" of visible, accessible, and popular community programs and services. These include multipurpose senior-citizen centers, nutrition programs (congregate settings and home-delivered meals), in-home services, residential repairs, housing assistance, ombudsman programs, and a host of social and supportive services.

The act is also an important source of funds for training, research, and discretionary projects and programs (Title IV). Title V of the act establishes community-service employment programs (administered by the Department of Labor) for people over 55 who are either unemployed or whose prospects for employment are limited. Title VI authorizes grants for Native Americans to develop social and nutritional services for the aged.

Notwithstanding its admirable intentions and many accomplishments, the Older Americans Act is under constant scrutiny because of its non-means-tested, universal entitlement features. Any person 60 years and over, regardless of income or need, is entitled to its benefits. The majority of these are in the form of social services administered by nonprofit organizations and local government under contract with area and state agencies on aging. Yet the act's relatively low level of funding requires it to "target" services to those with the "greatest economic and social needs." In recent years, this has increasingly come to mean low-income individuals, minority elderly, people in rural areas, and the frail aged. Targeting services and funding without politically alienating the healthier, more active elderly is a constant challenge.

In addition, the AoA is the only federal agency charged with overseeing federal policy for older Americans. The Social Security Administration, Health Care Financing Administration, National Institute on Aging (NIA), and other agencies involved in serving older people have no such mandate. However, AoA is small and buried deep in the bureaucracy. Historically, it has lacked the "political clout" to influence HHS and other federal agencies. With increasing demand for central leadership, attempts have been made to give AoA additional leverage by requiring that its commissioner report directly to the secretary of Health and Human Services.

In 1991 Secretary of Health and Human Services Louis Sullivan removed the Administration on Aging from the Office of Human Development Services (OHDS) and made it an independent agency in the Office of the Secretary. This move was greeted favorably by the aging network and congressional committees charged with overseeing the Older Americans Act (OAA) and gave Commissioner Joyce Berry the opportunity to influence aging policy at the highest levels of HHS. The feeling was that AoA would gain increased stature and authority to serve as a national advocate and leader for older persons, as stated in the OAA preamble. With its limited budget and staff and increasing statutory requirements, however, whether it will do so remains uncertain. In addition, AoA must face the reaction of certain family and children groups who believe AoA's promotion was at their expense and may signal generational competition within HHS.[4]

Housing

Publicly funded housing programs have been an important public benefit for low-income elderly and for those unable to afford to maintain their own homes or to live alone. The major housing programs are under Department of Housing and Urban Development (HUD) jurisdiction. They include public housing in which a portion of units are reserved for older people. The more popular public housing programs have been Section 8 and Section 202.

Section 8, authorized under the Housing and Community Development Act of 1974, encourages private market development of rental housing for middle- and low-income families. Section 8 provides a monthly rental allowance, subsidizing a tenant's maximum payment of 30 percent of adjusted income. Section 202, originally authorized under the Housing Act of 1959 and reinstated as part of the Housing and Community Development Act of 1974, provides low-interest federal loans to nonprofit sponsors for provision of rental housing for the elderly through new construction or rehabilitation of existing structures. Section 8, Section 202, and public housing have been primary sources of affordable housing for older people.

Funding for HUD-assisted housing programs took a beating during the 1980s, declining by 80 percent between 1981 and 1990 (U.S. Senate Special Committee on Aging 1990). Another problem may occur in the 1990s. Developers of low-income projects who obtained low-interest loans in the 1960s as part of the National Affordable Housing Act will be able to pay off long-term mortgages early, thus terminating their relationship with HUD. This jeopardizes low-income persons, including the elderly, who will face displacement, especially in the high-rent, metropolitan areas of California and New York. An estimated 645,000 low-income apartment units are at risk nationwide. In southern California, approximately half of the tenants affected are elderly (Garcia 1991).

Other Services: Transportation, Energy, Volunteer

Compared to housing programs, transportation services for the elderly are limited. Those that exist are via Section 16(b)(2) of the Urban Mass Transportation Act (UMTA), which provides grants to assist nonprofit organizations in aiding the elderly and handicapped (for example, subsidizing taxis, vans, specialized vehicles). UMTA also specifies that the elderly and handicapped have equal right to public transportation, thus serving as leverage for the installation of elevators at subway stations and hydraulic lifts on buses.

Two federal programs exist to assist low-income persons, including poor elderly, with the high cost of energy: the Low-Income Home Energy Assistance Program (LIHEAP), administered by HHS, and the Department of Energy's (DOE) Weatherization Assistance Program. These programs help low-income individuals weatherize their homes and obtain financial assistance for high energy costs (Gelfand 1988).

Civil Liberties

Social policies for the elderly go beyond services and benefits; they include a variety of legal safeguards and enforcement mechanisms. The Age Discrimination in Employment Act (ADEA), passed in 1967, is intended to promote employment of older people based on ability rather than age and to prohibit discrimination. Amendments provide individuals with the right to initiate action in claiming age discrimination after administrative remedies have been exhausted (Lowy 1980). Ageism in the workplace is a major target of the ADEA, which outlaws age-based discrimination (unless a bona fide requirement of the job) (Gelfand 1988). Amendments to the act have raised the original eligibility ages in private and nonfederal employment to 70 (1978), abolished mandatory retirement for most federal employees (1978), and, finally, eliminated mandatory retirement at any age (1986). The passage in the early 1990s of the Older Workers Protection Act overturned a Supreme Court decision that older employees' benefits are not protected by ADEA.

The Equal Employment Opportunity Commission (EEOC) is charged with enforcing the provisions of this act (along with Title VII of the Civil Rights Act of 1964 and Sections 501 and 505 of the Rehabilitation Act of 1973), and the U.S. Commission on Civil Rights is responsible for monitoring and studying civil rights abuses for all people, including the elderly. Throughout the 1980s, EEOC and the Civil Rights Commission were criticized for not enforcing these provisions or aggressively pursuing instances of age, race, and sex discrimination. The growing number of older workers and abolishment of mandatory retirement ensure that these two agencies and acts will be significant in the coming decades. A more recent law, the Americans with Disability Act, provides civil-rights safeguards to the disabled and handicapped.[5] As the number of older people with chronic and disabling conditions increases, this law might also be an important legislative tool.

State-Level Services

Notwithstanding the action at the federal level regarding social policies for the elderly, states play an increasingly important role in serving the elderly. In recent years, due largely to a deemphasis on federal leadership during the 1980s, states have become more prominent in the design and financing of health policies and social services, and the regulation of long-term care facilities (Lammers 1984). States also feel directly the pressure of an expanding constituency of Senior citizens, as well as federal mandates for cost-sharing and contributions to programs such as Medicaid, the Older Americans Act, and SSI.

In addition to federal Medicaid requirements, states must have a separate department on aging (a state unit on aging) and establish Area Agencies on Aging (AAA) for each Planning and Service Area (PSA).

States also expand indirect income support through tax assistance for both income- and property-tax liabilities and provision of free or reduced-cost services, including bus discounts and reduced fees for educational programs (Lammers 1984). Property tax relief for older people is an especially notable public policy benefit.

Two major avenues of state public policy action are program development and regulatory administration. States, for example, are vital innovators in developing case-management and long-term care techniques and have taken advantage of previous federal waivers (for example, Medicaid Section 2176 Home and Community-Based Waivers), which suspend Medicare and Medicaid restrictions for in-home services, case management, and services for the developmentally disabled. These waivers permitted states to use funds to demonstrate cost-effective systems for delivery of long-term care and to some extent have been supplanted by the option to use Medicaid funds for home- and community-based care for frail elderly.

States are also responsible for a variety of regulations and regulatory management. They oversee insurance plans, license professionals (occupational and physical therapists, marriage and family counselors), and certify board-and-care facilities and nursing homes. At the local level, cities and counties, through their land-use planning function, affect zoning laws that determine the location of health- and long-term care facilities and housing for the elderly.

During a period of decentralization, deregulation, and reduced federal funding, states have become important funding and regulatory instruments in government's response to the needs of older people. They are the first to feel pressure from politically active senior groups, and many now use "senior legislatures" to incorporate the elderly's input into the legislative process.

AGENCIES SERVING THE ELDERLY

Public policies are more than laws, regulations, and benefits. In the U.S. government, they form a vast and complex administrative structure composed of agencies, departments, institutions, and commissions at federal, regional, state, and local levels. These agencies are charged with administering and overseeing the provisions of law authorizing benefits and services to older people. They involve or employ thousands of civil servants and political appointees, countless consultants and contract agencies, and a growing number of people trained in gerontology and geriatrics.

There are several ways to view this administrative structure. The executive branch and its cabinet agencies are the primary sources of federal benefits and services. Figure 2.2 illustrates major cabinet-level agencies and their primary program responsibilities for aging services.

As the chart shows, each cabinet agency is somewhat involved in providing aging services and programs, but the Department of Health and Human Services carries the bulk of responsibility (Figure 2.3). Several independent agencies also handle aging issues.

HHS is divided into several principal operating components. Each of

Figure 2.2. Cabinet Agencies and Program Responsibilities

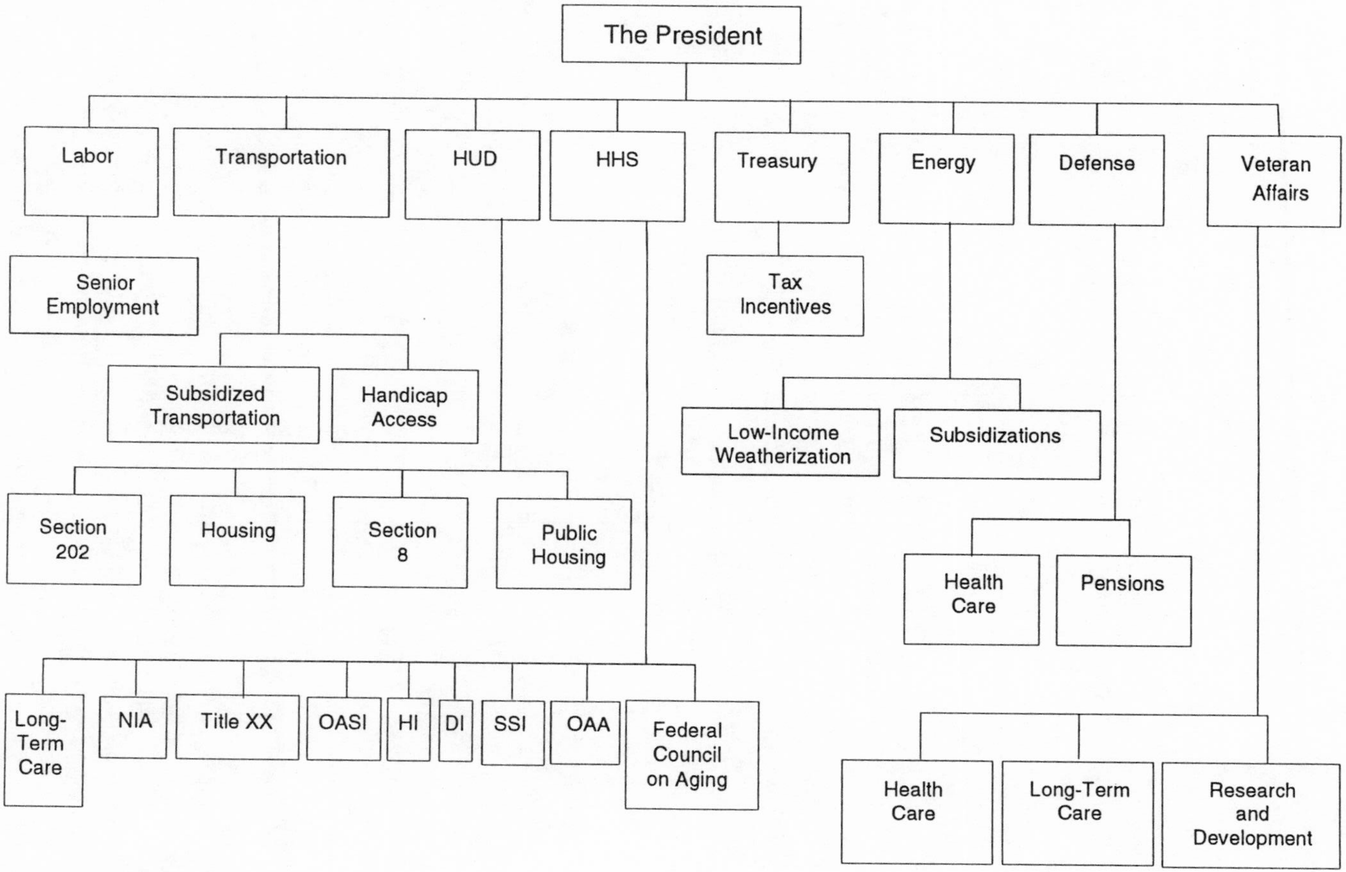

Illustration prepared by Brian Louis Lipshy.

Figure 2.3. Department of Health and Human Services

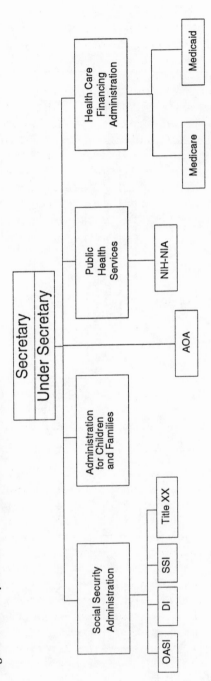

Illustration prepared by Brian Louis Lipshy.

these manages certain program areas. The largest is the Social Security Administration. It directs the OASI, DI, and SSI programs. It is the largest federal agency serving older people. The Office of Human Development Services, now known as the Administration for Children and Families, includes the Maternal and Child Health Block Grant and brings together children and family programs. The AoA implements the provisions of the Older Americans Act (see Figure 2.4). The Health Care Financing Administration (HCFA) administers Medicare and Medicaid benefits and regulations and is responsible for health-care policy and research. It is a major source of research and demonstration projects in long-term and nursing-home care, and health-care financing.

The Public Health Service (PHS) includes the National Institutes of Health (NIH), the nation's premier research center. Within NIH are eleven institutes, including the National Institute on Aging, which is charged with biomedical research on aging.

Discretionary dollars stem largely from the smaller budgets of NIH, including those geared toward research or available in the state domain, Social Services Block Grants, and Older Americans Act funds. Figure 2.4 illustrates the delivery system for OAA services. This three-level system of federal, state, and local agencies is sometimes referred to as the "aging network." The AoA provides grants to state units on aging (SUAs), which then allocate dollars to Area Agencies on Aging and local service providers.

The aging network provides important social services at the local level and enjoys considerable support from state and local governments and aging advocacy groups. It is a complete and autonomous administrative structure—separate from Social Security and other federal agencies—and has considerable independence in contracting for services.

States are part of the aging network but perform additional functions. Figure 2.5 uses California to illustrate state-level services and programs.

Each state has at least two departments charged with most of its aging services: a department on aging and a department on health. The aging department manages its share of OAA dollars and other state funding programs (e.g., ombudsman, case management). In California, long-term care is an important function of the aging department. The health department manages its portion of Medicaid funds and governs standards, licensing, and quality of care for local health-care agencies and facilities.

In most states, as in California, a Department of Social Services (DSS) administers its Social Services Block Grant, which provides for in-home services. Often, these funds are given to local government agencies who contract out for services. DSS also regulates the community-care industry and makes disability evaluations on behalf of the federal government for SSI/SSP (the state supplement to SSI), Medicare and Medi-Cal (Medicaid). In California, the DSS licenses two programs (Adult Day Care and

Figure 2.4. Older Americans Act Network

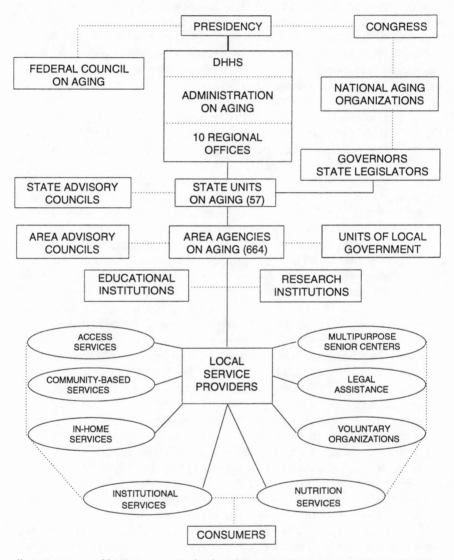

Illustration prepared by Brian Louis Lipshy, based on National Association of State Units on Aging, 1985.

Figure 2.5. State-Level Services in California

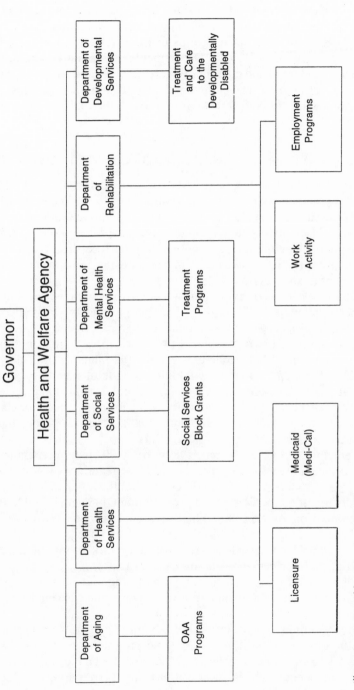

Social Day Care) providing respite for caregivers and enrichment for participants. In addition, Departments of Rehabilitation provide work activity and employment programs to the disabled, a group increasingly represented by older people. Departments of Mental Health are responsible for residential and community-care services and treatment programs. The Department of Developmental Services (DDS) administers care, treatment, and training for children and adults with developmental disabilities.

BENEFITS AND PROGRAMS: WHAT TO MAKE OF THEM

On the surface, it is easy to see why advocates, senior citizens, and family members despair in trying to obtain services. The system is a vast, complicated, fragmented, frustrating mass of bureaucracy, red tape, and, at times, insensitive public officials. Getting a Medicaid form processed, a hospital bill reimbursed, a meal delivered to a disabled person, or a board and care facility licensed can be confusing and can consume a great deal of time and energy.

After sixty years of evolution, we have a set of laws, regulations, and agencies developed for serving older people and their families with no coherent rationale. The system constitutes a piecemeal, political, narrow set of responses to congressional pressures, presidential interests, constituent lobbying, and public concern for the plight of the elderly.

In FY 1986, an estimated $270 billion of federal spending was of direct benefit to older Americans. Of every federal benefit dollar spent on the elderly that year, 54 cents went to Social Security and 27 cents went to Medicare and Medicaid (U.S. Senate 1988). Since 1960, the share of the federal budget spent on the elderly has nearly doubled, growing to 26 percent by 1986 (U.S. Senate 1989). By 1990, federal spending on the elderly accounted for 28.5 percent of total federal expenditures, representing over 46 percent of nondefense, noninterest spending in 1990, and equally about 6.6 percent of the gross national budget (U.S. House Select Committee on Aging 1991). This "aging enterprise" (Estes et al. 1983) has become costly, and it fails to serve well all people needing assistance. Each piece of legislation has particular paperwork requirements, eligibility criteria, and performance standards. Because it has become all but impossible for an individual to understand, negotiate, and access benefits and services, information and referral services and case management have become essential.

The system involves a myriad of administrative autonomies, each with jurisdiction and authority over specific programs and funds. Often, one agency knows nothing of what the others are doing. No single, overarching policy or agency wields responsibility for coordinating services or developing policy direction. Although the Older Americans Act gives the

AoA responsibility for coordinating federal policies on aging (and the Federal Council on Aging, an advisory group, responsibility for policy guidance), small size and low-level administrative placement inhibit its influence.

Changing this array of social policies will be difficult. We have invested a tremendous amount of money, manpower, and political initiative into the current set of programs. Advocacy groups, personnel, suppliers, elected officials, and constituencies each have a stake in the system. The administrative budgets of state and local governments are heavily composed of services and benefits to older people, a potent political bloc.

Notwithstanding this investment, we must ask: Can we afford such a fragmented, complex system? Is there a better way to coordinate services to older people and their families? Won't we exacerbate current problems if we respond to the growing number of elderly by simply expanding existing programs?

Already we see debates about reorganizing that system of agencies and programs. Repeated efforts have been made, for example, to move the Social Security Administration out of HHS and make it an independent agency. Supporters of such a move argue that it would "depoliticize" that agency by giving it greater administrative autonomy and shielding it from the vagaries of HHS budget politics. Others argue that SSA must remain within HHS in order to integrate aging-related programs and issues under one organizational umbrella. Efforts have also been made to elevate the Administration on Aging within HHS to give it more visibility and ability to coordinate HHS-related aging activities. A more dramatic proposal is to create a separate cabinet agency on aging (e.g., a Department of Elder Affairs) that would bring together old-age-related programs and benefits and have equal status with other cabinet agencies (including the newest, the Department of Veterans Affairs). Those organizational reforms, however, are often couched in the debates about bureaucratic influence and turf battles. Whether organizational restructuring of a particular agency would make the existing array of services and benefits more efficient remains an open question. The real issue might revolve around eligibility for benefits and how we pay for them.

The existing system, which is costly and in many ways inefficient, might actually work against those needing services most. In the New Aging, many older people might have no need for services entitled to them; others more needy might be deprived because of budget limitations. To prevent this, we must thoroughly understand the implementation and administration of existing social policies and programs for the elderly or risk overlooking an integral component of this nation's response to its aging society.

Later chapters suggest ways in which the existing system of programs, benefits, and services might be reformed. However, we must first examine how we came to have such a fascinating, albeit crazy, quilt of delivering services to the elderly. Why do we have so many different programs, agencies, and methods when, by all logic, assistance to the elderly could be handled more simply? In large part, the answer lies in the political evolution of principal laws authorizing benefits and services and the peculiar nature of American policy making and interest-group politics.

THE POLITICAL DEVELOPMENT OF AMERICAN SOCIAL POLICY

Origins

To understand the current political dilemma of old-age benefits and services we must look at the history of social policy and the escalation of old-age advocacy during this century. The origins of social welfare illustrate the evolution of programs for older people and the challenges in modifying them to meet the new realities of American society. Prior to the 1930s, unlike Europe, the United States developed no national social-welfare policy to handle social problems. Several reasons for this are: a tradition of rugged individualism; a classless society in which people and their families were expected to fend for themselves; constitutional limitations and restrictions on federal action; and the existence of a federal (federal/state partnership) rather than a powerful centralized national government (Lee and Benjamin 1983). We did, however, care about the less fortunate.

Our sense of compassion was reflected in the Elizabethan Poor Law of 1601 in England: welfare laws designed for children, able-bodied and indigent adults. The premises of this law—local financing and responsibility, minimization of costs, and distinction between the deserving and undeserving—influenced U.S. public charity during the eighteenth and nineteenth centuries (Lee and Benjamin 1983). The individual and the family bore financial, legal, and moral responsibility for their elderly and disabled. The local community, largely through almshouses and work farms (where the recipient of welfare worked for relief), cared for the indigent, but insisted that family members be accountable for their poor, sick, and elderly. War veterans (Civil War, Spanish American War), however, were considered a "deserving group" and received substantial government pensions beginning in the 1880s.

During this Young Aging period, little need existed for dealing with older people as a separate category. Federal and state governments played a minimal role in serving needy older adults. Life expectancy was relatively low; older people constituted a very small proportion of the population; and most were cared for by family or private charity. Older people were expected to work through old age and remain active in their communities. Except among the very rich, the concept of leisure and retirement was nonexistent. Thus, a lack of federal welfare for older people was not an issue in a mainly agrarian, provincial, and conservative society.

In addition, American politics of the eighteenth and nineteenth century were not constituency-based, although government was heavily influenced by special-interest groups such as bankers, industrialists, and railroads. With notable exceptions—Revolutionary and Civil War veterans and farmers—few instances of groups organizing around specific social-welfare issues, much less age, occurred.

From its inception, the United States has prided itself on being a "youthful" nation with boundless opportunities for the energetic and ambitious—attributes of the young. Nevertheless, older people in eighteenth- and nineteenth-century America were accorded a large measure of influence and respect, particularly older men, who were more likely to have accumulated economic, religious, and political power. This status was common in generally agrarian societies throughout world history. From the time of ancient Greece, China, and Rome, older men enjoyed the benefits of a patriarchal society—power and material assets handed down to the oldest son (Williamson et al. 1982). Maintaining traditions and customs, ancestral worship, preserving the history of a society, and property ownership gave the elderly an advantage socially. Unfortunately, women and the poor elderly throughout history were consistently excluded.

In early American history too, older people were not regarded as a separate group socially or politically. This began to change in the latter nineteenth century and shifted dramatically during the twentieth. By the turn of the century, the United States was transforming from an agrarian to an urbanized industry-based economy. This diminished farming as an occupation, led to the growth of an urban society and a middle class, emphasized routine and repetitive tasks rather than individual skills, and enhanced social and economic mobility. These factors, coupled with westward expansion, a democratic system based on merit rather than seniority, scientific progress overshadowing tradition, and the rise of professionalism and mass education served to dilute the customary credibility and influence of old age (Achenbaum 1978). Individual progress, youthful energy, and a focus on the future instead of the past served to deemphasize the hallmarks of old age, stability and security.

The Politics of the Modern Aging

By 1920, this transition led to what Andrew Achenbaum calls the "fundamental modernization of old age in America" (Achenbaum 1983). This modernization includes four major shifts critical to understanding the public policy dilemma we now face: demographic trends (such as increases in life expectancy), changing images of old age (older people increasingly viewed as a social problem), group action among the old (interest-group politics), and new directions in social welfare.

The 1920s were a time of prosperity, youthful optimism, and cultural change in the United States. We had won a war; incomes and stock-market investments were rising; and social and upward mobility inspired young people to educate themselves and move to the cities. Rural communities, a rapidly emerging middle class, and the new industrialists (for example, Andrew Carnegie and John D. Rockefeller) saw little need for federal government intervention, socially or economically, except to remedy the excesses of an unregulated economy. Poverty and social ills did exist. Chinese, blacks, Mexicans, new immigrants, the poor elderly in rural areas, and the poor of all ages in urban centers faced deprivation and isolation. But, by and large, no collective call for government to step in and alter what appeared to be increasingly good times was voiced.

By the early 1930s, of course, this changed dramatically. The Depression decimated middle-class stability. People lost their lifesavings and homes. The marketplace was unable to deal with economic collapse. Older people, in particular, were hard hit. Inordinate numbers lost their homes and retirement incomes. Their families moved away or had problems of their own. Faith in self-reliance and social stability was shaken. The Great Depression, in many respects, fundamentally altered not only our view of the poor and vulnerable, but the political role of the elderly.

The genesis of senior-citizen activism occurred in the period of the Modern Aging with the Townsend Movement of the 1930s. Dr. Francis Townsend, moved by the elderly's impoverishment, organized thousands of older people to push for a national pension system giving every person over 65 years $200 a month, provided they spend this amount within thirty days (Pratt 1983).

The idea of old-age pensions spurred political organizing in the 1920s as well. Three organizations were especially active in the 1920s in urging adoption of old-age pensions: American Association for Old Age Security (AAOAS), The American Association for Labor Legislation (AALL), and the Fraternal Order of the Eagles (Day 1990). Their efforts, although failing to result in actual policies, set a precedent for government responsibility for old-age security, an idea advanced by the Townsend Movement.

Never before in United States or world history had mass movements organized by older people pushed for old-age benefits. In 1935, the Social Security Act was created. Originally formulated to deal with the broader concerns of unemployment and poverty and to further President Franklin Roosevelt's political agenda of greater federal control, this law was, nevertheless, passed with the help of liberal groups, urban politicians, labor, as well as Townsend and other old-age groups.[6]

The war years of the 1940s saw the retreat of senior activism. An over-reliance on charismatic individuals such as Townsend (as opposed to organizational continuity), a newly prosperous economy, postwar concerns, and economic dislocations overshadowed elderly issues.[7]

Throughout the 1950s, however, and by the early 1960s, senior-citizen activism once again flourished. Better organized old-age groups, including the National Council on the Aging (1950), the American Association of Retired Persons (1958), the National Retired Teachers Association (1947), and the National Council of Senior Citizens (1961) formed to push for a variety of programs and benefits.

By the mid-1960s, a liberal political climate, a popular young president supportive of old-age programs, and the involvement of labor and civil-rights groups pushing for expanded social programs, led to the next major social policy advancements for senior citizens: the passage of Medicare, Medicaid, and the Older Americans Act in 1965. These victories came on the heels of the 1961 White House Conference on Aging, an event demonstrating the executive branch's formal recognition of senior citizens as warranting special attention. Although President Harry Truman convened a "National Conference on Aging" in 1950, the White House Conference was the first to directly involve senior-citizen organizations in lobbying the federal government (Torres-Gil 1987).

By the end of the 1960s, older people were an important political element and lobbying force in American public policy as a result of several factors: the early organizing efforts of the 1930s; a strong popular belief that government could serve the public good (especially among survivors of the Great Depression); increased life expectancy; and mandatory retirement at age 65. Ever-growing groups of retirees realized they had old-age based issues in common and that to advance them they could and should associate with like-minded older people. A fundamental change in U.S. heritage, the creation of an old-age constituency, would have an important bearing on American politics in later decades. The swing generation had become the first age cohort to make old age a rallying cry, and their leaders would influence public policy through the 1990s.

By the 1971 White House Conference on Aging, old-age benefits and politics were accepted as an important part of federal government and social policy. Few disagreed that older people deserved such services or that government should develop separate programs for older people. Senior organizations became larger and more influential. Presidents courted senior-citizen favor, especially knowing that a high percentage would vote. Within five years of the conference, at which President Richard Nixon publicly committed himself to expanded benefits and services to older people, the Older Americans Act was expanded to include a nutrition program and a state and local network of agencies to contract for social services. In addition, the Supplemental Security Income program and Title XX Social Services were enacted, and the National Institute on Aging was created to promote research on aging.

By the latter years of the Modern Aging period, the situation began to change. The election of Ronald Reagan in 1980 signaled a retrenchment in federal leadership and a growing disenchantment with the public sector. Influenced by Vietnam, Watergate, the recession of the 1970s, and the antigovernment mood promoted by President Jimmy Carter, most of the public no longer believed that federal government could or should solve social problems. A new neoconservative philosophy emphasized family, community groups, nonprofit agencies, and the private sector in responding to social needs.

This philosophy of privatization involved a growing backlash against groups perceived as special interest, particularly those representing the poor, minorities, civil rights, and women (although other special-interest groups—savings-and-loan industry, oil companies, defense industry—were accorded political access). The success of these groups in pressing Congress and the executive branch to develop and expand programs and increase expenditures caused important segments of the electorate to believe their tax dollars were being spent by an out-of-control bureaucracy influenced by narrow, self-interested groups.

The 1981 White House Conference pitted a new administration committed to less government and federal spending limits against leaders of aging advocacy groups. Political controversy at the conference (e.g., debates about expanding or restricting Social Security) and the lack of any meaningful policy or program recommendations represented the high-water mark for the politics of the Modern Aging, leaving a political stalemate: no major expansions of old-age benefits, but no significant dismantlement of old-age programs.

The remainder of the decade saw cutbacks in social-welfare programs (especially those perceived as benefiting the poor), proposals to eliminate or restrict other benefits (e.g., Disability Insurance, Social Security, cost of living increases), and a holding of the line for other entitlement programs (e.g., the Older Americans Act). Established senior-citizen organizations battled constantly to preserve benefits and services and to be acknowledged by a conservative administration.

The politics of the period faced their greatest challenge with the rise of "intergenerational conflict," first as an idea, then as an answer for the decade's budget problems. Academics, policy analysts, opinion writers, and elected officials began viewing older people as an interest group whose success overshadowed and undermined other needy groups (such as children and the poor). A decrease in poverty rates among the elderly, an even larger increase among poor children and families, and a dramatic rise in Social Security, Medicare, and Medicaid funding created a backlash against old-age lobbies and programs.

In the early phase of the New Aging period, an uneasy political climate existed for older people. The retrenchment and consolidation of the 1980s had taken a toll on the elderly and old-age organizations. Senior citizens worried about the security of their benefits. Old-age lobbies faced new and powerful competitors (pharmaceutical firms, hospitals, children's groups). Amid a "revenue neutral" climate (no new expenditures without reductions elsewhere), advocates were forced to justify proposals. During the late 1980s, however, there were some achievements: expanded Medicaid benefits to poor children and women; expanded home health and long-term-care benefits in Medicare and the Older Americans Act. However, the Medicare Catastrophic Coverage Act of 1988, potentially the greatest triumph of the period, became, instead, its worst defeat. Senior citizens revolted against the surtax that would have protected older people against the high cost of hospital care. The 1990s began with an uneasy stalemate between those who would continue special treatment for the elderly (developing since the Townsend Movement), and those who increasingly viewed older people as one more special interest group competing for scarce resources.

Success and Dilemmas

What does the history of the politics of aging tell us about the pressure for change now confronting our system of social policies for the elderly? What lessons does it provide for addressing the problems of an increasingly diverse older population in the New Aging?

The last sixty years represent a new form of generational politics in American history. Based on interest groups, where organized constituencies compete for public resources, the system has exhibited a phenomenon never before seen—the organizing of people considered old around issues for their age group. The success of old-age politics in America has been due to a constituency with few counterparts elsewhere. Its activism has led to a vast system of services and benefits at all levels of government with largely age-based eligibility criteria.

The irony of the New Aging is that it took shape because the politics and policy developments of the Modern Aging were successful, not because they failed. The benefits and services established led to a dramatic reduction in poverty among the elderly and the empowerment of older voters. By shouldering much of the burden of elder care, government provided children and grandchildren with increased freedom and social mobility. Countless programs, agencies, and services created thousands of jobs for people working with the elderly. The need to understand the social, behavioral, biomedical, and economic aspects of aging created a new academic and research area—gerontology and geriatrics. The sheer number of older people demonstrating their new-found identity led to a new political force in the United States. The increased health, activism, and productivity of older people gave positive meaning to being old.

In the New Aging, older people and society at large are victims of this success. Proliferation of fragmented, largely uncoordinated social policies and their organizations has gone unchecked. No single agency or department has had responsibility for coordinating and overseeing this expansion. Services and benefits may be obtained at any level of government—federal, regional, state, local—as well as from the private sector. Paperwork requirements and a multitude of standards and regulations make the system frustrating, impersonal, and difficult to use.

More important, most programs have benefited middle-income people and not the most needy. The poor elderly have been forced to rely on SSI and Medicaid (whose resources have been increasingly diverted to middle-income elderly). Any attempt to modify benefits and their eligibility requirements, however, faces the opposition of powerful interest groups with a personal stake in the status quo. The overall cost of funding programs (particularly Medicare, Medicaid, and Social Security), however justified, has become so great in the face of severe budget deficits that the general public and elected officials have been forced to question the value of these programs.

The old-age lobbies, too, have become victims of their own success. Other groups—environmentalists, welfare-rights groups, children's advocates, health-care activists—argue that other social problems require attention and attempt to emulate the senior-citizen organizations. Intergenerational tensions between young and old, and affluent and poor elders intensify concern about the allocation of scarce resources. The plight of the homeless and the poor raises questions about expanding services for groups already commanding a large portion of federal and state budgets. Fear about the growing number of older people and the aging of the baby boomers prompts proposals to restrict entitlement. These factors, however inaccurate or misconstrued, have combined to create a sense of urgency for reform. The onset of the 1990s has become an important transition period. On entering a new century, policy makers, providers, and the public will need to reassess the system and consider how it might be changed to better address the realities of the New Aging. In doing so, a set of philosophical and ideological dilemmas arise.

PHILOSOPHICAL AND IDEOLOGICAL DILEMMAS

We must also address philosophical and ideological issues fundamental to any decisions or proposals changing existing services. The historical development of today's social policies reflects American values about individualism, the role of government and the family, and caring for dependent and vulnerable populations. No change will be successful or proceed smoothly unless these values are considered and incorporated in the process. There are, however, tensions and contradictions in these values.

Achenbaum (1983) identifies seven sets of dual-value systems inherent in societal institutions and public policy:

1. Self-reliance and interdependence—pride in taking care of oneself, versus relying on others (e.g., government) for financial, public, and social support.
2. Expectation/entitlement—the expectation of receipt of certain benefits if earned or if specific criteria have been met (e.g., a means test), versus assurance of benefit receipt by broadly defined categorization (e.g., being old).
3. Public/private—reliance on the private sector (family, church, business), versus dependency on the public sector (government, publicly funded institutions).
4. Individual/family—the expected freedom to seek individual pursuits, versus the responsibility of caring for family members (e.g., sick and elderly relatives).
5. Work/leisure—the work ethic applies to all regardless of age, versus the more recent phenomenon of leisure lifestyle during retirement.
6. Tradition/novelty—reliance on traditional approaches to social policy (such as the Elizabethan tradition of workfarms seen in the civilian conservation corps), versus new and innovative solutions (for example, social insurance, reverse annuity programs).
7. Equity/adequacy—providing a minimal level of benefits based on need, versus a fair and adequate return based on contribution (through payroll taxes, for instance).

Although Achenbaum uses these dual-values sets mainly to illustrate contradictions and tensions inherent in the Social Security program, they apply to many social policies. As Americans, we preach self-reliance, but demand that government step in during moments of crisis (such as an earthquake, or a drug epidemic). As individuals, we want the opportunity to build a career, to travel, to have an active social life, but face the reality that our parents and grandparents might need extensive health and home care. As a society, we recognize the need to help the poor, especially if they are seen as deserving (i.e., children, the elderly), but resent having our tax dollars go to those we perceive as undeserving (i.e., welfare families, ex-convicts, the able-bodied unemployed).

In other countries, national health and welfare policies represent a consensus that people are universally entitled to have certain needs met. No such consensus exists in the United States with the exception of public education and veteran's benefits. The contradictions and tensions within our value systems help explain why national health care and gun control remain elusive.

These conflicts have affected and continue to influence development of our old-age policies. Social policies for the elderly are, by their nature, highly personal, raising questions of how we take care of our parents, grandparents, and ourselves. How we shape and reform those social policies requires answering a series of questions addressing philosophical and ideological issues:

- How should we involve a growing older population in American society?
- How do we view dependency?
- Can we afford to view the elderly solely as needy or greedy?
- How can we balance public and private responsibility?
- Where do federal control end, and states' rights begin?
- How can we prepare our young people for aging?

Involving the elderly. The last sixty years of politics and policy represent a movement toward segregating older people. The origins of this approach were benign and meant to focus attention on the poor and disadvantaged. However, creation of separate services for the elderly (e.g., nutrition programs), separate benefits (e.g., Medicare), and special recreation and housing programs (e.g., Leisure World) has instead divided society. The political power of senior citizens encourages many older people in the belief that they belong exclusively to an old-age constituency. Can we afford to continue down this path, segregating the 22 percent of the population expected to be 65 years and over by the year 2030? Is there a limit to expanding and creating programs only for the elderly? At what point should we reintegrate older people in overall social policy, especially considering our redefinition of being old?

Perceptions of dependency. Americans value individualism and self-reliance. As individuals we are socialized to care for ourselves, pull ourselves up by the bootstrap, and remain physically and mentally fit. Much of this relates to our regard for youth with its attendant vigor and strength. If we are ill or disabled we expect to recover and become active again. We have difficulty accepting frailty, disability, and dependence on others. As a nation, we avoid vaguely "collective" or "socialist" programs or policies that take responsibility for others, be they poor, homeless, or sick. Present social policies reflect these views. We pay for acute care, but not for long-term care in the home or community. We willingly spend huge sums of scarce public dollars on expensive medical technology that keeps the terminally ill alive, but won't pay to provide Medicare and Medicaid beneficiaries with rehabilitation treatment promoting physical function.

Only recently have the disabled garnered public attention, but they still face difficulties getting public buildings and transportation made accessible to the handicapped. What will happen when a growing proportion of our population—especially the rapidly increasing 85-and-over segment—becomes frail and requires extensive and expensive home health and community-based services? How will we care for the growing number of babies suffering long-term effects from alcohol and drug addictions? Our values and social policies refuse to respond to the fact that increasing segments of our population depend on health and social services, on others, and on government.

Needy vs. greedy argument. Our views of the elderly have shifted since the 1930s. At first, stereotypes portrayed them as needy; now some see them as greedy. The fallacy of these views is obvious, but public perceptions and media images tend to generalize and thus influence public policy. Portraying all older people as poor and needy once served the purpose of advocates for the elderly. The new image serves the purpose of those who want to reduce or dismantle hard-won entitlement programs. How can we incorporate the dramatic diversity of the older population into social policy? How can advocates for the aging acknowledge that some older (as well as younger) people do want something for nothing and will demand benefits but refuse to pay for them? How can we merge the needs of both disadvantaged older and younger groups? A major challenge in the next decade will be to present a complex picture of a diverse elder population in a simple, marketable way while avoiding stereotypes.

Balancing responsibility. The history of American politics has been a constant battle between those stressing public (government) responsibility and those who feel the private sector (family, business, the community) should be primary. Who should be responsible for addressing social problems in an effective and efficient manner? What can government do best? For what role is the private sector best suited? Each must take part, and a balance is necessary. Measuring and incorporating the respective roles of each into public policy is very difficult and is usually hostage to ideological differences. Increasingly, the public recognizes the need for activist government but fears an expensive, inefficient, and impersonal bureaucracy. The private sector has proven both cost-effective and efficient in addressing some social needs (such as hospital care for private pay patients), but is unable or unwilling to respond to others (nursing-home and home health care for the poor). By the early 1990s, the private sector was pressured to assume public sector responsibilities. Federal and state governments began to push for requirements on businesses to provide employees with health-care coverage and to allow workers leave to care for younger and older disabled relatives. This caused an increasing number of small businesses and large corporations to reconsider their opposition to national health care and public intervention. A key obstacle in the next decade will be to determine the strengths of both government and the private sector and where a balance lies between public and private responsibility.

Federal control vs. states rights. Ongoing debates about public/private responsibility are accompanied by constant tension between federal leadership and control and states' rights. During the Great Society era of the 1960s, most federal anti-poverty programs were conceived, implemented, and overseen by the federal government. This created resentment among state and local officials who felt their prerogatives were being ignored. The Reagan era reversed the role of federal government to some degree. States were given more responsibility (although fewer dollars) in the form of social services and community development block grants. They were also given more flexibility by way of federal Medicare and Medicaid waivers, allowing them to innovate in the provision of health care to older people. Most social policies for older people, however, remain at the national level, although certain programs—Medicaid and the Older Americans Act—involve a federal/state partnership in terms of funding and administration. In an aging society, where health, income, and social need require a comprehensive solution (that is, a national health care system), what role will states play? Will they be implementers and innovators, or will they be forced to follow federal dictates? What kind of balance can ensure national standards and accountability, yet take into account the tremendous differences among states and reward them for initiative and innovation? How can a federal approach avoid a vast and complex set of procedures, requirements, and agencies, while still providing supervision and leadership? How can local government foster loyalty and commitment to programs requiring federal dollars and requirements? Any proposed changes to benefits and services must address the relationships between the federal and state governments.

Preparing the youth. If we do not prepare younger groups for a longer life span, much of the energy we spend finding solutions to present problems will be in vain. Dependency on government and others can be minimized if young people are educated to prepare for the social, emotional, physical, and economic requirements of a 100-year life span. We cannot afford to concern ourselves only with youth and we do not have the luxury to focus entirely on modifying old-age benefits. We must parallel our efforts to reform policies for the elderly with teaching younger and middle-aged people to skillfully manage extended life expectancies.

Ideological and philosophical issues strongly influence our responses to the pressures of an aging society and the need to reform our existing system of benefits and services. Conflicting opinions make finding solutions difficult. Any proposal, idea, or legislative initiative must confront contradictions in our value systems and ideological and philosophical debates concerning our views of older people, government, the private sector, and need. We have in place a complex, expensive, and huge system, the product of sixty years of politics, policy, and demographics. Although specific policies reflect a shift in opinion, the system has, by and large, been successful in ameliorating the worst aspects of poverty among the elderly. Yet its success has engendered other problems. In many respects, the system has matured to a point of obsolescence.

We have prepared and created policies using increasingly outdated ideals, values, and assumptions about older people. Today people live longer and are healthier. At the same time, many more are sick and dependent. A more sophisticated set of interest groups uses political power skillfully, but we also have a sophisticated population that might not need them. In short, the New Aging requires modification of existing social policies, in large measure because our definitions of being old and our philosophical and ideological views are changing. We must build and reform from the existing system, however, because of our huge investment and stake in its programs and benefits.

The 1990s might be our last chance to make the difficult political decisions required in reforming the policies of the Modern Aging. In just twenty years, the baby boomers will reach retirement. We must be ready with social policies that respond to increased life expectancies, new definitions of old age, and immeasurable diversity. We must welcome and nurture changing attitudes about government, the individual, and the family.

NOTES

1. Aging is not as inevitable for populations as it is for individuals. A population ages when it experiences a decline in death rates and/or birthrates (the two primary determinants of population dynamics) (Wyatt 1990). When mortality rates decline, a population ages, reflected in a rising median age and an increase in the proportion of elderly. A population also ages when its fertility declines (fewer children). Population aging has major implications on a nation's work force, its economy, human resource policies, and public spending and taxes. For an analysis of the societal impact of population aging, see the 1990 series of articles by the Wyatt Company.

2. Social policies can also be evaluated using recipients' characteristics (Nelson 1982). For example, older people can be classified into three categories based on their need for benefits: poor or marginal elderly (e.g., living alone, female, minority, very old); downwardly mobile elderly (e.g., middle- and lower-middle-class older people with limited or fixed incomes and limited private resources); and integrated elderly (middle- and upper-income elderly with multiple sources of income, such as assets, pensions, public benefits).

3. Although DI is not age based, the Social Security disability program recognizes that individuals over 55 may have diminished capacities. Disability determinations give the age factor considerable weight.

4. Secretary Sullivan's reorganization also resulted in the merging of OHDS with the Family Support Administration (FSA), and formation of a new Administration for Children and Families, which includes the Maternal and Child Health Block Grant. The fate of the existing Low-Income Home Energy Assistance and Community Services Block Grants is uncertain.

5. The Americans with Disabilities Act (ADA) is a far-reaching civil-rights measure providing a variety of safeguards for persons with disabilities. The ADA has an intergenerational aspect, in that it benefits both older and younger disabled people. The act requires that employers with fifteen or more employees may not discriminate against qualified disabled individuals. Employers must reasonably accommodate the disabilities of qualified applicants or employees, unless undue hardship would result. State and local governments may not discriminate against qualified disabled individuals and must make facilities accessible to them. Public transportation must also be accessible (e.g., new buses, rail vehicles, transit stations). In addition, public accommodations such as restaurants, hotels, theaters, doctors' offices, libraries, and day-care centers may not discriminate on the basis of disability and must ensure the absence of physical barriers.

6. Many scholars (Pratt 1983; Day 1990; Williamson et al. 1982) believe the Townsend Movement and old-age groups of the time played no major role in the formulation and adoption of Social Security and, at best, were peripheral players in the politics of the time. In fact, the Social Security Act of 1935 was a disappointment to senior-citizen groups because it included no health insurance and relied on a regressive payroll tax. Nevertheless, the old-age groups of the 1920s and 1930s are credited with elevating the political status of the elderly and forcing government to consider establishing entitlement programs based on age.

7. Henry Pratt's insightful analysis of "national interest groups among the elderly" reveals that senior-citizen groups of the 1930s and 1940s had several fundamental flaws that explain their demise. They relied on the personality and charisma of an individual whose death or departure led to the group's decline, and they emphasized political and legislative accomplishments over membership services (Pratt 1983). Contemporary old-age organizations such as AARP, NCSC, and NCOA maintain long-term stability by relying on an organizational infrastructure made up of lobbyists, professional staff, local chapters, and group services.

BIBLIOGRAPHY

AARP. "A Profile of Older Americans: 1987." Washington, D.C.: American Association of Retired Persons, 1987.
———. "A Profile of Older Americans: 1990." Washington, D.C.: American Association of Retired Persons, 1990.
Achenbaum, Andrew. *Old Age in the New Land: The American Experience since 1790*. Baltimore: The Johns Hopkins University Press, 1978.
———. *Shades of Gray: Old Age, American Values, and Federal Policies Since 1920*. Boston: Little, Brown and Company, 1983.
Day, Christine. *What Older Americans Think: Interest Groups and Aging Policy*. Princeton, N.J.: Princeton University Press, 1990.
Detlefs, Dale, and Robert Myers. *1989 Guide to Social Security*. Louisville, Ky.: William M. Mercer-Meidinger-Hansen, Inc., November 1988.
Estes, Carroll, Robert J. Newcomer, and Associates. *Fiscal Austerity and Aging*. Beverly Hills, Calif.: Sage Publications, 1983.
Garcia, Kenneth. "Law May Force Loss of Low-Income Apartments." *Los Angeles Times*, June 4, 1991.

Gelfand, Donald. *The Aging Network*. 3d ed. New York: Springer Publishing Company, 1988.

Gibson, Rose. "Defining Retirement for Black Americans." In *Ethnic Dimensions of Aging*, edited by Donald Gelfand and Charles Barresi. New York: Springer Publishing Company, 1987: 224–38.

Lammers, William, and David Klingman. *State Policies and the Aging*. Lexington, Mass.: Lexington Books, 1984.

Lee, Philip, and A. E. Benjamin. "Intergovernmental Relations: Historical and Contemporary Perspectives." In *Fiscal Austerity and Aging: Shifting Government Responsibility for the Elderly*, edited by Carroll Estes, Robert Newcomer and Associates. Beverly Hills, Calif.: Sage Publications, 1983, 59–81.

Lowy, Louis. *Social Policies and Programs on Aging*. Lexington, Mass.: D.C. Heath and Company, 1980.

Nelson, Gary. "Social Class and Public Policy for the Elderly." In *Age or Need?: Public Policies for Older People*, edited by Bernice Neugarten. Beverly Hills, Calif.: Sage Publications, 1982, pp. 101–30.

"Older, Slower-Growing America Predicted." *The Washington Post*, Feb. 1, 1989.

Pratt, Henry. "National Interest Groups among the Elderly: Consolidation and Constraint." In *Aging and Public Policy: The Politics of Growing Old in America*, edited by William P. Browne and Laura Katz Olson. Westport, Conn.: Greenwood Press, 1983: 145–80.

Rosenblatt, Robert. "Bankruptcy of Part of Medicare Feared." *Los Angeles Times*, May 18, 1991.

Social Security Administration. U.S. Department of Health and Human Services. *Social Security Bulletin: Annual Statistical Supplement*. Washington, D.C.: U.S. Government Printing Office, 1990, p. 124.

Torres-Gil, Fernando. "White House Conferences on Aging." In *The Encyclopedia of Aging*, Ed. George Maddox. New York: Springer, 1987: 692–93.

U.S. Bureau of the Census. *Statistical Abstract of the United States*. 109th Ed. Washington, D.C.: U.S. Government Printing Office, 1989.

U.S. House of Representatives. Select Committee on Aging. Subcommittee on Retirement Income and Employment, "Supplemental Security Income (SSI): Current Program Characteristics and Alternatives for Future Reform." Washington, D.C.: U.S. Government Printing Office, 1988.

———. Working documents, 1991.

"U.S. Payment of Disability Claims Faulted." *Los Angeles Times*, May 20, 1991.

U.S. Senate. *Aging America: Trends and Projections*. Washington, D.C.: U.S. Government Printing Office, 1986.

———. *Aging America: Trends and Projections*. Washington, D.C.: U.S. Government Printing Office, 1989.

U.S. Senate Special Committee on Aging. "Developments in Aging: 1990." Vol. 1. Washington, D.C.: U.S. Government Printing Office, 1991.

Williamson, J. B., L. Evans, and L. A. Powell. *Politics of Aging*. Springfield, Ill. Charles C. Thomas, 1982.

The Wyatt Company. "Population Aging: A Misunderstood Phenomenon." *Wyatt Newsletter* 6, 4 (April 1990): 1–2.

3
THE POLITICS OF THE
NEW AGING

Politics is not an exact science.

Otto von Bismarck

Since the Townsend Movement of the 1930s, senior citizens have strongly influenced public policies and political decisions. Their political activism pressured Franklin Roosevelt to pass Social Security, and their alliance with President John Kennedy, labor unions, and the Democratic party helped establish Medicare and Medicaid. Senior citizens might not always have been the principal player, but they have been an important one.

Today, high voting rates and sophisticated old-age organizations give senior citizens a high degree of political visibility and influence among elected officials. Questions arise, however, about the appropriateness and effectiveness of older people as a political interest group. The politics of aging—participation by and for the elderly in the political process—evoke positive and negative views.

Advocates see the empowerment of senior citizens as a means of preserving hard-won benefits for the elderly. Organizations such as the American Association of Retired Persons and the National Council on Aging view the high voting rates of people over 65 years as an opportunity to influence elections. The increased political visibility of older people seems the embodiment of American democracy.

Others, however, argue that the elderly are simply another narrow interest group out to protect their gains. Groups such as the now-disbanded Americans for Generational Equity (AGE), who think that the elderly receive too great a proportion of the federal budget, promote an image of them as "selfish, greedy geezers." Others argue that the elderly, as a highly diverse age group, exercise a "political bluff," presuming more political influence than they actually have.

Regardless of how one views the political participation of older people, their activism over the last sixty years demonstrates their importance as a political constituency. Elected and government officials carefully avoid alienating them. Organized aging groups have proven that they can force Congress to repeal unpopular legislation (witness the Medicare Catastrophic Coverage debate of the late 1980s) or alter budget priorities (as they did with the 1990 budget debates). Their "old"-style political involvement, based on a propensity to vote in large numbers, an evolving group identity, and a proliferation of organizations with the sole purpose of representing them, has been very successful. It has enabled senior citizens to pressure federal and state government to expand benefits and programs and protect those benefits from serious erosion. By the beginning of the 1990s, notwithstanding the political battles of the 1980s (or because of them), the elderly had reached what Christine Day describes as "the pinnacle of their organizational success and ha[d] achieved Washington insider status" (Day 1990, 33). Organizational growth and activity during the Modern Aging period resulted in a political system that now recognized the elderly as a formidable political force. The political backlash generated by their success might have diminished their moral credibility, but they were, nevertheless, more powerful than most. Where they must merge with other groups (civil-rights, women, children) they are now the senior partner rather than a peripheral player.

The politics of aging, however, will undergo dramatic change in the coming years. Older people will be denied the automatic legitimacy granted them when the public assumed most were poor and needy. Their political clout already engenders resistance among other interest groups less successful (e.g., children, disabled, minorities). The public is increasingly reluctant to pay the escalating cost of public programs for low-income and affluent elderly.

Longevity, diversity, and generational issues will influence the politics of the New Aging. A new political climate will affect changes in strategies for and approaches to political involvement by older people. Former methods of pressuring government will change.

The extent to which the elderly will compete successfully with other groups and exercise political power in the future is unknown. Future politics of aging will differ in many ways from the political developments of the last sixty years. New alliances will form. A breakdown of traditional coalitions will occur, and a new political climate within which older people must operate as a political group will emerge. Senior citizens and their organizations will be forced to reassess the manner in which they compete with other constituencies. This chapter examines the changes facing older people as an organized political force and their future ability to influence policy decisions.

POLITICAL PARTICIPATION

What constitutes political influence on the part of senior citizens? What factors in the politics of the Modern Aging have enabled the elderly to manipulate the political process to their advantage? Over the last sixty years, three factors have contributed to the successful political role of the elderly: a propensity to vote in large numbers; group identity; and the proliferation of age-based organizations.

Higher Voting Rates

Older people vote at a higher rate than those in other age groups. For example, in the 1988 presidential election, 68.8 percent of those 65 years and over voted, compared to 54 percent of those 25 to 44, and 36.2 percent of those 18 to 24 years old. This ratio has increased over time. Since the 1964 elections, the percentage of voters 65 years of age and over has increased from 66.3 percent to 68.8 percent, while the 18- to 24-year-old category has dropped from 50.9 to 36.2 percent. Voters 25 to 44 years have also decreased from 69 to 54 percent. This imbalance holds for congressional elections from 1974 to 1986, with the number of elderly voters increasing, and the number of those 18 to 44 years old decreasing (U.S. Bureau of the Census 1989).

The elderly's propensity to vote extends to minority groups who, generally, have lower rates of voting. While only 51.5 percent of blacks voted in the 1988 presidential election compared to 59.1 percent of whites, elderly blacks, aged 65 to 74, participated in greater numbers (69.5 percent) than other age groups in the black population. Hispanics exhibited the lowest overall participation rate in the 1988 elections (28.8 percent). Older Hispanics, 65 to 74 years, however, had a much higher voting rate (50.1 percent) than those younger (U.S. Bureau of the Census 1989).

The consistently high registration and voting rates among elderly of all races remain a powerful political tool. That the voting rates of older voters have increased compared to that of younger voters does not go unnoticed by politicians.

Identity as Senior Citizens

Another factor contributing to the political influence of the elderly has been their growing identity as a group. Supporting issues as a part of an old-age group is a phenomenon unique to this century. In the past, the elderly were too few to form a constituency. Elders were more likely to be part of intergenerational economic and social systems.

Studies show that the elderly's interest in politics steadily increases with age. They become more attentive to political campaigns and devote more time to news and public affairs. Studies also show that older people favor government action in health care and efforts promoting employment and a high standard of living more than other age groups (Hudson & Strate 1985). This mounting interest fortifies the historical legacy of their generation: enduring support for the New Deal approach to addressing social issues. The establishment of Social Security, Medicare, the Older Americans Act, and other public programs gives the elderly impetus to use their collective political strength to preserve these benefits of old age.

The political organizing of older people for their own purposes during the past sixty years has shown senior citizens the benefit of viewing themselves as older people. The growth of AARP to over 30 million members and increased media interest in the elderly demonstrate that older people today do view themselves as members of an alliance. Older people, however, do have allegiances to others—their families, neighborhoods, political parties—and do not always single out for their support age-related issues. Nonetheless, they do identify as members of an age group, and this phenomenon contributes to their political clout as a special-interest group.

Age identification and allegiance will grow among upcoming cohorts of older people. Tomorrow's elderly are already aware of the potential politics of age and will spend an increasing portion of their life span conscious of their status as senior citizens (Bengston et al. 1985). The prevalence and threat to the existence of entitlement programs reserved for the elderly, the private sector's courting of the senior-citizen market, and increases in life expectancy will heighten age-based consciousness.

Age-Based Organizations

The political influence of older people is also a function of the growth of age-based organizations and their position as a center of political activity for many senior citizens. Francis Townsend of the Townsend Movement and George McLain of the California Pension Movement crystalized the fear and disenchantment of the elderly during the Depression. At its peak, the Townsend Movement had as many as 2 million members, and the McLain organization reached about 100,000 (Hudson, & Strate 1985). Although they disappeared by the 1950s, many other groups have taken their place. The number of older people involved in old-age groups has, consequently, jumped dramatically.

Today, three categories of interest groups representing the elderly exist (Ficke 1985):

1. *Mass membership organizations representing older persons*: the American Association of Retired Persons (AARP), the National Council on Aging (NCOA), the Families, USA advocacy group, the National Association of Retired Federal Employees (NARFE), the National Council of Senior Citizens (NCSC), the National Indian Council on Aging (NICOA), the National Hispanic Council on Aging (NHCOA), the National Caucus and Center on Black Aged, the Older Womens League (OWL), and the National Committee to Preserve Social Security and Medicare (NCPSSM).

2. *Professional associations representing people who act for or on behalf of the elderly*: the Gerontological Society of America (GSA), the American Society on Aging (ASA), the Association for Gerontology in Higher Education (AGHE), the National Senior Citizens Law Center (NSCLC).

3. *Public-interest organizations representing the constituent concerns of public and provider groups*: the National Association of State Units on Aging (NASUA), the National Association of Area Agencies on Aging (NAAAA), the National Association of Foster Grandparent Programs, the National Association of Meals Programs, the American Association of Homes for the Aging (AAHA).

These groups provide numerous opportunities for older people, family members, and those working with the elderly to participate in organized activities. Questions still persist, however, about the real ability of these groups to exercise political clout as opposed to their perceived influence. Some groups are accused of exercising a "political bluff," claiming they represent many voters when in actuality they cannot deliver those votes. Others are seen as organized fronts for direct-mail fundraising. Still others are perceived as more interested in protecting jobs. Nonetheless, the proliferation of old-age organizations can only add to the political influence of older people and their advocates. At the very least, those groups are considered a highly visible and politicized set of lobbying groups.

Beyond the political role old-age groups perform, the political activity of and social policies for the elderly affect others. Diverse interest groups, constituencies, and organizations increasingly seek to influence political decisions regarding benefits for the elderly: small businesses faced with increasing Social Security payroll taxes; large corporations paying for elder care and long-term care insurance for their employees; pharmaceutical companies faced with cost controls over prescription drugs; lawyers handling age-discrimination cases; and the health-care industry facing large numbers of elderly patients. All of these have a stake in the politics of aging.

In some cases, groups not representing the elderly have more political muscle than old-age organizations. Some argue that elderly groups were never principal players in influencing policy decisions (Williamson et al. 1982). During debates over Medicare and Medicaid, for example, key groups supporting passage included the AFL-CIO, the American Nurses

Association, the Council of Jewish Foundations, the National Association of Social Workers, the National Farmers Union, and the American Geriatrics Society. Opponents included the American Hospital Association, the Life Insurance Association of America, the National Association of Manufacturers, the National Association of Blue Shield Plans, the Chamber of Commerce, and the American Legion (Williamson et al. 1982).

We expect that many other groups will want to influence political developments in aging and, together, they might well have more political influence than the elderly. This will complicate further the future political role of the elderly. Regardless of how we view the elderly and their influence, questions remain: Will the elderly be more powerful in the future, or will their influence dissipate? How will their growing number shape politics and change in social policies for the elderly? Where will old age fit in the constellation of new players participating in senior-citizen policies?

POLITICAL ISSUES OF THE NEW AGING

The Case of Medicare Catastrophic Health Insurance

In 1988, a law was passed—the Medicare Catastrophic Coverage Act (MCCA)—providing expanded benefits for older people. The passage and, later, repeal of this bill and its aftermath reveal much about the future of the politics of aging. The repeal of the MCCA serves as the political divide between the politics of the Modern Aging and the politics of the New Aging.

The MCCA was passed by an overwhelming bipartisan vote and was supported by a Republican administration. The bill capped the annual out-of-pocket expense Medicare beneficiaries could incur ($1930 for the first year), expanded coverage (home health care and skilled nursing facilities, mammograph screening, prescription drugs), and provided greater protection for the spouses of nursing home patients and the very poor elderly. The bill was hailed as the greatest expansion since Medicare was enacted. Passage of the bill seemed a win-win situation.

The financing of the MCCA, however, radically differed from previous public benefits packages: the elderly were required to pay for the new benefits. The bill imposed a self-financing surtax based on income (up to $800 a person the first year) and increased the Part B premium.

Less than a year later the elderly revolted. Widespread opposition to the surtax pressured Congress to repeal the bill by an equally large margin. Although only a small percentage of the elderly would actually have had to pay the maximum surtax, many claimed they were already protected by Medi-gap insurance or retiree health care coverage, and others preferred long-term-care coverage.

Reversal of the MCCA revealed that the elderly had come a long way since the Townsend Movement. On one hand, older people as a political constituency demonstrated political clout. No other major legislation had ever been enacted and repealed within a year due to political pressure. On the other hand, older people were perceived, as a result, as a selfish interest group wanting expanded benefits without the burden of paying for them.

Repeal of the MCCA also showed deepening divisions within the elderly community. Not all older people opposed the bill. Only the most vocal and articulate were heard. The millions of poor elderly who stood to gain the most were absent in the debates. Aging organizations that supported the bill, most notably the American Association of Retired Persons, were castigated by grassroots aging organizations and other older individuals opposing the bill.

Whether the case of the MCCA is a harbinger of the future remains to be seen, but it does demonstrate how the future politics of aging will differ from the past, and how longevity, diversity, and generational issues will affect the political influence of future cohorts of older people.[1]

In retrospect, the MCCA episode might not be considered a milestone. It might not foreshadow a demise in the political influence of older people, but merely a temporary setback (events since show the elderly can successfully pressure the political system). The MCCA, however, can be considered an important transition from the politics of the Modern Aging to the politics of the New Aging because it signifies a shift in the perception of older people by the public and the political system—a shift from automatic legitimacy to political justification for senior-citizen benefits.

Longevity and Politics

The downfall of the MCCA clearly demonstrates what can occur when greater numbers of older people become politically active. Further, it illustrates what happens when people live longer: they have added years within which to take a direct interest in old-age issues, and so do their family members.

In general, people living longer means that aging issues will affect both the old and young. An increasing life expectancy means an individual can anticipate up to 25 years in retirement—a sufficient enough time for worrying about pensions and health benefits. Family members, too—spouses, children—cannot help but become concerned about caring for the needs of an aging relative and related cost. Longevity not only increases the number in that constituency affected by public benefits and political decisions, but alters its composition as well. In short, the children and grandchildren of the elderly become honorary members of the senior-citizen constituency.

In the case of the MCCA, the surtax would have motivated husband and wife to be equally concerned, because each would have been subject to it (the maximum $800 × 2 = $1600). The offspring would have had to become directly involved when health- and long-term-care costs unmet by the government or the elders themselves required payment.

In addition, longevity might change our view of aging, and consequently, reduce the political effectiveness of older people. As people live longer, and as the elderly, in general, become healthier and more educated, they might consider themselves young at increasingly older ages. In addition, pressures are building to raise the eligibility ages for retirement and pension plans. When this occurs, the overall number of people who now consider themselves members of senior-citizen groups will drop sharply. How this will balance out against the increasing number of people interested in the politics of aging is uncertain.

As their number increases, the elderly's prestige and moral authority might diminish. If they are viewed as a narrow interest group, as opposed to "elders" providing a source of leadership and wisdom to a community, their political clout could deteriorate.

In general, longevity (coupled with diversity) might dilute the aggregate political influence of older people. In the politics of the Modern Aging period it was possible to maintain a consensus demanding and protecting benefits and services for older people. In the politics of the New Aging, longevity might split that consensus.[2]

Longevity and its implications will prompt some difficult political decisions for the population. When up to 25 percent of the population reaches 60 years and over, the private sector will discontinue senior-citizen discounts for restaurants, transportation, theaters, and other businesses. State and local government will be unable to afford property-tax relief for senior citizens.

The meeting of longevity and politics, then, creates something of a contradiction: more older people, more electoral influence, but less political credibility. On the other hand, the pendulum might shift over time. The overall improvement of the health and financial status of older persons might not last. With increasing life expectancy, most older persons will spend their savings and personal assets. In the absence of comprehensive governmental health- and long-term-care coverage, older people will have to use their assets to pay for expensive care. A lack of inflation protection for most pension and retirement plans means time will erode their value. A greater homogenization of economic and social status among the elderly will occur.

Longevity, then, will alter the politics of aging by diminishing the aggregate political influence of the elderly, despite their greater numbers. On the other hand, it might create a set of common concerns among older people as time affects their personal and social status. A longer life span might become the great equalizer.

Diversity

Increasing diversity among the elderly will serve to further dilute their political effectiveness and cohesiveness. The case of the MCCA revealed a stark division between affluent and low-income older people. An income gap is one sign of change in the social, economic, and political profile of the older population in the politics of the New Aging. Although this can and will generate conflict among the elderly, it might also create opportunities for alliances and coalitions with nonelderly groups. In the politics of the New Aging, a splintering of the elderly lobby will occur, and new constituencies and interest groups will form. As noted in Chapter 1, the older population will be divided by gender, income, race, and social diversity. Older women, a group more likely to be poor, frail, and isolated, will be greater in number, and pressure to address their needs will be brought to bear. Increased longevity will boost the number of frail and disabled older people demanding comprehensive health- and long-term-care coverage. The growing gap between relatively affluent older people and the elderly poor will heighten differences in policy objectives. Lifestyle changes, variable definitions of old, and geographic mobility will serve to alter the view that older people comprise a homogeneous group.

Perhaps the greatest source of diversity will be a rapid increase in the racial and ethnic diversity of the elderly. Blacks, Hispanics, Asian and Pacific Islanders, as well as Native Americans, are living longer and will constitute a much larger proportion of the elderly early in the next century. Concerns about immigration, culture, language, discrimination, and poverty will add new political dimensions to old-age politics.

What does increasing diversity mean for the politics of the New Aging? It means increased complexity and divisiveness. It means intensified competition for scarce public resources (i.e., taxes, services). Diversity means more age/income/race stratification where poor elderly and young minority groups might be pitted against affluent white retirees.

While a wealthy white retiree, for example, might be concerned with protecting pension and retirement income and might seek a secluded life-care retirement community, the poor and minority elderly are forced to survive on diminishing social services. Older women, as they organize politically, will promote legislation and benefits that account for their greater life expectancy and lower lifetime earnings. Organizations (such as the AARP) that seek to recruit low-income and minority people, might find it difficult to maintain solidarity among their large membership.

The MCCA demonstrated what can happen when affluent elders refuse to subsidize benefits for disadvantaged older people. Their political weight buried a bill that would have helped older women, the poor, and the disabled elderly. It showed that not all the elderly are represented in one powerful and forceful constituency. Instead, several constituencies began emerging.

Questions about policymaking and politics in the 1990s arise: How will the different interests of the aged play out? Will elder groups begin infighting, with the more economically secure—who are protected by private and retiree health insurance—opposing the cost of expanded public services in these areas, and those representing poorer people seeking to expand them?

Can political differences be overcome, and a political agenda uniting differing elderly constituencies be established? Judging by the changing profile of the older population, this will not be easy. The political process and differing opinions of the elderly constituency will instead become more intense and divisive, resulting in a more complicated process and dialogue.

A realignment of political positions and coalitions among diverse segments of older people is possible, with low-income elderly consolidating with reformist groups and the more affluent elderly with conservatives. Older women will join with younger disabled groups to secure quality home care. Minority political organizations will unite with liberal senior-citizen groups to fight for national health care.

Realignment signifies a major change from the modern politics period to the politics of the New Aging. In the modern politics of aging, elderly groups allied horizontally: old-age groups lobbied for and supported old-age positions. In the new politics, vertical alliances between aging and nonaging groups will become the norm: the poor old and the poor young, the elderly disabled and the younger disabled. Vertical alliances will replace the horizontal politics characteristic of the last 60 years. The elderly will cease to be the homogeneous, monolithic force they might have been.

In the politics of the New Aging, diversity will bring both bad and good news. It might undermine the existing political influence of older people and their organizations, but it will absorb many more groups with a stake in aging and related public policies. Pluralism and interest-group politics will increase, but so will a demand that public policies serve those traditionally denied access to benefits and services. Diversity, therefore, in creating a more complicated set of politics for future generations of older people, might also increase the political participation of the disadvantaged.

Generational Tensions

The controversy surrounding the MCCA illustrates the generational backlash that can occur in politics. The elderly opposing that bill were perceived by many as a selfish, well-off group demanding that the taxpayer finance their benefits. The media image of the "greedy geezer" caused many political commentators to predict that the more affluent elderly would pay a political price.

That political price was a shift in priorities among many members of Congress toward children, the poor, and the medically uninsured. A feeling that Congress had been had by supporting a bill senior citizens detested (at least in their most vocal groups) caused many legislators and appointed officials to shift their attention (at least in the short term) from such aging issues as long-term care to the health, education, and social needs of children and their families.

The residual effects of MCCA also benefited low-income and minority elderly. It caused many legislators at the federal and state level to give more attention to disadvantaged senior citizens on the premise that not only would scarce resources go to the most needy, but poor elderly would be more appreciative. By the early 1990s, congressional attention was shifting toward targeting services toward low-income older people and children in low-income households.

The generational tensions that political choices between the old and the young can create did not originate with MCCA, however. Throughout the 1980s, they were developing. Generational tradeoffs simply reflect the effects of increasing longevity and diversity among the aging population when the old and the young feel they must compete with one another.

Perhaps generational issues illustrate best what the politics of the New Aging might bring and how it will differ from the old.

Debates over generational conflicts began developing in the early 1980s (Minkler 1986). Samuel Preston's article, "Children and the Elderly in the United States" (1984), presented the views of many researchers and policy analysts. Preston compared the dramatic decrease in poverty among the elderly with its even more dramatic increase among children in poverty households. He suggested that the elderly were gaining at the expense of poor children and pointed to the increasing proportion of federal benefits awarded the elderly while aid to low-income families declined.

The political viewpoint of Preston's article was picked up by Americans for Generational Equity (AGE) (a group founded in the mid–1980s but since disbanded and merged with the Association of Baby Boomers [ABB]). AGE and its founders argued that federal programs, including Social Security and Medicare, should be reduced so that resources could go to groups more needy. Furthermore, they projected that the growth of retirement, health, and social programs for older people would "indenture" younger generations, creating conflict among different age groups. The argument and a well-orchestrated educational campaign garnered great media interest. Articles like "The Coming Conflict As We

Soak the Young to Enrich the Old" (1986), "Consuming Our Children" (1988), "Justice between Generations" (1985), and "Young vs. Old" (1984), warned of impending generational conflict as a result of older people wielding their political leverage to the detriment of the young.

Others disagreed, of course, and used public opinion polls to show that old-age programs such as Social Security and Medicare enjoyed widespread support among younger groups. Advocates for the elderly viewed generational conflict as a false notion "scapegoating" the elderly for a society and government that ignored the needs of children and the poor. They argued that the elderly were unfairly criticized for their success in preserving their benefits while programs for the poor were being scaled back by a conservative administration. Equity between generations and intergenerational policies (e.g., long-term care for the young and old) became strategies for responding to the real problems facing children and the poor. Generations United, an organization composed of elderly, consumer, and children's groups, was formed to promote intergenerational activities.

Legislative initiatives in the late–1980s reflected the controversy. The self-financing aspect of the MCCA—where the elderly were to pay for their own benefits—merely attempted to shift the burden from younger to older taxpayers. On the other hand, legislation to provide home care for all age groups and a "Parental and Family Leave" bill, allowing workers to take time off for the care of young and older family members, reflected intergenerational solutions. The issue of how age cohorts might fare in the New Aging was given impetus by Senator Daniel Moynihan's proposal in 1990 that Social Security payroll taxes be reduced to help younger workers and to expose the use of the Social Security surplus in reducing the federal deficit.

The extent of the conflict between the old and young remains questionable, and whether or not the elderly should sacrifice their programs on behalf of other pressing social needs remains high on the public agenda. The two opposing viewpoints—the old are selfish and already have too much, versus intergenerational conflict is nonexistent—continue to trouble politicians, intellectuals, and the public.

The effect of the generational debate of the 1980s was to create tremendous consternation and soul-searching among advocates for the elderly. Spurious at best, the notion of generational conflict initially relied on limited data and overgeneralizations of the true economic status of the elderly. It added two plus two and came up with seven or eight by connecting the true demise of children to the relative improvement among older people, and concluding that the elderly were somehow responsible for the nation's neglect of younger people. The generational equity debate of the time fed off the "Darwinian" nature of the 1980s, where survival of the economically fittest (big business, affluent professionals, successful speculators, the highly educated) and cutbacks in social programs (maternal and child health, public education, health care, subsidized housing) caused fighting among needy groups. Senior-citizen groups were victimized for having successfully exercised their right as politically active citizens, and political analysts ignored the high poverty rates among many older people (e.g., women, minorities, rural residents).

Nonetheless, proponents of generational conflict provided an important public service by forcing advocates, gerontologists, and the public to look at the future of younger groups and question whether aging lobbies were too complacent and smug in protecting their programs. They forced recognition that we are, in fact, mortgaging the future of large segments of the U.S. population by passing costs on to later generations. In addition, they caused political analysts and decision makers to recognize the tradeoffs inherent in responding to interest group pressures when funds are limited.

The reality of generational differences falls somewhere between the two opposing viewpoints. Despite the efforts of gerontologists to discount the generational conflict thesis as counterproductive and a narrow way of viewing social problems, tensions are increasing between generations and subgroups of the elderly population. The MCCA and budget debates of 1990s made this fact clear. By the early 1990s, political commentators were once again predicting "age-old strife" and generational divisions. This time their predictions were based on the growing political power of baby boomers and federal budgeting procedures requiring tax hikes or cutting existing entitlement programs (such as Medicare) for new domestic initiatives (such as long-term care) (Barnes 1991).

In addition, other points illustrate the possibility of real generational tension:

• The elderly are continuing to be used as scapegoats for social ills. The affluent senior citizen, in particular, is being viewed as selfish and concerned only with personal pension and income benefits.

• The zero-sum politics of the 1980s and 1990s, where national administrations refused to raise taxes, while increasing deficits pit groups against one another for scarce public resources.

• The success of the older lobby in protecting their entitlement make them an easy target for groups less successful.

This tension, however, lies more with organizations purporting to represent younger generations (e.g., ABB) and senior citizens (e.g., AARP) than among individuals or within families. These organizations center their arguments around resolving the budget and political problems facing the United States as a whole through a system of tradeoffs. Do we reduce cost-of-living increases in Social Security to pay for prenatal and maternal health care programs? Do we scale back pension benefits to support education for minorities? This energy might be better spent studying ways in which to increase the economic pie so that we avoid tradeoffs among needy groups altogether.

Tension also exists among those who must pay for benefits and those who receive them. Younger workers question the future solvency of Social Security. Will they recoup what they have contributed through increasing payroll taxes? How will they afford long-term care for their parents when government puts its dollars into Medicare's hospital insurance program?

At present, no measurable conflict exists, at least between today's senior citizens and young and middle-aged groups. Public opinion polls today show a reservoir of support for older people (R L Associates 1987). An aura of gratitude to the swing generation, whose members (now in their 60s, 70s, and 80s) sacrificed dearly for their children and country, persists. Overcoming the Depression of the 1930s, fighting Fascism and Communism during World War II and the Korean War, and building a strong and prosperous nation, remain appreciated. Most senior citizens have children, and for the most part, children are bound by reciprocity to their parents and grandparents. This minimizes conflict.

The reality tomorrow, however, is that we are likely to have generational conflict unless we acknowledge and identify today the sources of growing tension between subgroups of the elderly and generational cohorts. The following are likely to create conflict among future cohorts of older and younger people:

- More older people will be without children, a reflection of the tendency today for people to remain childless or single into old age. Many more older people will be supported by children from other families. The sense of obligation between young and old may diminish.

- Bonds of reciprocity will weaken with increased geographic and social mobility.

- Future cohorts of older people will not have the societal gratitude and sense of accomplishments enjoyed by the swing generation. The Vietnam War, the Civil Rights era, and the Persian Gulf War are not considered on par with victory in World War II.

- Resentment toward affluent elders, who are seen as well-off and unconcerned about the needs of other disadvantaged groups, will escalate.

- The old-age lobby will subdivide. Diversity will create subgroups of older women, affluent retirees, minorities, and the disabled competing for public attention and resources.

- Other constituent groups with an interest in aging—industry, business, hospitals, professionals—will compete to influence age-related political decisions.

- The economics of aging, with greater expenditures for older people and higher taxes for younger groups, will create resentment between various age cohorts.

A wild card in future generational conflict will be the influence and political activity of the baby-boom generation, which will become the nation's largest group of elders ever. Baby boomers are likely to have greater age identification and allegiance, thus giving them tremendous political influence on issues of common interest (for example, protecting pension and retirement plans, strong law and order measures). If, however, baby boomers use their political muscle to raise taxes and expand their own benefits to the detriment of other special-interest groups, resentment toward them will develop. Minorities and a young labor force, in particular, will be affected by the choices baby boomers make regarding public expenditures.

On the other hand, cohort pluralism—heterogeneity within the baby-boom cohort—will factor in greatly for that generation. Baby boomers have always been comprised of a diverse population with tremendous differences. If baby boomers find few common interests and identify primarily with diverse subgroups—affluent, blue-collar, educated, minority, Sunbelt, liberal, conservative, etc.—their numbers might not translate into greater political influence. In either event, however, as this post–World War II population ages, the baby boomers and baby busters will be the source of great interest and concern for generations older and younger (Light 1988).

LESSONS FOR THE POLITICS OF THE NEW AGING

The key to understanding the politics of the New Aging for the next several decades is anticipating a greater likelihood of tension and conflict. Although they might not have sprouted, the seeds are planted. We can forestall and minimize conflict among generations and among subgroups of the elderly population if:

1. *We move away from the interest-group nature of the politics of the Modern Aging period.* The sixty years since the Townsend Movement have been dominated by an old-age lobby primarily concerned with expanding benefits only for senior citizens. This approach was necessary and successful when most older people were poor and disadvantaged, but that is no longer the case.

    Today, the needs of subgroups of the elderly who are already poor or likely to become poor—minorities, women, the frail and disabled, people living in rural areas—are eclipsed by the political power of middle- and upper-middle income, white elderly. The interest-group approach of the old politics will not help these or younger disadvantaged groups.

2. *We move away from age-segregated policies and programs.* The age-segregated nature of public policies is becoming obsolete. With up to a quarter of the population already qualifying for age-related benefits, this approach cannot help but become economically and politically unfeasible. Age-related programs were necessary when the elderly lacked political influence, were fewer in

number, and were mostly poor. Now, however, as people live longer and
increasingly regard themselves as younger at older ages, such programs become
counterproductive and fuel resentment among younger groups.

3. *Elders and their old-age organizations support non-aging issues.* Elders and
their advocacy groups must resume the traditional role of older people: providing leadership and wisdom for entire communities. In the politics of the
New Aging, they must provide the leadership and strength necessary to address
the serious problems facing America: homelessness, drugs, housing, poverty,
economic productivity. Senior-citizen organizations can play an extraordinarily
positive and influential role by supporting public funding for inner-city schools,
employment and training programs for young and older workers, health care
for all Americans, and other such broad-based concerns.

   The role of old-age organizations must change if they are to avoid contributing
to rising tension and conflict. They must gain support of elders for nonaging
issues. Establishing coalitions with nonelderly on nonaged issues is a first step.

4. *We educate young persons about a long life span.* To minimize generational
conflict and to prepare for increased life expectancy, younger people must be
educated about aging, a long life span, and the problems of ageism and age
discrimination. Stereotypes, myths, and discomfort in the presence of older
people and about aging is endemic in the young and contributes to political
polarization among age groups. Providing gerontology programs at the primary
and secondary level will better prepare children for their role in an older society
and will underscore the importance of intergenerational cooperation.

The history of political activity among older people is unique to this
century and country. Only since the 1930s have we seen senior citizens
organize to support political issues for the elderly. The age-segregated
nature of interest-group politics by senior citizens was extraordinarily
successful. The passage of Social Security and other federal and state
programs for older people, decreasing poverty among the old, and the
high political participation rates among elders testify to the success of
politics during the period of the Modern Aging.

However, social, cultural, and political changes now facing a rapidly
aging society require a change in the practice of political activities. Today,
we feel the strain of generational tensions. Although the media might
overstate the conflict that exists among young and old—and such views
are inaccurate and polarizing—we are, in fact, likely to see conflict between and among various older and younger groups in the future.

Longevity, diversity, and generational changes will further fragment an
already competitive political climate. More groups will fight for fewer
public resources. To minimize divisiveness and conflict, our approach to
the politics of aging must change.

The politics of the New Aging must deemphasize age and old-age interest groups and promote vertical alliances as foundations for advocacy
and political organizing. Politics must be based more on vertical com-

monalities representing need rather than on political influence. The poor, the disabled, minorities, women, and other disadvantaged groups of all ages will find more in common with each other than with those who simply share their age.

The old style of politics in which senior citizens, through their extraordinary political influence, could demand public support based on age is fast disappearing. Political influence must shift focus to nonaging issues. The elderly's greater numbers, which in the past implied political clout and legitimacy, might actually hinder their effectiveness in the future. In the new politics, class and need, rather than age, will be overriding factors. Low-income and disadvantaged groups among the elderly will find more in common with younger groups facing similar problems than with their age peers.

Because future politics will be based more on vertical commonalities, old-age organizations must represent the needs and problems of nonaging groups requiring health care, income security, and protection from discrimination (ageism, nativism, sexism, and racism). Since class will be more predominant in the new politics, the well-off elderly must avoid engendering resentment because they are perceived as uncaring toward those less fortunate. Despite the increased electoral strength of future cohorts of older people, politicians must exercise caution and courage in seeking the vote of the elderly. The changing nature of the politics of New Aging will require age-based organizations to change their approach to advocacy and politics if they are to retain and expand their membership. The American Association of Retired Persons, for example, must gravitate toward older minority communities if they are to increase their membership.

We are on the brink of tremendous political change that will be driven by diversity, longevity, and generational relationships, underwritten by economic challenges, and crowded with pressing social needs and competing interests. Can we rise above the fray and develop common cause? Chapter 4 suggests that one step toward social stability might be making better sense of our finances and using them not to secure the desires of a few, but to satisfy the needs of the many.

NOTES

1. For a comprehensive historical overview of events leading to the passage and repeal of the Medicare Catastrophic Coverage Act of 1988 see F. Torres-Gil, "The Politics of Catastrophic and Long-Term Care Coverage," *Journal of Aging and Social Policy* 1, no. 1/2 (1989): 61–86.

2. McKenzie also noted that diversity and the high cost of benefits may undercut the elderly's political clout (1991). He refers to the "law of the few," where smaller numbers allow for a more cohesive, participatory constituent group that

can more effectively influence politics and distribute income and benefits among fewer constituents (e.g., farmers). Where numbers are greater, the "law of the many" prevails, cohesiveness and unity deteriorate, and the aggregate cost of supporting a larger constituency makes it a political target.

BIBLIOGRAPHY

Barnes, James. "Age-Old Strife." *National Journal* 4 (Jan. 26, 1991): 216–19.
Chakravarty, Subrata, and Katherine Wesman. "Consuming Our Children?" *Forbes*, Nov. 14, 1988, 222–32.
"The Coming Conflict as We Soak the Young to Enrich the Old." *The Washington Post*, Jan. 5, 1986.
Ficke, Susan, ed. "An Orientation to the Older Americans Act." Washington, D.C.: National Association of State Units on Aging, July 1985.
Hudson, Robert, and John Strate. "Aging and Political Systems." In *Handbook of Aging and the Social Sciences*, 2d ed., edited by Robert Binstock and Ethel Shanas. New York: Van Nostrand Reinhold Company, 1985. 554–88.
Kosterlitz, Julie. "Young vs. Old." *National Journal* (December 10, 1988): 3160.
Longman, Phillip. "Justice between Generations." *The Atlantic Monthly*, June 1985, 73–81.
McKenzie, Richard. "The Retreat of the Elderly Welfare State." *Wall Street Journal*, March 12, 1991.
Minkler, Meredith. "Generational Equity and the New Victim Blaming: An Emerging Public Policy Issue." *International Journal of Health Services* 16, 4 (1986): 539–51.
Preston, Samuel. "Children and the Elderly in the United States." *Scientific American* 251, 6 (1984): 44–49.
R L Associates. "The American Public Views of Long-Term Care." Princeton, N. J.: R L Associates, October 1987.
Torres-Gil, Fernando. "The Politics of Catastrophic and Long-Term Care Coverage." *Journal of Aging and Social Policy*, 1, no. 1/2 (1989): 61–86.
U.S. Bureau of the Census. Voting and Registration in the Election of November 1988 (Advance Report). *Current Population Reports*, ser. P–20, no. 435. Washington, D.C.: U.S. Government Printing Office, 1989.
Williamson, J. B., L. Evans, and L. A. Powell. *Politics of Aging*. Springfield, Ill.: Charles C. Thomas, 1982.

4
ECONOMICS OF THE
NEW AGING

Any government, like any family, can for a year spend a little more than it earns. But you and I know that a continuance of that habit means the poorhouse.

Franklin Delano Roosevelt

Financial support for benefits and programs for older people and the increasing cost of entitlement programs are central to the New Aging. Can we afford the current array of public benefits and services? How will we finance services for an anticipated larger cohort of older people?

As the U.S. population ages, tension and debate escalate over the allocation of public and private resources among generations and within subgroups of the elderly. Are too many resources being spent on today's older population? How do we prepare for more poor and low-income older people?

Generational issues, increasing life expectancies, and diversification of the aged population in the coming decades will directly affect the economics of aging. The economics of the New Aging reflect circumstances now impacting the financial security of individuals as they age, and raise unsettling questions about the financial status of future generations of older people.

This chapter examines the present and future economic situation of the elderly and the ongoing debate about paying for old-age benefits, and explores economic factors defining income security, as well as ways in which the economics of the New Aging will redefine our view of financial security in old age.

INCOME SECURITY IN OLD AGE

How do the elderly support themselves? How do individuals prepare for retirement? In what ways has our view of what constitutes sufficient income and financial resources in old age changed over time?

Income security means many things. It involves what children do for their parents and what parents expect from their children. It also has to do with one generation's dependence on another for funding of large-scale entitlement programs. Income security is about fear of impoverishment in old age and society's ability or inability to afford benefits for large segments of an elderly population.

The threat of dependency among the elderly has been a concern for a long time. With increasing life expectancies, it becomes a more central issue for society. It wasn't until the beginning of this century that retirement and leisure in the later years became a societal expectation. In this century, the United States and much of the industrialized world encountered the need to provide financial support for older people unable to support themselves and not fully supported by their families. Industrialization, bureaucratization, urbanization, economic prosperity, individualism, and increasing life expectancy led to the phenomena of "retirement" and "leisure" years. Older people were either better able to leave the work force or had outlived their usefulness as workers. Mandatory retirement laws forced the elderly to leave their jobs. Changes in family structure and social mobility meant more elderly living independently or apart from family members. Thus, the question of how older people could provide for their own income security arose.

By the 1930s, the first major federal attempt to provide income security to older people occurred with the passage of the Social Security Act of 1935. At the time, individuals were expected to rely on a "three-legged stool" for their retirement income. This stool presupposed using three sources of retirement income: (1) private and/or public retirement and pension plans; (2) personal assets (investments, home equity, savings); and (3) Social Security as a supplement to the other two. The three-legged stool has defined the economics of aging over the last sixty years, but is now undergoing major changes. Those changes will, in the New Aging, lead to a "four-legged chair" of retirement income, where pensions, personal assets, and Social Security will be supplemented by whatever public benefits (e.g., SSI, DI, OAA) are available at that time.

Today, income security in old age is a variation of the three-legged stool. Private pensions are viewed by some analysts as a major source of funding future retirement income. Since 1974, the number of plans has more than doubled from 340,000 to over 870,000 (Population Reference Bureau 1990). In 1984, private pensions covered over 40 million people accounting for 49 percent of workers. By 1990, 50 million workers were covered by an employer-sponsored pension plan. Nearly 60 percent of workers in 1990 were eligible to participate in an employer-sponsored pension plan, although only half had enough years of service to be fully vested in a plan and thus entitled to future benefits (Population Reference Bureau 1990). Private pensions and retirement programs continue to be a major source of income security, and will increase in importance in the future. They are also a major source of private capital. In 1990 private pension funds totalled $2 trillion. In 1988, pension plans owed $566 billion in equities, 18 percent of all equities in the United States (U.S. Senate, 1991).

Reliance on personal assets is changing dramatically. Many view home equity as a major financial luxury enjoyed by the aged, since over 80 percent of elderly couples own their home, and many parts of the country have enjoyed high rates of home appreciation during the 1970s and 1980s. By 1984, almost 70 percent of the elderly had at least $20,000 in home equity (Schulz 1988, 39). On the other hand, during the same period, older people had few other financial assets. Among married couples over 65 years of age, only 28 percent had assets over $100,000. This trend continues. Most middle-aged people have very low savings rates and assume their home equity will provide for their retirement, as it has for many older people.

The role of savings in providing income in retirement has increased over the last decades. In 1986, 26 percent of elderly income came from assets, compared with only 16 percent in 1962. The distribution of asset income, however, varies for different elderly subgroups, demonstrating how longevity and diversity affect savings. The old-old are less likely to have asset income than the younger elderly. In 1986, for example, only 62 percent of those 80 and older had asset income, compared with 68 percent of those in the 65–69 age group. In 1986, 71 percent of elderly men had asset income, compared with 66 percent of elderly women. Seventy-one percent of elderly whites had asset income, compared to only 30 percent for blacks and 31 percent for Hispanic elderly (U.S. Senate, 1991).

Personal assets include family contributions. Interfamily and intrafamily transfer of financial resources (gifts or loans) have traditionally been a major source of economic support for the elderly (Schulz 1988). This will change over time, as individuals have fewer children and, later, outlive them.

Today, Social Security more than supplements the income of older people. For many it is their primary source of income. In 1984, for example, 62 percent of white senior citizens relied on Social Security for 50 percent or more of their income—24 percent of them relied on it for 90 percent of their income. Dependence on Social Security is even greater for minority older people. Among the black elderly, 78 percent rely on it for 50 percent or more of their income—39 percent of that group rely on it for 90 percent or more of their income. For Hispanic elderly, 72 percent rely on Social Security for 50 percent or more of their income, and 38 percent for 90 percent or more of their income (National Council of La Raza 1987). If the percentage of senior citizens in poverty increases, Social Security income will become a more important leg of the stool.

At present, the stool has a fourth leg, making it more of a "chair" of retirement income. Public benefits and services, including Medicare and Medicaid health-care coverage, services provided under the Older Americans Act and Social Services Block Grant, income accruing from Disability and Supplemental Security Income, Title V Employment and Training, and volunteer programs (e.g., Foster Grandparents) represent an increasingly large segment of income and support. Many older people, particularly the poor and lower-middle income elderly, rely on nutrition programs for their primary meal, or on the limited dollars of SSI.[1]

The economic circumstances facing the elderly today reflect changes in our earlier view of retirement income. Characteristic are the increasing reliance on Social Security and the added leg of public benefits and services. As Social Security and public benefits become more important, the importance of the first leg—retirement and pension programs—will diminish.

Formerly the primary source of old-age income, this first leg could become weak and vulnerable to economic disruption. Recent years have seen serious problems in private pensions. In 1986, for example, three pension plans covering LTV Corporation's steel operations were discontinued (when LTV filed for Chapter 11 bankruptcy) with unfunded pension benefits of about $2 billion dollars (Schmitt and Solomon 1987). Only the intervention of the Pension Benefit Guaranty Corporation assured distribution of at least some benefits. Even at that, it took a Supreme Court decision in 1990 to give PBGC the authority to restore LTV's pension obligation back to the corporation. Many more private and public (e.g., municipal governments) pensions face substantial unfunded pension liabilities, and the vulnerability of firms in other declining industries is growing. If private pensions and public retirement programs prove vulnerable, the first leg becomes undependable and future cohorts of retirees are forced to rely more heavily on Social Security and personal savings, and to continue working ("Company-Financed Pensions are Failing to Fulfill Promise" 1990).

The economics of the New Aging, however, will encompass more than how individuals should accrue retirement income or on what public benefits they can depend in old age. Income security will involve a host of issues complicating our approach to its reform.

Income security will be about working and being able to work. Living longer and retiring earlier—the trend today—will mean that inflation will erode even the most secure pension plan. Increases in the cost of living will shrink retirement dollars. Individuals might want to continue to work in retirement or might have no choice. Age discrimination, flexible work opportunities, late-life education, and post-retirement benefits will become major issues.

The economics of the New Aging will include distribution of economic resources. Public benefits and pensions comprise a large portion of the federal budget. The elderly, in comparison to other groups (the disabled; welfare recipients), protected their programs during funding reductions in the 1980s. Reallocating domestic funding among the elderly and other needy groups will become very controversial politically.

Income security will also involve one generation's reliance on another for benefits and support. Taxing younger workers to pay for Social Security benefits, passing bond measures that will obligate future taxpayers financially, drawing on the elderly's political influence to impose new taxes to pay for expanded old-age benefits, and handling younger people's concerns about what awaits them, highlight generational issues related to income security. It is what Hugh Heclo calls generational politics between those paying taxes and those receiving benefits (Heclo 1988).

Thus, the economics of the New Aging goes beyond changes in the three-legged stool of retirement income. It involves a set of complex factors affecting not only the income security of today's elderly but tomorrow's as well. The political and economic decisions we make in addressing these cannot help but be affected by our view of the economic status of the elderly. As long as we view the elderly as "them" against everyone else, economic controversies will revolve around old-age benefits. Moving away from age-segregated programs and creating intergenerational coalitions among organizations representing the old and young are indispensable in avoiding economic conflicts. Shifting stereotypes about the elderly make this a paramount concern.

Needy vs. Greedy

In recent years, misperceptions and stereotypes about the economic status of the elderly have clouded the public's view. During most of the past sixty years—the politics of the Modern Aging period—the elderly were portrayed as needy and dependent. In making its case for public pensions, the Townsend Movement highlighted the despair and destitution of older people. The architects of Social Security were responding as much to the distressing situation of elderly who had lost homes and savings as to creating job opportunities for younger workers. Advocates for the elderly throughout the 1950s, 1960s, and 1970s portrayed older people as a needy group facing serious problems (with income, transportation, housing, food, and health care), among other things.

That advocacy, most pronounced during the White House Conferences on Aging in 1961, 1971, and 1981, served a useful political purpose. It generated public sympathy and congressional support. It accorded legitimacy to demands for expanded benefits. The dramatic expansion in old-age services during the 1960s and 1970s was supported in large measure because older people were perceived as a "deserving" constituency.

In the 1980s, that view changed. Almost overnight, the elderly began being portrayed as well-off, healthy, enjoying multiple pension and retirement benefits, and retiring in leisure and affluence. In "Grays on the Go," *Time* magazine portrayed retirees relaxing in hot tubs at luxurious retirement communities (1988). *The New Republic* ran a cover story on the "greedy geezers" who demanded more benefits than they needed (Fairlie 1988). This portrait of the affluent elder served as a pretext to push for reducing benefits and to force the elderly to pay for their expansion (as in the case of the Medicare Catastrophic Coverage Act).

By the 1990s, the shifting view of the economic status of older people became part of national budget debates. Some viewed entitlement programs for older people as a luxury the nation could not afford and a potential source of generational divisiveness. Even the savings and loan debacle had an air of economic and generational tensions, with one argument put forth "that the money transfer is between generations: from fuzzy-cheeked, hard-working taxpayers to older folk who put their nest eggs into failed S & Ls" (Starobin 1990).[2] Thus, the economics of the New Aging reflect shifting stereotypes characterizing the financial condition of older people. These views, in turn, influence political decisions.

Where does the truth lie? Are nearly all of the elderly as well-off or as poor as they are portrayed? Have we achieved a measure of income security allowing today's elders to be better off financially than their children? Can middle-aged and younger people expect an adequate income, Social Security, and other old-age services in their later years? What can we expect from the economics of the New Aging?

ECONOMIC STATUS OF THE AGED: FACT AND FICTION

Older people, as a group, have improved their economic status. During the 1930s and 1940s, approximately 75 percent of people 65 and over were poor (Smolensky et al. 1988). That proportion dropped to 35 percent in 1959, 24 percent in 1970, and 12.2 percent in 1986 (U.S. Senate 1988; Preston 1984; Villers 1987). In addition, older people enjoy tax benefits and public transfers. The nontaxability of most Social Security benefits, a tax credit for elderly persons with retirement income, and the capital gains tax credit earned in selling one's home, augment public benefits the elderly have acquired since the 1930s.

Notwithstanding these relative gains, the elderly as a group are less well-off than aggregate figures might suggest. Many are poor or susceptible to impoverishment. Compared strictly on the basis of income, people 65 and older, on average, earn less than those under 65. In 1986, the median income of families with heads age 65 or older was $19,932—about 62 percent of the median income ($32,368) of families with heads age 25 to 64 (U.S. Senate 1988). By 1990, the median income for families with a householder age 65 and older had increased to $21,676 (Social Security Administration 1990).

Further, the elderly are much more likely to have incomes just above the poverty level. In 1986, 15.5 percent of people 65 and older were in families with incomes ranging between the poverty level and one-and-a-half times it. Only 8.5 percent of those under age 65 were members of families with incomes within this range (U.S. Senate 1988).

Wide income and poverty variations occur within elderly groups. Poverty is high among minority elderly: blacks, 31.5 percent; Hispanics, 23.9 percent; women, 15.6 percent; and those 85 years and older, 18.7 percent (Villers 1987). The Census Bureau's use of a lower index for the elderly must also be taken into account in comparing poverty rates based on age. In 1986, for example, poverty was defined as $5,255 for an individual over 65, compared to $5,701 for a person under 65 (U.S. Senate 1988).

In recent years, the definition of poverty has become a subject of debate. Richard Margolis (1990) vividly describes the real-life poverty confronting many of America's elderly, particularly those who are female, black, Hispanic, and near poor. He also points out that, since 1969, the federal government has used two measures to determine poverty: a lower poverty threshold for those over 65 ($5447 in 1987 for a single person), and a higher level for those under 65 ($5909 for a single person). The result of this two-tier system is to artificially lower the number of older persons considered poor. The official poverty threshold focuses primarily on what families spend for food and assumes that older persons will spend a smaller proportion of their income on food.

Organizations such as Families USA argue that if the poverty lines used for the elderly were the same as for everyone else, the elderly poverty rate would exceed the poverty rate of the population as a whole (O'Hare et al. 1990). Based on an extensive public opinion poll asking what Americans consider "real life poverty," Families USA suggests that the average poverty line for a family of four (based on 1988 dollars) be $15,017, rather than $12,092, the official government poverty line. This would raise the percentage of Americans said to be poor from 13 percent to 18 percent. The real life poverty rate for the elderly would be 24 percent, or 3 million persons. During the 1990s, poverty specialists, advocates for the poor, and some politicians will probably attempt to update the federal poverty measure to reflect changes in the cost of necessities. Others will argue that the value of in-kind welfare benefits (e.g., food stamps, housing subsidies, and health-care coverage) should be included, and that revising the official poverty index would dramatically increase fiscal demands to aid the newly proclaimed poor (Kosterlitz 1990).

Despite the income diversity within the elderly population, a large proportion of public resources are devoted to older people. Social Security and Medicare, the two largest components of social spending on the elderly, comprise 6.6 percent of the GNP (Gould and Palmer 1988). Nationally, by 1990, we spent at least $358 billion dollars a year for benefits to the elderly, comprising approximately 28 percent of federal spending, and representing roughly five times what was spent on this age group 25 years earlier, in real terms. Granted, those figures include programs funded largely by people who will benefit by them (Social Security, public pension and retirement systems).

Even with a large proportion of federal and state revenues going to the elderly, the poorest and most vulnerable are not benefiting. Stephen Crystal, in his prescient book describing *America's Old Age Crisis* (1982), argues that existing old-age policies are inequitable, inefficient, and ineffective. His book describes how large public expenditures for the elderly subsidize the greater number of healthy and well-off at the expense of the fewer really poor and old, and isolate the aged (via age-specific requirements) from the central institutions of society (i.e., family, community).

Robert Binstock has long argued that "many older persons remain highly vulnerable with respect to income, health, functional status, and other dimensions of fundamental well-being" (1990, 76). Despite massive public expenditures, close to 4 million elderly live in poverty, with an additional 4.4 million within 150 percent of the poverty index. Poverty rates for older minorities and older women living alone are extraordinarily high. Even with the SSI program and its minimum guaranteed federal income payment, upwards of 50 percent of those eligible are not enrolled. Medicaid, a program intended for the medically indigent of all ages, has become a de facto nursing-home program for middle- and upper-income elderly who have spent down to the poverty level. Social support programs such as the Older Americans Act and senior volunteer programs are most heavily used by middle-income and English-speaking older people and are under-used by the minority and poor.

In examining the economic status of the elderly today, we find large amounts of public resources available to older people, but a high level of poverty and economic vulnerability among those individuals. In the economics of the New Aging we face a paradox: certain groups of older people—middle-income, English-speaking, relatively well-educated, and middle-class—are well served, while others—poor, non-English-speaking, sick, and isolated—remain vulnerable. Why are so many in need of health, income, and social services when we spend such a large proportion of the federal and state budgets for the elderly?

Answers vary. For many poor older people, the rising cost of health care, housing, and transportation outstrip their retirement income. For others, Social Security's relatively low benefits are their primary source of income. Still others (immigrants, undocumented people, non-English-speaking) find qualifying difficult and are intimidated by the complicated set of existing social programs and benefits. A basic feature of social policies for older people is that, with some exceptions (e.g., SSI) programs and services for the elderly are not intended to focus on the very poor (although they do to a large extent), but to enable middle-income people to enjoy greater independence and assistance in later life. Programs serving the poor (Medicaid, Supplemental Security Income, Social Services Block Grants, Aid to Families with Dependent Children) enjoyed less political support and faced greater reductions during the 1980s.

Many retirement benefits, particularly government and private pensions, have gone to those best able to obtain high wages: educated, skilled, white males. Women, minorities, the poor, sick, uneducated, and those working in small businesses are much less likely to participate in high-paying jobs that lead to higher levels of retirement income. Women and minorities, in particular, have only in the last two decades entered the labor force in large numbers and begun to enjoy promotions and salary increases. Ironically for them, their upward mobility occurs at a time when union wages and protections are declining and many companies are trimming their pension and retiree health care coverage.

This economic state of affairs creates fertile breeding grounds for "doom-and-gloom" scenarios about the economy and generational relationships. Futurists and editorialists ask, "Who Will Pay?" (Kosterlitz 1986), and speculate that Social Security will go broke before the baby boomers retire. Others portray a picture of an indentured generation of younger workers "born to pay" (Longman 1987) and predict war between young and old. Editorialists depict younger Americans as downwardly mobile, while today's senior citizens are the richest in history. Other writers, most notably Peter Peterson (1987), point to "The Morning After," when we as a nation discover that while spending huge sums on the elderly population, our economy has declined, and we are unable to meet our domestic and foreign obligations.

Dire predictions about our inability to afford benefits to the elderly create an emotional and reactionary climate ripe for drastic solutions. The same writers answer their fear-laden predictions with proposals to privatize Social Security, reduce benefits for the elderly, ration health care to the very old, and eliminate universal entitlement in favor of means-tested programs.

No one knows if these predictions will prove true. However, the solutions proposed are extreme and misguided at best. They reflect a classic case of scapegoating the elderly for the real problems of poverty, budget deficits, loss of competitiveness and productivity to other countries, and a political unwillingness to tackle social problems. They perpetuate divisiveness and generational conflict and do little to address the real culprit: a lack of national will to address the needs of all groups, regardless of age. In many respects, the elderly are blamed for one of the few successes in American social policy: the relative decline of poverty among them and their increased life expectancy. Unfortunately, much of the debate about America's aging and domestic concerns revolves around the cost of providing services to older persons. Notwithstanding large public expenditures for the elderly, policy solutions often assume that serving other population groups requires draconian cuts in existing entitlements for the elderly and their families. Schulz, Borowski, and Crown (1991) say the key to serving an aging population lies in the economy's performance, not the cost of providing for legitimate needs. Population aging presents manageable economic issues, but the debate about paying for services has us looking for solutions in the wrong places. Our inability to go beyond the bottom-line in addressing an aging society's needs generates what Schulz, Borowski, and Crown term "voodoo demographics," wherein both the problem and solution focus on lost opportunities and an intolerable economic burden. The debate and political options must expand beyond what is possible. The issue is whether public opinion and the political system can look beyond their fascination with old age and its attendant costs.

Although views presented by those who feel too much is done for the elderly at the expense of the economy are unfair and at times extreme, real economic problems related to aging are afoot in the United States; problems complicating both benefits reform and ways of preparing baby boomers for retirement.

Fiscal Tensions in Aging Policy

Providers and advocates for the elderly must recognize that fiscal tensions do exist in aging policy. Although fears provoked and extremist solutions put forth by those who would retract social programs for the elderly are unwarranted, fiscal tensions leading to those views are real. Financing the current costly system of public benefits for older people (using current eligibility criteria) is becoming a heavy burden for state and federal governments.

John Palmer and Stephanie Gould estimate federal budget outlays required to support existing pension and health-care programs will increase dramatically during the period of the New Aging. Their projections show that, using 1985 federal budget assumptions, without reform, the health-care sector's share of GNP would more than double in fifty years, rising from 3 to 6 percent of GNP. Pension programs would increase from 6.1

percent of GNP in 1990 to 7 percent by 2025. Total expenditures would increase from 24.6 percent of GNP in 1990 to 29.4 percent in 2050 (1986).

Palmer and Gould conclude that, if current commitments continued, we face a major tax increase. Without such an increase we will encounter some painful choices: cut programs and entitlements, pit groups against each other for dwindling resources, means-test programs only for the poor and lose political support among the middle class, or take away from other domestic programs (such as food stamps, job-training programs, education). These choices will create winners and losers and exacerbate conflict, competition, and tension among subgroups of elderly and other age cohorts. They will do little to stem the growing incidence of poverty among the elderly or the even greater economic disparity between the older poor and their affluent counterparts.

Efforts during the early 1990s to control spending and reduce the deficit may actually create generational tensions. The Omnibus Budget Reconciliation Act of 1990 (OBRA 90) included new rules to curb taxes and spending options for fiscal years 1991 to 1995 (ASAP 1991). OBRA 90 created, for example, three categories for discretionary spending (not including Medicare, Medicaid, and Social Security): domestic programs, defense, and international (primarily foreign) aid. Spending and cuts cannot be shifted among these categories. The domestic category includes programs for older persons and ensures that entitlement programs grow naturally as new beneficiaries become eligible for them. It also allows for inflation. It forbids expansion of programs (e.g., adding long-term health care for the elderly), unless new benefits are offset by entitlement cuts elsewhere (within the domestic category), or taxes are raised. Otherwise, across-the-board cuts will occur within the category. Thus, programs (e.g., student loans vs. expanding Medicare) and interest groups (e.g., poor children and poor elderly vs. the better-off elderly) may compete unless public reluctance to increase taxes declines markedly.

Unfortunately, we have been in a period of fiscal conservatism fostering an unwillingness to fund social programs, fiscal cutbacks (primarily in programs for younger groups), and a persistent budget deficit. This deficit exacerbates the financing of old-age benefits. Its existence is used as an excuse for not expanding benefits to the needy elderly and other groups.

On a personal level, even with the large public expenditures on behalf of older people, individuals fear impoverishment in old age. Increasing life expectancy, the fact that few private or public pension and retirement programs are adjusted for inflation, and the incidence of reductions and bankruptcy among pension and retiree health-care plans, further the concern among many individuals that they could become destitute. Although poverty rates for older people (65 years and over) as a group are around 13 percent, they increase to 19 percent or more for those age 85 and over (Villers 1987).

Medicaid is another example. To qualify for nursing-home care, older people must deplete much of their assets to the poverty level. This is easy to do. With the cost of nursing homes averaging $30,000 a year (upwards of $60,000 for quality institutions), an older person with substantial personal assets (e.g., savings and property) would see their resources rapidly erode. A major study in Massachusetts showed that the income of seven in ten elderly living alone was spent down to the federal poverty level after only thirteen weeks in a nursing home (U.S. House Select Committee on Aging 1987).

Fear of impoverishment, the failure of public expenditures to address poverty among the elderly, and the almost certain rapid escalation of costs for old-age programs dramatize the serious fiscal tension inherent in social policies for the elderly. No public program underscores these better than the Social Security System.

Social Security and the Economics of the New Aging

Social Security reflects both the overall success in the economic position of the elderly and our shortcomings in providing for the financial security of an aging population. It demonstrates why generational pressures, longevity, and diversity will prompt changes in economics and financing. In the economics of the New Aging, the Social Security System and all other social policies for the elderly will require modifications. These changes will have a bearing on the federal deficit, the economy, and future generations.

Social Security was passed in 1935 (a time when many young men were seeking work) to create jobs and provide a minimum income to the elderly. The image of destitute and homeless older people forced to scrounge for food was a powerful motivator in creating the nation's first social insurance program. The system was predicated on several key features: an eligibility age of 65, pay-as-you-go financing wherein contributions equaled outlays, government-sponsorship, and compulsory contributions.

Social Security evolved over the years to become a comprehensive social, health, and income security program for the elderly, their widows and survivors, the disabled of all ages, students, domestic workers, and the self-employed. Robert Gray and Joan Szabo characterize Social Security today as really four programs: a pay-as-you go retirement program; a welfare program that provides proportionately higher benefits to those with lower contributions; a program that provides medical benefits; and a program whose surplus is used to fund current government operations (1990). To pay for these diverse benefits and financing schemes, payroll taxes to workers and employers rose from 1 percent back in 1950 to 7.65 percent for individuals and for employers (or a total of 15 percent for the self-employed) on a maximum taxable income of $51,300 by 1990 (with the wages subject to the 1.45 percent Medicare Part A payroll contribution slated to increase to a maximum taxable income of $125,000 beginning in 1991).

Social Security became the most politically popular of social policies. Its social insurance mechanisms enjoyed widespread support among young and old. Fully 95 percent of the work force participates in the program. Approximately 40 million people in 1990, including retired workers and their survivors, as well as the disabled, receive benefits (that figure will rise to 50 million beneficiaries in 2010 and 75 million beneficiaries in 2050, assuming current eligibility criteria) (Gray and Szabo 1990; U.S. Senate 1991). Social Security is the primary reason poverty has decreased among the elderly from 28.5 percent in 1966 to 12.4 percent in 1986 (U.S. Senate 1989). Throughout most of its history the Social Security Administration has been viewed as a well-managed and efficient federal agency providing benefits in a timely and consistent manner (in 1990 administrative expenses were around one percent of the total benefits paid during that period).

On the other hand, Social Security dramatizes the intersection of generational pressures, longevity, and diversity. Although it was never intended to be more than supplemental to personal assets, pension and retirement programs, and savings, Social Security is the primary source of retirement income for many low-income and minority older people. Who could have guessed that the average life expectancy would increase to over 75 years of age while, at the same time, the average retirement age decreased to 62 years of age? That divergence meant that the ratio of workers paying into the system and individuals receiving benefits would decrease from 16.5 to 1 in 1950, to the present 3 to 1. Unless retirement trends reverse, the ratio will further decrease to 2.4 to 1 by 2020, and 1.9 to 1 by 2035 ("Social Security at 50 Faces New Crossroads" 1985).

The need to increase payroll taxes to offset demographic changes has raised serious generational tensions among younger workers paying a large portion of their income to Social Security but doubting they will benefit ("Social Security Drain Worries Under–45 Set" 1990). Polls show that, although most Americans of all ages support the Social Security program, serious concerns about the future of Social Security proliferate. One survey, for example, showed that 70 percent oppose reducing benefits to current beneficiaries ("Social Security at 50 Faces New Crossroads" 1985), while, at the same time, fully 40 percent were unsure if they would receive their Social Security benefits. Another poll, conducted in 1990 by the National Taxpayers Union Foundation, found that 63 percent supported the idea of reducing Social Security and Medicare benefits for high-income persons to ensure payments for future retirees, while 80 percent believed government should provide tax deductions to encourage people to save for retirement (Rich 1991).

Ironically, this crisis of confidence among younger workers might increase as a result of the 1983 reforms that created a growing Social Security surplus. In 1983, because the pay-as-you-go system was proving
insufficient, Congress instituted several major reforms, including raising
the eligibility age, increasing payroll tax, subjecting partial Social Security
benefits to income taxation, and instituting a surplus revenue system.

These reforms have worked spectacularly well. As of 1990, Social Security reserves totalled an estimated $226 billion, compared with $163
billion in 1989 (U.S. Senate 1991). Unfortunately, until 1991, this surplus
was used to offset the federal deficit and meet the deficit reduction requirements of the Gramm-Rudman-Hollings legislation. In 1990 alone, for
example, the inclusion of Social Security reserves offset an estimated $63
billion in the general revenue deficit.

The use of Social Security to mask the federal deficit at that time, and
the continuing practice of investing Social Security reserves in interest-
paying Treasury securities, meant that at some-time the federal treasury
would have to repay the Social Security trust fund. According to the U.S.
Senate Special Committee on Aging, the assets Social Security accrues
represent internally held federal debt (1991). The growing trust-fund re-
serve enables Congress to spend more money elsewhere without raising
taxes or borrowing from private markets. At some point, general revenues
will have to increase, or spending will have to be cut, when the debt to
Social Security comes due. Either the economy would be so prosperous
that the federal budget would generate huge surpluses, or new taxes would
be required. Some would argue, however, that there was little to worry
about, given the fact that the federal government's "full faith and credit"
was backing those treasury IOUs. However, those huge sums of projected
surpluses are difficult for future Social Security beneficiaries to ignore.

By 1990, Congress and the president were forced to confront this co-
nundrum. Senator Moynihan was one of the first to propose that Social
Security return to a pay-as-you-go system and that payroll taxes be reduced. His plan would have reduced the Social Security contribution rate
from 6.2 to 5.2 percent over five years and raise the wages subject to the
payroll deduction from $53,400 in 1990 to $82,000 in 1996. He criticized
the regressive nature of the program and the use of the surplus for purposes other than saving for the baby boomers' retirement. President
George Bush and some members of Congress (Republican and Democrat)
vehemently opposed this proposal, fearing that reducing the surplus would
force them to raise other taxes or further reduce domestic and defense
programs to cover the deficit.

The Moynihan proposal was initially defeated on a Senate procedural
vote during the budget debates of 1990. However, the Budget Enforcement Act of 1990 unintentionally made the Moynihan proposal viable
again. With implementation of the budget accord, Social Security Re-

serves will not be used to offset the deficit amounts. Yet, the reserves are still being invested in treasury securities. Thus, a combination of not needing the reserves to hide the true size of the deficit and continuing fears that those securities might not be paid back emboldened sufficient members of Congress to revisit the idea in 1991. Congress again defeated the Moynihan proposal on a procedural motion (by a larger margin than the year before). Arguments for and against revealed further political and ideological divisions not necessarily based on partisan politics. The president, many Democrats and Republicans, and some senior-citizen organizations (e.g., AARP) were against the proposal, ostensibly to avoid undercutting the public's already tenuous faith in the Social Security system. They did, however, acknowledge that cutting payroll taxes would exacerbate the federal deficit and hurt the economy, since no other sources of revenue were available to restore such cuts. Republicans and Democrats voting with Moynihan felt it was unfair to use reserves to reduce the federal deficit. The Democrats, however, also saw the Moynihan proposal as *the* political issue to demonstrate the regressive effect of raising Social Security taxes on the middle class while lowering income taxes on upper-income taxpayers.

The political firestorm sparked by this proposal to alter the manner in which Social Security collects and disburses contributions is symptomatic of fiscal tensions in the economics of the New Aging. It reflects the high stakes millions of Americans of all ages have in protecting public programs affecting their future income security.

Whether or not payroll taxes are reduced, the pressures of longevity, the growing number of older people, a trend toward early retirement, and changing worker-beneficiary ratios will continue to generate controversial proposals to change the system. Some have proposed, for example, that Social Security be a voluntary program. Individuals could choose to contribute to the system or invest their payroll taxes elsewhere. Others argue that Social Security should be means-tested and serve only the poor and needy. Even conservative voices, such as *Business Week*, argue that "it makes little sense to give Social Security benefits to the many elderly households with sizable earnings and assets," and the United States will be forced to "replace Social Security systems in their present form with systems of benefits only for the needy elderly" ("Social Security Should Benefit Only the Elderly Poor" 1989).

By the 1990s, the Social Security program had become an object of social engineering for purposes other than the original intent of the program. Some economists and policy analysts, for example, would add "social investing" as a basic construct by using the reserves to fund programs for children as an investment in the future, using the Social Security surplus to increase national savings by investing in public infrastructure and human capital, and raising the mandatory retirement age.

Others have proposed using Social Security to promote inter-generational approaches. In the early 1990s, Congressman Bill Hughes (D–N.J.) proposed an "Intergenerational Earnings Test Elimination Act" that would drop the Social Security earnings test for older workers providing child-care services.

Any proposal to change the basic nature of the Social Security system is guaranteed to excite major political controversy and a vehement backlash from the current cohort of elderly (as the MCCA of 1988 demonstrated).[3] Social Security, however, will serve as a case study on how a proven method of providing economic security to the elderly in the Modern Aging might not serve them in the future. The original intent of the program—to provide a supplemental income to workers—has changed drastically. Many more people rely on the program for basic financial support. Others no longer believe it will serve their retirement needs. All the while, political constituencies benefiting from the current structure fear any change that might affect what they receive. Changing demographics and the overall aging of the population create pressures unforeseen by the program's architects in the 1930s. What we will find is that Social Security, in its present form, will be unable to fully satisfy the needs of an increasingly diverse and rapidly growing older population. The important issue to note in focusing on Social Security as an illustration of the changing economics of the New Aging is that the structure of Social Security might require modifications, but not its basic principles. How we administer benefits and develop eligibility criteria will change. However, the concept of social insurance, the underlying rationale, must remain. To use the program's difficulties in meeting the demographic pressures of the New Aging to dismantle or privatize Social Security is wrong. The concept of sharing risks and requiring universal contributions remains sound.

An examination of generational pressures, diversity, and longevity will further reveal the reasons economic reform is required if we are to avoid problems. Further, it will provide recommendations for reforms in Social Security and other programs that will ensure income security for the elderly into the future.

GENERATIONAL CLAIMS

The economics of the New Aging will spotlight generational differences among the elderly, past, present, and future. Today's generation of elderly are a product of the economics of aging in earlier times. Tomorrow's economics will dictate a different set of fiscal and income policies for the next generation of elderly. One aspect of these is the changing attitudes and expectations individuals have toward preparing for retirement.

For example, today's elderly have been influenced by the Great Depres-

sion of the 1930s and World War II. The poverty, joblessness, and economic insecurity they might have experienced bred a set of attitudes: self-
reliance, saving for the future, and expecting the government to step in
as a last resort. Victory in World War II created faith and trust in big
government's ability to benefit the social welfare. These attitudes might
seem contradictory, but they help to explain why many older people today
hold conservative social values (e.g., patriotism, faith in religion and
family) but remain liberal in their view of government (e.g., supporting
Social Security and Medicare).

In addition, the present generation of elderly benefited from peacetime
prosperity in the 1950s and 1960s, an accumulation of Social Security
surpluses, and the dramatic growth and generosity of pension plans with
few claimants. Many now enjoy multiple pensions (for example, veteran's
pension, civil-service retirement income, and Social Security), as well as
home equity and income from appreciated stocks. The image of a retired
couple driving cross-country in a roomy RV to their home in southern
Florida might be somewhat exaggerated, but it is true that many older
people today enjoy substantial benefits and maintain an active and independent lifestyle in retirement.

Similarly, the elder generation of the 1990s will continue to benefit.
Their retirement will remain relatively secure, although an increasing
number of pension and retirement programs face fiscal pressures, retiree
health-insurance programs are being scaled back, and public benefits are
under budget constraints. In large measure, this continued security is due
to a drop in birthrates during the 1930s and 1940s. Those reaching old age
in the 1990s enter at a time when the increase in the older population will
plateau and the baby boomers will be at their most productive.

It will be the baby boomers of the next century and the baby busters
who will face the "generational economics" of the New Aging. The fiscal
tensions in today's system of public benefits and programs may become
serious financial problems by the time these generations reach retirement.

The expectations of the baby boomers and busters are different than
those of their parents and grandparents. Raised during the economic affluence of the 1950s, 1960s, and 1970s, they were indulged by parents who
wanted their children to have the material benefits they themselves lacked
in their youth. Consequently, the baby boomers and busters are not as
likely to have worried about their future and the need to save for old age.
They expect to do better than their parents and to carry relatively affluent
lifestyles into their retirement years.

For example, unlike their parents, whose homeownership pattern was
to trade up from a small to a larger, more comfortable home, children
and grandchildren today expect to start off with a large, expensive home
in a nice neighborhood. Further, they expect to acquire the high home
equity their parents enjoyed. Yet, if real-estate predictions prove accurate,

the baby boomers are in for a rude awakening when home prices decline because the baby-buster cohort provides fewer homebuyers. Even now, we are beginning to see downward mobility among some baby boomers who face job layoffs, erosion of health benefits, and lower wages.

Much of the prevailing uncertainty and potential for problems revolves around pensions, the solvency of retirement plans, and the ability to save for retirement. Pension-system stability, the financing of private and public pensions, and pension regulation will be crucial to a comfortable retirement lifestyle in the future. Will pensions go bankrupt? Will future cohorts of older people find themselves vulnerable and impoverished as a result?

In the economics of the New Aging, the four-legged chair heavily emphasizes private and public pensions rather than savings or home equity. Thus, the future state of pensions and retirement systems will largely determine the income security of later generations. Pensions held $2 trillion in assets in 1990. That huge stockpile of income security for future retirees is beginning to show some cracks. A number of issues have begun to raise concerns, including the high turnover rates of investment portfolios, the adequacy of U.S. Department of Labor monitoring activities, the disposition of surplus assets of terminated plans, the use of employee stock ownership plans in leveraged buyouts, the attempted involvement of public pensions in corporate governance, and the voting of proxies (EBRI News 1990).

The greatest concern, however, is the solvency of those pension assets. Through the 1960s and 1970s, these pension programs were sound, having benefited from a healthy stock market. That situation began to change in the 1980s. By 1987, the General Accounting Office (GAO) found that 3,351 of the 14,581 plans they examined were underfunded by about $21 billion (Schmitt and Solomon 1987). Furthermore, the Pension Benefit Guaranty Corporation, charged with providing restitution in the event a private pension plan fails, faces a large unfunded liability. In 1986, for example, the PBGC's deficit equaled $3.8 billion, nearly three times the PBGC's deficit at the end of FY 1985. Most of that deficit was attributable to plan terminations in the steel industry. (Schmitt and Solomon 1987).

Further large-scale fund closures will severely tax the ability of PBGC to replace lost retirement income. A congressional subcommittee in 1989 heard warnings that $1.7 trillion in assets in private pensions were inadequately supervised by the Department of Labor, prompting fears that insolvent pension plans might someday become the savings and loans crisis for aging baby boomers (Gerth 1989). In addition, many corporations are now scaling back pension-fund contributions or forcing employees to shift from defined benefits plans (where the worker is guaranteed a specific amount of retirement income), to less regulated, defined contribution plans (where retirement income is dependent on level of contributions and performance of pension investments). In addition, because few private pensions provide inflation protection (one in four) and workers are retiring earlier and living longer, pension income, no matter how secure, will erode (Uchitelle, 1991; Schulz, 1988). The precariousness of some pension systems was illustrated by the failure of Executive Life Insurance Company in 1991, whose large portfolio of junk bonds led to losses among 250,000 life-insurance and annuity policyholders. This incident reflected the trend in the 1980s for companies to terminate pension plans and use the surplus for other purposes. Many companies replaced their pension plans with higher-paying annuities, policies from insurance firms such as Executive Life that provided for monthly payment of retirement benefits. The failure of Executive Life called into question the lack of regulation on this practice and whether firms should compensate workers and retirees when life insurance companies are unable to fulfill their obligations.

Then, there is the matter of publicly funded pension plans. Federal, state, and municipal pension plans, as well as state and local teachers' pension systems, are a major source of retirement income. State and local government pension plans cover 11.4 million active and 3.1 million retired participants in more than 6,600 plans. In 1989, state and local pension plans had assets of $727 billion (U.S. Senate 1991). Public pension systems such as the Civil Service Retirement System (CSRS) and the Military Retirement System rely primarily on current worker contributions to pay for retiree benefits.[4] Unlike Social Security, they do not accrue a surplus but provide generous cost-of-living adjustments. These programs are facing increasingly large unfunded liabilities (in 1985 CSRS had a $500 billion unfunded liability) dependent on the willingness and ability of the existing labor force to pay for retiree benefits (Longman 1987).

What about those unable to acquire pension and retirement coverage? Many workers lack the luxury of worrying about the solvency of retirement plans. Although the number of workers covered under private pension plans has increased greatly in recent decades, a large proportion remain uncovered. Ominously, the growth in pension coverage has leveled off and shows signs of decreasing. Sixty percent of those without pension coverage work in two industries: trade and service. Almost all are nonunion and work for small businesses (Schulz 1988). Only certain segments of the work force (primarily those in larger firms) have substantial pension coverage. In 1988, for example, among private firms with 250 employees or more, 83 percent provided pensions. Only 18 percent of private companies with 25 employees or less provided pension coverage for their workers (Sanchez 1991).[5] The changing labor structure in this country is toward fewer union benefits and increased jobs in service and retail industries where pension coverage is limited or nonexistent. Workers, predominantly among younger generations, without college education, and minority or recently immigrated, will be unlikely to accrue pension coverage.

Social Security will then be even more crucial for many of tomorrow's elderly, although today all agree that its purpose is to supplement income. Low-income workers will increasingly rely on Social Security as their primary income in retirement. Consequently, current debates about the Social Security surplus, its availability in the future, the restructuring of the system, increasing taxes, or altering benefits, will directly affect future generations of retirees.

Because future retirees will rely more on Social Security, we must avoid changes that could erode its solvency or discourage public support. This means Social Security must maintain its social insurance approach. It cannot be means-tested without losing the political support of those who pay into it through payroll taxes. The great fear is that Social Security will become income- and race-stratified. Only the poor and minorities will rely on its programs for their retirement. In this scenario, the more affluent and educated will depend on personal savings, asset accumulation, and private pensions. They will lose interest in preserving the basic structure of the Social Security system. Using Social Security benefits to serve only the needy, however laudable that might seem, will unwittingly put future poor elderly in a more precarious situation.

Already, the seeds of generational tension are brewing among younger groups. They resent the high payroll tax. Intergenerational taxation is a perilous tightrope for political decision makers. To prevent the surplus from being heavily invested in Treasury Securities (with the uncertainty of how and when it might be paid back) or used for other purposes (such as funding infrastructure improvements), we must reduce payroll taxes and return to pay-as-you-go financing, much as Senator Moynihan proposed in 1990. This will mean higher taxes at the turn of the century, but the likelihood is that future generations would have to pay higher taxes anyway to redeem Treasury Securities. Some suggest that the surplus be used for capital improvements (rebuilding highways, for instance) or social purposes (funding education and job training), as a national investment, replacing current federal expenditures. The reality is that the political system cannot be trusted to make rational and long-range decisions, free from the pressures of narrow-interest groups, with such a huge amount of money. Returning to a self-financing system would have another benefit. It would reduce the extremely inequitable nature of Social Security payroll taxes, where lower-income groups pay a higher proportion in taxes.

Beyond Social Security, other generational issues arise in the economics of the New Aging. Relying on the work force to pay taxes for Social Security and other old-age programs for seemingly affluent retirees is raising fears that "we are witnessing nothing less than a massive transfer of income and wealth from the younger generations to the older" (Kosterlitz 1988).

Phillip Longman's book, *Born to Pay: The New Politics of Aging in America*, is a harbinger of blame directed at the elderly for the increasing problems younger taxpayers will have to face (1987). Longman pointed to the growing downward mobility of younger Americans unable to afford a home, facing stiff competition in the work force for high-paying jobs, witnessing reductions in their health and pension plans, and unable to save—even with both married partners working. Comparing this state of affairs to the relatively prosperous retirement of many older people, Longman and others prophesize a growing rebellion by younger workers against "backdoor borrowing" (increasing benefits for today's elderly by placing the tax burden on future taxpayers).

Many will argue against Longman's thesis and the alarmist fears he raises. As a pragmatic liberal believing in the social vision of the programs developed during the Modern Aging period, this author might be expected to discount Longman's views as heresy, as many gerontologists have done. However, I must acknowledge the contributions Longman and other gero-revisionists have made in reassessing the basic premises underlying today's system of public benefits for the elderly. Longman's warnings that real fiscal tensions today might create generational conflict as economic circumstances change are sound. Our response should not be to dismiss those warnings as ideologically incompatible with the principles of social insurance and public entitlement, but rather to incorporate them in restructuring public benefits while maintaining the social vision of their early architects.

To avoid potential generational tensions, it is imperative to move away from age-segregated expansion of benefits and toward intergenerational and age-integrated solutions. The existing system of benefits, including Medicare, is largely predicated on serving only older people. Continuing on this route would require vastly increasing taxes or scaling back benefits. Either approach is politically difficult. Without restructuring the present age-segregated approach, benefits will be expanded by a powerful fiscal interest group composed of politically influential, educated, and well-off elderly. The interests of the more vulnerable young and old will be unrepresented.

Therefore, a central premise of the economics of the New Aging is to gradually integrate benefits of the young, middle-aged, and old in the 1990s. One example of age-integration is providing long-term care for the frail elderly as well as the younger disabled. Social Security is another, providing benefits to young and old through SSI, DI, and OASI. Chapter 6 contains other areas well-suited to age-integration. Avoiding single-generation financing and moving toward intergenerational programs will prevent many of the tensions and conflicts otherwise possible in the economics of the New Aging.

DIVERSITY

A diverse aging population adds to the economic complexity of the New Aging. Greater differences among the older population mean greater income variation. Chapter 1 described the increasing diversity of the elderly with respect to class, income, race, and economics. Future generations of elderly will be less homogeneous. There will be a greater number of ethnic and minority elderly, older women, elderly living alone, and the very old. Further, changes in family and social support ratios (fewer children to care for elders) will be evident.

The economic status of the elderly will vary greatly, with many more better off and many more poor. Through much of the last sixty years, the elderly have been portrayed as economically homogeneous. Reliance on mean and median income and a single age breakdown (those 65 and over) to statistically represent the economic status of the elderly has led to stereotyping them as an affluent age cohort. In reality, as shown earlier, many poor and marginally poor elderly subgroups exist.

These groups, in all likelihood, will be worse off in the future. Older women, older minorities, retirees with limited pension and retirement coverage, the frail, and those living alone will remain economically vulnerable. The better educated and healthy, as well as those who planned well or were able to save, will be more economically secure. One of the most comprehensive studies on the subject, conducted by the Commonwealth Commission on Elderly People Living Alone, indicates that the high incidence of poverty among elderly women living alone will continue unabated or grow (Commonwealth Fund Commission 1988). The growing number of black and Hispanic elderly (whose poverty rates are high) will increase the number of poor older people. What we will likely see in future years is a growing gap between the have-not elderly and the haves.

Income diversity will also be reflected geographically. The poor will concentrate in inner cities and the Snowbelt areas of the Midwest and Northeast. The affluent will live in retirement communities and the Sunbelt.

We will also see increased downward mobility and impoverishment among middle-income and marginally well-off older people as their life span lengthens and inflation takes its toll on public and private retirement systems. The Commonwealth Fund Commission study also examined the income distribution among future elderly populations and reveals an ironic convergence of interest among the poor and middle-income elderly. Findings show the reduction in retirement earnings and a reliance on Social Security income are contributing to a greater homogenization of income among these groups in the later years (Commonwealth Fund Commission 1988).

The central message here is that growing income differences among subgroups of elderly must be factored into policy decisions. We must recognize the deepening economic schism among the have-not elders of the future (women, minorities, the poor or frail, and those living in rural areas) and the haves (the educated, affluent, white, and equity-rich), or we will face tensions not only between generations but also among subgroups of elderly.

For example, in 1969, families in the top 20 percent of the nation's income distribution accounted for 41 percent of all income; by 1989, they held 45 percent. Meanwhile, families at the bottom 20 percent of the income scale lost ground, declining from 5.6 percent to 4.6 percent (Population Reference Bureau 1990). If we fail to reverse these trends in the 1990s, we will see a gap developing among elders in the early part of next century.

This recognition must guide political decisions in the 1990s. For example, not only must the OASI program remain a social insurance system, but we must expand the benefits levels in the Supplemental Security Income program and improve Disability Insurance. SSI and DI will be crucial to later generations of low-income elderly. Medicaid will be the primary health care program for many elderly unless we develop universal health-care coverage. To the extent we restrict Medicaid coverage, we jeopardize the health care of the next generation of older people. The middle class has a stake in preserving these programs or they run the risk that in their retirement, however well-planned, they will be eligible for programs perceived as serving only the poor.

To gauge the future economic diversity of the elderly, we need only look at today's younger population. The growing underclass of young minorities and the "truly disadvantaged," the illiterate, the homeless, those afflicted by drug use and violence, and drug- and alcohol-addicted babies will comprise the future disadvantaged elderly (Wilson 1987). Today, one-fifth of all children live in households classified as poor, a level not seen since the Great Depression. What will they be like in old age? What chance do they have to obtain income security in their retirement?

Economic diversity raises the important issue of whether or not the labor force can support, through taxes, a larger elderly population. Will a declining labor force, affected by lower birthrates, be able and willing to afford the high level of taxes required to pay for current old-age benefits? Will it be able to pay for expanded benefits for the growing number of poor elderly? The labor force will increasingly be composed of members of minority and immigrant communities. Who will educate, train, and prepare them to be productive members of the work force? If we do not make drastic changes in our educational, social, and health programs, and reverse the growing incidence of illiteracy, school dropout, drugs, and crime, we might find this racially diverse work force unable to support future retirees. In the economics of the New Aging, we will depend on other people's children to support whatever old-age programs exist in the next century (Rauch 1989).

Thus, diversity will complicate the economics of the New Aging. How we pay for benefits will dictate whether tensions and conflicts arise among diverse groups. We must come to terms with increasing taxes to improve our education system, develop a national health-insurance program, and reinvest in the social needs of our young. The future economic circumstances of the elderly require our using the 1990s to reduce the federal deficit so we can use tax revenues to develop age-integrated programs serving both young and old. Otherwise, the growing economic disparity occurring among the young in the 1980s will appear among the old at the turn of the century.

LONGEVITY

A longer life span raises the issue of how to prepare younger people to plan for their retirement security. Retirement planning and saving will become increasingly important. With the "emergence of retirement as a normative expectation" (Schulz 1988, 14) and the uncertainties of retirement systems, individuals and governments must promote—and require, if necessary—retirement planning and preparation. Retirement planning includes teaching young people at the primary and secondary levels about the demographic dimensions of aging and longevity and the complex pension and public benefit systems for retirees and the elderly.

Retirement preparation requires savings incentives such as tax credits and Individual Retirement Accounts and the use of personal assets for retirement income. Reverse annuity mortgages, for example, can provide a monthly income by returning a portion of the equity the homeowner has accumulated. Encouraging purchase of long-term health insurance and providing public subsidies so low-income workers can afford such insurance are important elements in preparing for a long retirement. At a personal level, health promotion efforts must increase (toward better exercise, nutrition, and the avoidance of drugs and alcohol) if we are to reduce chronic illness and the high cost of long-term care in old age.

A longer life span forces us to confront the retirement age and its economic consequences. The age of 65, carried over from Germany's social insurance system of the late nineteenth century, is obsolete. The 1983 Social Security reforms will raise the age for receipt of full benefits from 65 to 67 by early in the next century. This trend should prevail in private and public retirement systems, mitigating the fiscal tensions inherent in our current approach to pensions. Of course, arguments will persist that raising the retirement age goes against the trend toward early retirement. The reality in the New Aging, though, is that people are generally living longer and maintaining their health better, and we are pushing back the definition of old age. We cannot subsidize those who can afford to retire early at the risk of further burdening Social Security.

How high should we raise the retirement age? Yung-Ping Chen, in developing equivalent retirement ages accounting for life expectancy increases, has calculated that if 65 was the old age standard in 1940, it would be 70 years in 1995 and 73 years in 2045 (Chen 1987). Raising the retirement age to 70 by 2040 is not unrealistic, but it must be done in conjunction with expanding benefits and provisions in Disability Insurance programs and state Workmen's Compensation programs. Many individuals employed in physically demanding or dangerous occupations require an earlier retirement. Some racial and ethnic groups have lower life expectancies. Any increase in the retirement age must provide for these occupations and groups. For this reason, we should retain Social Security's early retirement age of 62 but provide a phase-in of partial benefits at ages 62 and 65 with a premium for those working after age 70.[6]

To work, not to work, and having to work in old age will be important longevity issues. Malcolm Morrison argues for "reconceptualizing work and retirement" by placing "a higher social value on using the creativity, talent, and motivation of people throughout their lives (1986, 363). A work-retirement continuum for a population with a longer life span would involve lifelong education and training.

The abolishment of mandatory retirement through amendments in the Age Discrimination in Employment Act creates opportunities for older workers to remain in the work force. Yet, the work/leisure tradeoff creates dilemmas for business and retirees. Businesses are recognizing older workers and retirees as valued employees, especially as a worker shortage develops. By the year 2000, the median age of the labor force is projected to increase from 36 years to 39. By that time there will be an increase in the number of workers age 55 and over, and a decrease of one million in the number of workers age 16 to 24 (U.S. Senate 1991). However, businesses might not want or be able to afford health insurance and other benefits for older workers. Further, certain work environments might be unsuitable for the elderly. Retirees will seek flexible work opportunities (e.g., part-time or home-based). Public incentives for business to meet the employment requirements of an older population should accompany expansion of the Title V Senior Employment Program and use of volunteer programs such as Senior Executives. Deleting the earnings limitation test of Social Security is a step in the direction of better using older workers in the work force.[7] Late-life reeducation and career changes should become commonplace.

The watchword for the New Aging will be productivity—how to utilize older people to contribute to the economy, to their own income security, and to lifting the burden off other generations. Harry Moody argues, "Advocates for the elderly have dwelt too long on the 'failure model' of old age and cast the elderly in an outdated stereotype of a vulnerable or needy group to justify entitlement programs" (Moody 1990, 136). This view portrays a vast, useless mass of retirees with nothing to contribute. In contrast, he suggests a "politics of productivity," where the elderly are viewed as a critical pool of skilled, talented workers whose energy can reduce fiscal tensions in the New Aging. If more older people were in the work force, for example, their productivity could render the need to increase the retirement age inconsequential.

Going hand in hand with a reconceptualization of the elderly's role in economic productivity is the need to protect pension and entitlement programs to prevent dependency on public benefits. This requires better enforcement of ERISA provisions and a strengthening of the oversight provisions of PBGC.[8] Returning the financing of Social Security to a pay-as-you-go system will heighten the credibility of that program among younger workers, and making the Social Security trust fund "off budget" (to prevent funds from being calculated as part of the federal budget) will restore organizational integrity to a program that has become highly politicized. Given expected increases in longevity and economic diversity among the elderly, and the need to maintain Social Security's solvency, Social Security benefits must be taxed. We are already partially taxing some benefits (as a result of the 1983 Social Security reforms) for upper-income individuals. The logical extension would be to tax these fully. Some will argue that this is merely a "back-door" way of means-testing the program and weakening public support for Social Security. This is not the case, however, since upper-income persons will continue to be eligible for programs and services (e.g., disability insurance, cost-of-living increases, Medicare) and can receive Social Security income benefits.

Longevity will force change in our daily lives and public policy. The sooner we accept this, the better. Providing greater incentives to save, raising the retirement age, promoting productivity among older workers, reversing the trend toward early retirement, and protecting pension and retirement programs will be essential to the economics of the New Aging.

CONCLUSIONS

The economics of the New Aging expose the fiscal consequences of being unprepared for the demographic revolution. Examining the current economic status of the elderly unveils fiscal pressures that will require significant changes if we are to afford programs for future generations of older people. We are unable to afford the current system of financing benefits. To provide economic security for later generations, difficult choices must be made in the 1990s, while time remains to prepare for the aging of the baby boomers.

If we ignore the warning signs—the escalating cost of health and social programs for the elderly, the increasing reluctance of taxpayers to pay for age-segregated services—dire predictions of "age wars" and fears of "the old burdening the young" could materialize. With the current structure of benefits largely geared toward the middle- and upper-income elderly, we are likely to see tremendous economic disparity among the future elderly, particularly a growing gap between the haves and have-nots.

This chapter has identified several avenues for change, including raising the eligibility age for retirement while buttressing the SSI and DI programs, eliminating the earnings-limitation test in Social Security but retaining its partial retirement benefit (at a slightly lower rate), and revising our view of older people from dependent to productive. To reinstall confidence in pension and retirement systems, we must strengthen oversight of private pensions and address unfunded liabilities within public retirement programs. Either the Social Security surplus should be used exclusively for future retirement needs and correcting inequities for women and minorities, or we should return to a pay-as-you-go system by reducing payroll taxes.

Our response to the fiscal pressures of old-age benefits cannot be divorced from the economy as a whole. Frank Levy's book, *Dollars and Dreams*, describes the demographic debt that will come due because one-fifth of our children are now raised in poverty (1987). Yet, developing social programs to assist people at the bottom of the distribution ladder is linked to economic productivity. "Rising productivity is the ultimate source of rising living standards"; rising incomes will help fund a larger welfare state (Levy 1987, 4). Likewise, our ability to afford an expansion of benefits for the elderly will in large part be determined by the state of the American economy. If we reduce the deficit and maintain prosperity, we can afford to continue many of today's benefits as well as others, such as long-term care.

Prosperity is dependent on our investment in a declining labor force. Health care, educational improvement, and job-training programs are essential to a young immigrant and minority population. However, we must avoid imposing burdens or creating disincentives to the corporate and business sectors that might discourage productivity and competition. In this regard, we should not impose mandated health benefits on business if it works against economic productivity and providing jobs. We must recognize where the public and the private sector's responsibilities begin and end in an aging society.

The private sector must be charged not only with economic productivity but with the creativity and flexibility to employ older workers and retirees.

Further, it must protect pension and retirement programs. We must prohibit, for example, the tendency of investors and corporations to reduce or overturn pension plans to capture excess surpluses. On the other hand, the private sector can play an important and creative role by demonstrating the productive capacity of older workers and by instituting personnel benefits such as elder care.

The marketplace cannot be trusted to allocate social benefits equitably, however. Government must reassert its responsibility to provide for the basic social welfare by assuring all citizens basic health and long-term care. The for-profit and proprietary sectors have shown during the 1980s that, if left up to them, nursing-home care, home health services, case management, and other such services will serve only a limited segment of the population, excluding the poorest and most needy. This chapter has demonstrated the economic disparity developing within an increasingly diverse elderly population. Public benefits and services will be required by more senior citizens. To this extent, the public sector will play a larger role as the baby boomers age.

This quid pro quo between public and private sectors—business is not saddled with social benefits, and the for-profit sector is restricted in the extent to which it provides publicly funded social services—will require major reforms and ideological changes throughout the 1990s. Medicare and Medicaid, for example, and their implementing agency, HCFA, should revise requirements so that nonprofit organizations and voluntary organizations are the major contractors for publicly funded programs for the elderly. On the other hand, we must develop a social insurance form of health and long-term care that frees employers from the burden of providing health coverage to their workers.

We must acknowledge that major changes in our present system of paying for benefits and entitlement will be required. Conservatives and liberals alike agree that we can no longer afford our current approach. The escalating number and intensifying social needs of the elderly require major reforms now, while they are still possible. The 1990s are our last opportunity to make difficult and controversial changes and decisions. Afterwards, the baby boomers will have too much at stake to allow changes that might restrict their benefits. Raising the eligibility age in 2010, for example, would face tremendous resistence from older workers preparing to retire at that time.

If we continue along our present path, keeping the current level of benefits without eliminating the deficit and raising taxes, we will be forced to means-test entitlement programs, including Social Security, Medicare, and the Older Americans Act. The resulting welfare-type programs will create tremendous disenchantment and loss of public support. Instead, we must restructure public benefits so that only the truly old receive universal entitlement to social, health and long-term care, while basing other programs on need, functional limitations, and disability. (Chapter 6 will describe such a system in greater detail.)

In addition, we must raise taxes. The federal deficit has escaped all reduction efforts by Congress and tempered any major social initiative. Increasing revenue will be imperative in the 1990s, or we will surely burden future generations with today's debts. The purpose and rationale for tax increases must be clear and convincing to middle-class taxpayers. They are the most important barometer of what is politically saleable. They have shown a willingness to support clearly defined social needs such as public education, transportation, and long-term care.

Unfortunately, reform remains grudging. Throughout the 1980s, only incremental relief was applied. The federal budget reconciliation process, designed solely to readjust budget targets with legislative modifications, was the main source of policy solutions to the pressures of the demographic revolution. The 1990s will require major changes and structural reforms if we are to prepare for the exigencies of the New Aging.

NOTES

1. Keith Morris, a student in my USC ethnicity course, characterized the economic status of minority elderly as a "pole." Because they have no pension plan, are unable to save or acquire assets, and may be ineligible for Social Security (due to immigrant, occupational, and disability barriers), they rely on only one leg of the four-legged chair—public benefits.

2. The seriousness of the Savings and Loan crisis, however, was brought home to senior citizens with the proposal to limit FDIC (Federal Deposit Insurance Corporation) coverage to $100,000. The American Association of Retired Persons opposed this proposal, since 34.9 percent of those with $100,000-plus bank accounts are elderly (Knight 1991).

3. See *Social Security and the Budget* for an overview of differing opinions about the political and economic status of the Social Security program (Aaron 1990). This book contains the proceedings of the first conference of the National Academy of Social Insurance.

4. The Civil Service Retirement System (CSRS) is the largest pension plan in the country, a pay-as-you-go system financed partially by employees' payroll taxes and the employing agency, but primarily by federal general revenues. In 1990, the annual cost of the retirement system was a total of $31 billion with 2.2 million annuitants. The Federal Employees' Retirement System Act of 1986 replaces CSRS with the Federal Employees Retirement System (FERS). FERS covers all Federal employees hired on or after January 1, 1984. CSRS covers all employees hired before January 1, 1984, who did not transfer to FERS by December 31, 1987. CSRS will cease to exist when the last employee of that system dies (U.S. Senate 1991).

In 1987, 1.6 million retirees and survivors received military retirement benefits. For fiscal year 1988, total Federal military retirement outlays have been estimated at $18.9 billion. The Military Retirement Reform Act of 1986 changes the computation formula for military personnel who enter military service on or before August 1, 1986. Since a participant becomes vested in the military retirement program after 20 years of service, the first retirees affected by the new law will be those with 20 years of service retiring on August 1, 2006 (U.S. Senate Special Committee on Aging 1991).

5. In 1991, the Labor Department proposed a simplified low-cost retirement plan for small firms. This would allow small firms (with fewer than 100 workers) to save up to $8,300 tax free annually through employer and employee contributions, encourage government agencies and nonprofit firms to set up tax-free retirement savings or 401K plans for employees, and make it easier for workers to place their pension savings into new retirement accounts without penalty (Sanchez 1991).

6. Sam Sadin, Deputy Director, Brookdale Center on Aging, Hunter College, suggests that recipients at early retirement receive 70 percent of the NRA at age 62, 85 percent at age 65, 100 percent at age 70, and receive a premium increase in their benefits for working after age 70.

7. In 1990, Social Security beneficiaries under age 65 had their benefits reduced by $1 for every $2 earned above $6,840, rising to $7080 in 1991. In 1990, beneficiaries aged 65 to 69 years had benefits reduced $1 for each $3 earned above $9,360, rising to $9,720 in 1991. The exempt amounts are adjusted each year to rise in proportion to beneficiaries who have reached age 70.

8. The 1990 Omnibus Budget Reconciliation Act (OBRA 90) attempts to improve supervision of private pension systems. It discourages plan terminations. Businesses with pension funds exceeding those needed to pay retiree benefits may cease the plan's operation, as long as they offer alternatives to workers already covered. To discourage abuses, Congress raised the excise tax from 20 percent to 50 percent on reversions of excess pension assets. OBRA 90 also allows companies limited transfers, without taxation, from ongoing pension plans to pay for retiree health benefits. OBRA 90 also raises the premiums corporations pay to the PBGC (Hughes 1991).

BIBLIOGRAPHY

Aaron, Henry, ed. *Social Security and the Budget.* Washington, D.C.: The National Academy of Social Insurance, University Press of America, 1990.

Aaron, Henry, Barry Bosworth, and Gary Burtless. *Can America Afford to Grow Old?* Washington, D.C.: The Brookings Institution, 1989.

"America's Best Graduate and Professional Schools." *U.S. News and World Report,* March 19, 1990, 65.

ASAP. *Advocates Senior Alert Process,* Vol. 7, no. 6 (March 1991).

Binstock, Robert. "The Politics and Economics of Aging and Diversity." In *Diversity in Aging,* edited by S. Bass, E. Kutza, and F. Torres-Gil. Glenview, Ill. Scott, Foresman & Company, 1990.

Carlson, Allan. "Depopulation Bomb: The Withering of the Western World." *The Washington Post,* April 13, 1986.

Chen, Yung-Ping. "Making Assets out of Tomorrow's Elderly." *The Gerontologist* 27, 4 (1987): 410–16.

Commonwealth Fund Commission. "Aging Alone: Profiles and Projections." A report of the Commonwealth Fund Commission of Elderly People Living Alone, Baltimore, Md. Prepared by Judith D. Kasper, 1988.

"Company-Financed Pensions Are Failing to Fulfill Promise." *New York Times*, May 29, 1990, A1.

EBRI News. "U.S. Pension Funds Attract Policymakers' Attention." Washington D.C.: Employee Benefit Research Institute, May 9, 1990.

Fairlie, Henry. "Talkin' bout My Generation." *The New Republic*, March 28, 1988, 19–22.

Gerth, Jeff. "Panel Is Told of Lax Monitoring of Pension Plans." *The New York Times*, August 3, 1989.

Gould, Stephanie, and John Palmer. "Outcomes, Interpretations, and Policy Implications." In *The Vulnerable*, edited by John Palmer, Timothy Smeeding, and Barbara Boyle Torrey. Washington, D.C.: The Urban Institute Press, 1988: 413–42.

Gray, Robert, and Joan Szabo. "Social Security: Hard Choices Ahead." *Nation's Business*, April 1990, 18–25.

"Grays on the Go." *Time*, February 22, 1988.

Heclo, Hugh. "Generational Politics." In *The Vulnerable*, edited by John Palmer, Timothy Smeeding, and Barbara Boyle Torrey. Washington, D.C.: The Urban Institute Press, 1988: 381–412.

Hughes, William. "Private Pension Coverage Declining." *Aging Today* (February/March 1991): 9.

Knight, Jerry. "Protesting All the Way to the Bank." *The Washington Post, National Weekly Edition*, March 25–31, 1991.

Kosterlitz, Julie. "Measuring Misery." *National Journal*, (August 4, 1990): 1892–96.

———. "Who Will Pay?" *National Journal* (March 6, 1986): 570–74.

———. "Young vs. Old." *National Journal* (December 10, 1988): 3160.

Levy, Frank. *Dollars and Dreams: The Changing American Income Distribution*. New York: Russell Sage Foundation, 1987.

Longman, Phillip. "Age Wars." *The Futurist*, January-February 1986, 8–10.

———. *Born to Pay: The New Politics of Aging in America*. Boston: Houghton Mifflin Company, 1987.

———. "Justice between Generations." *The Atlantic Monthly*, June 1985, 73–81.

Margolis, Richard. *Risking Old Age in America*. Boulder, Colo.: Westview Press, 1990.

Moody, Harry. "The Politics of Entitlement and the Politics of Productivity." In *Diversity in Aging*, edited by S. Bass, E. Kutza, and F. Torres-Gil. Glenview, Ill. Scott, Foresman & Company, 1990.

Morrison, Malcolm. "Work and Retirement in an Older Society." In *Our Aging Society*, edited by Alan Pifer and Lydia Bronte. New York: W.W. Norton & Company, 1986, 341–66.

"Moynihan Urges Social Security Tax Cut, Return to Pay-as-You-Go Benefits System." *The Los Angeles Times* Dec. 20, 1989.

National Council of La Raza. *The Hispanic Elderly: A Demographic Profile*. Washington, D.C.: National Council of La Raza, October 1987.

O'Hare, William, Taynia Mann, Kathryn Porter, and Robert Greenstein. "Real

Life Poverty in America." A report of the Center on Budget and Policy Priorities and the Families USA Foundation, Washington, D.C., July 1990.

Peterson, Peter. "The Morning After," *The Atlantic Monthly*, October 1987, 43–69.

Population Reference Bureau. "America in the 21st Century: Social and Economic Support Systems." Washington, D.C.: Population Reference Bureau and the Population Resource Center, December 1990.

"The Power of the Pension Funds." *Business Week*, Nov. 6, 1989.

Preston, Samuel. "Children and the Elderly in the United States." *Scientific American* 251, 6 (1984): 44–49.

Rauch, Jonathan. "Kids as Capital." *The Atlantic Monthly*, August 1989, 56–61.

Rich, Spencer. "Hearing Told U.S. Stymies the Helpless," *The Washington Post*, April 6, 1990, A18.

————. "Lower Benefits Backed for Well-to-Do." *Washington Post*, Feb. 27, 1991.

Sanchez, Jesus. "Tension over Pension Reform." *Los Angeles Times*, May 23, 1991, p. B1.

Schmitt, Ray, and Carmen Solomon. "Meeting the Pension Obligation: Underfunding and Overfunding Issues." Washington D.C.: Congressional Research Service, Library of Congress. May 8, 1987.

Schulz, J., A. Borowski, and W. H. Crown. *Economics of Population Aging: The "Graying of Australia, Japan, and the United States."* New York: Auburn House, 1991.

Schulz, James. *The Economic of Aging.* 4th ed. Dover, Mass. Auburn House Publishing Company, 1988.

Shipp, R. "Paying for the Baby Boom's Retirement." Washington, D.C.: Congressional Research Service, Library of Congress, 1988.

Smith, Lee. "The War between the Generations." *Fortune*, July 20, 1987, 78–82.

Smolensky, Eugene, Sheldon Danziger, and Peter Gottschalk. "The Declining Significance of Age in the United States: Trends in the Well-Being of Children and the Elderly since 1939." In *The Vulnerable*, edited by John Palmer, Timothy Smeeding, and Barbara Boyle Torrey. Washington, D.C.: The Urban Institute Press, 1988: 29–54.

Social Security Administration. U.S. Department of Health and Human Services. *Social Security Bulletin: Annual Statistical Supplement*. Washington, D.C.: U.S. Government Printing Office, 1990.

"Social Security at 50 Faces New Crossroads." *U.S. News & World Report*, Aug. 12, 1985.

"Social Security Drain Worries under-45 Set." *Chicago Sun-Times*, January 1990.

"Social Security Should Benefit Only the Elderly Poor." *Business Week*, Jan. 16, 1989, 20.

Starobin, Paul. "Who Comes Out Ahead?" *The National Journal*, Sept. 22, 1990, 2255–58.

"300 Billion Whopper." *U.S. News and World Report*, Feb. 11, 1991, 51–53.

Uchitelle, Louis. "Company-Financed Pensions Are Failing to Fulfill Promise." *The New York Times*, May 29, 1991.

U.S. Department of Health and Human Services. "Fast Facts and Figures about Social Security." Washington, D.C.: Social Security Administration, 1988.

U.S. House Select Committee on Aging. "Long-Term Care and Personal Impoverishment: Seven in Ten Elderly Living Alone Are at Risk." Comm. Pub. No. 100–631. Washington, D.C.: U.S. Government Printing Office, 1987.

U.S. Senate Special Committee on Aging. "Developments in Aging: 1989." Vol. I. Washington, D.C.: U.S. Government Printing Office, 1990.

———. "Developments in Aging: 1990." Vol. 1. Washington, D.C.: U.S. Government Printing Office, 1991.

U.S. Senate. *Aging America: Trends and Projections*. Washington, D.C.: U.S. Government Printing Office, 1986.

———. *Aging America: Trends and Projections*. Washington, D.C.: U.S. Government Printing Office, 1988.

Villers Foundation. *On the Other Side of Easy Street: Myths and Facts about the Economics of Old Age*. Washington, D.C.: The Villers Foundation, 1987.

Wilson, William Julius. *The Truly Disadvantaged*. Chicago: The University of Chicago Press, 1987.

5
THE AGING OF THE
BABY BOOMERS

They who would be young when they are old, must be old when they
are young.

John Ray, *English Proverbs*

The baby boomers illustrate the challenges and opportunities of the New
Aging. In the final analysis, their generation is the basis for the New
Aging. Baby boomers will be the elderly of the period. As we pass through
the transitional Modern Aging to the New Aging, baby boomers will have
to adjust more than others to a redefinition of age and a new set of policies
and benefits. They will also exhibit most the full effects of living longer
in a more diverse society replete with competing generational claims. The
actions of the baby boomers in transition will affect generations both
preceding and following them.

MYTHS AND FACTS

Much has been written and discussed about this huge post–World War
II cohort. Their lives and actions have been dissected, popularized, and
criticized. The baby boomers are, for better or worse, a "trend generation." Moving through the life cycle, they establish new trends by virtue
of sheer number (Torres-Gil 1988). Unfortunately, they are also saddled
with numerous misconceptions and stereotypes. Baby boomers are often
viewed as liberal, antigovernment, and selfish. They are often portrayed
as an homogeneous group whose social and political behavior can be
generalized. They are variously credited (or blamed) for ending a war,

promoting civil rights, creating new lifestyles and popular fads, and making competition among different age groups difficult in the workplace.

The baby-boom generation includes people born from 1946 through 1964. Shortly after World War II's end, the annual number of births hit new highs, with 3.4 million in 1946, and 3.8 million in 1947. Numbers fell in the late 1940s, then rose again during the 1950s. In 1961, more than 4.2 million babies were born. This number did not fall below 4 million until 1965 (Russell 1982). The impact of these numbers on society can be measured by the percent of change among 18- to 24-year-olds. The largest increase (23 percent) in this group prior to 1970 occurred in 1910, then fell dramatically. Before 1960, 18- to 24-year-olds as a group never increased more than 7 percent annually. By 1970, however, babies born just after World War II had reached adolescence. The number of people 18 to 24 years of age increased by an astonishing 53 percent. In 1980, this number dropped to 19 percent. It is expected to continue dropping until the early 1990s (Jones 1980), after which we can expect an upsurge of births among the baby boomlet cohort. Thus, baby boomers represent the largest age segment of the U.S. population, numbering approximately 77 million. Those at the leading edge of the group are now in their middle 40s, and, at the tail end, entering their 30s.

Not surprisingly, the group's dramatic increase in size led to some unsettling, even radical changes in American life as its members reached adolescence and young adulthood. Unprecedented growth in elementary and secondary school enrollment (between 1950 and 1960, enrollment rose from 28 million to 42 million students) occurred, followed by explosive growth in higher education (Russell 1982). Correspondingly, the labor force grew by more than 30 million workers between 1965 and 1980, largely fueled by baby boomers (Russell 1982). Consumption patterns altered dramatically as the generation aged. Housing construction (and prices) hit new highs during the 1970s and 1980s. New products and markets proliferated in areas such as toys, leisure, computers. Baby boomers created nothing short of a cultural revolution in the 1960s. Throughout its history, this trend generation has shaped and reshaped American life.

The fact that they are reaching middle age is no reason to expect this to change. Those changes may be different, however. As they move into middle age, we can expect less consumer spending and more saving, cheaper housing, and perhaps a more stable work force. On the other hand, their longevity may bring surprises. The baby boomers' life expectancy is the longest ever. The length of their retirement will exceed that of their parents. Baby boomers might be the first generation in recorded history to achieve what Alan Pifer terms the four quarters of life (Pifer and Bronte 1986), a time in which the third quarter (ages 50–75) can be as active and productive as the first two, and the fourth a new "golden age."

Unquestionably, the generation is diverse. Notwithstanding myths and stereotypes characterizing its affluence, activism, and idealism, it is highly heterogeneous. Most are not affluent; only about 3.5 million have household incomes of $50,000 or more. In comparison, the income of 12.7 million averages between $18,000 and $20,000 ("After the Boom" 1990). The group is, however, relatively well-educated, with one in three having had at least some college education. Baby boomers are, in general, more educated than previous age cohorts. In 1988, nearly 90 percent of the population 25 to 44 years of age, primarily baby boomers, completed high school, 48 percent attended some college, and 25 percent completed college (Scholz 1990). Baby boomers span occupational, ideological, and class structures. Twenty-five million are what are called "new collars," with at least a year of college and incomes between $20,000 and $40,000. Many are poor; in 1985, four out of ten made less than $10,000 a year (Light 1988).

They do, however, share common historical and sociogenetic experiences. The Civil Rights Movement of the 1950s and 1960s affected their view of individuals and government, making them more tolerant of differences. The death of President John F. Kennedy inflicted a psychic wound. Watergate, Vietnam, and the Iran-Contra scandal deepened their mistrust of government, public authority, and bureaucracies (e.g., business, labor unions). Blatant pandering by the media and advertisers makes this group a barometer and creator of American tastes, values, and lifestyles. For all these reasons, the baby boomers have become the most age-segregated generation of the century, drawing on their huge numbers and history to view their youth and upcoming middle age as a shared experience (witness "thirtysomething," a popular TV program of the early 1990s).

Ideologically, the group's political views span the full spectrum. They are far from being the liberal and radical generation painted in the '60s. Most, during that time, did not demonstrate or protest. They were busy going to school, working, raising families, and, for many young people, joining the military. As a group, they share the values of their parents; they are generally patriotic and relatively moderate in their social views. Baby boomers voted two to one for Ronald Reagan in the 1984 presidential election (Light, 1988). They tend to be more flexible politically, however, and are more likely to act on issues and personalities rather than political parties or partisan politics.

At least three mini-cohorts within the group exhibit the ideological fluctuations of the 1960s, 1970s, and 1990s. Members of the oldest subgroup—those who were teenagers or young adults in the 1960s—share one set of historical and political experiences. (This mini-cohort tends to represent the stereotypical baby boomer.) Members of the middle mini-cohort—those coming of age in the 1970s—reacted against the perceived excesses of their older brothers and sisters by moderating their own social and political behavior. The third and youngest mini-cohort—socialized in the 1980s—has come to epitomize the stereotypical, career-oriented, materialistic "yuppie." How these mini-cohorts and the baby boomers as a group will exercise political power remains to be seen. Baby boomers, as a political force, have yet to voice their needs and choose causes. During the 1990s, however, as they reach peak voting years, we can expect their positions to become clearer.

AGING AND THE BABY BOOMERS

The baby-boom generation is only now contemplating aging, and gerontologists are beginning to recognize the extraordinary impact their numbers will have on an aging society.[1] Unfortunately, accompanying their passage into aging are debates about generational equity: Which generation wins, and which loses? Baby boomers have been characterized as the first downwardly mobile generation in U.S. history, faced with a lower standard of living than that of their parents. An article in *Mother Jones* captured the plaintive cry of a baby boomer who said, "The competition with our parents is over. We lost" (Butler 1989, 33). In this highly personal account of the trials and tribulations of baby boomers unable to afford their parents' lifestyle, Katy Butler criticizes her own generation for "failing to defend its interests politically" (Butler 1989, 36).

This type of analysis reveals the generational conflict thesis at its core and has the potential to create a great schism in the political landscape. In large part, it reflects the media's absorption with the baby boomers' effect on society. Members of this trend generation have often been placed at odds with their parents and grandparents. (Remember the "generation gap" of the 1960s, where parents and their kids argued over lifestyle, politics, and a war?) Phillip Longman first captured this intrafamily and intergenerational competition with the notion that parents of baby boomers were "taking America to the cleaners" by accepting generous federal benefits (such as the GI bill, federally subsidized home loans, and old-age benefits) that their children were unlikely to get (Longman 1982). The establishment of groups such as Americans for Generational Equity and the Association of Baby Boomers confirms this growing view.

In reality, baby boomers are in relatively good shape compared to their parents and grandparents at comparable periods. They will, however, face a set of advantages and disadvantages different from that of today's elders and the elderly that will follow later in the twenty-first century. Because husbands and wives both tend to work, baby boomers, as a cohort, have earning power and high employment rates but fewer children. They might pay more for their possessions, but they possess more material goods (cars, stereos, appliances, clothes, homes) than their parents did at a comparable age.

Baby boomers, to their disadvantage, are also the product of reverse destiny. They were raised in a time of unparalleled prosperity and benefited from sacrifices made by their parents. During their formative years (with the exception of those who fought in Vietnam), they faced no serious economic or social dislocation, such as the Great Depression and the world wars of their parents and grandparents. Thus, the swing generation enjoys the fruits of its labor in old age, while the baby-boom generation will face its greatest challenges. All things being equal, the baby boomers will have a chance to prove their mettle in the latter stages of their lives.

Another disadvantage for baby boomers is their great number, which creates constant competition for jobs, education, homes, and retirement benefits. Their aging follows a time of serious economic problems in the United States that is accompanied by the public's demand for less government involvement. Rather than an advantage, their long life span might become problematic if they fail to prepare for it and they exhibit the indicators of problems in old age.

Baby boomers as a group possess several indicators that may make their old-age more of a challenge than that of their parents and grandparents. Members of that cohort are getting married at later ages, and thus remaining single longer. They have a higher divorce rate than that of preceding generations, a higher proportion of people living alone, and more households headed by single parents, especially women. Last, that group is having fewer children than their parents. The combination of those factors demonstrates that baby boomers have moved away from the traditional patterns of extended families and supportive networks of children and friends, the things that allow older persons to remain in their homes and their community. Hence, to the extent they become frail, sick, or dependent, they must recreate supportive relationships or rely on public sources of assistance.

Unfortunately, the media often suggest that "baby boomers are jealous of the Gold in Golden years" (Craeger 1989), as if any generation had an automatic right to peace, prosperity, and material rewards (without earning them). The real issue, however, has more to do with the unrealistically high expectations members of the trend generation have acquired by comparing themselves to their parents and peers. This tyranny of expectations and comparisons will create conflict among cohorts if it is allowed to fester over the next ten to twenty years when major public sacrifices will be required.

The baby boomers' rendezvous with destiny is around the corner. Up until now, they have remained unconcerned with aging and retirement. They have thought of themselves as ever youthful. This Peter Pan syndrome has led many to delay marriage and children, and spend more time pursuing education, seeking self-fulfillment, and otherwise avoiding "settling down" until well into their 30s and 40s (a time when their parents were already worrying about retirement and the empty nest).

Baby boomers have had little time to worry about old age because they were and are preoccupied with establishing careers, delaying childbearing, and affording a home. Something unanticipated is happening though; their parents are getting old. The paradox is that, in the 1990s, senior-citizen issues will become a personal matter to baby boomers not because they themselves are growing old but because they will need to care for elderly grandparents and parents and pay for Social Security and Medicare.

In providing home-health care and long-term care to increasingly frail relatives, baby boomers will discover the gaps in and fragmented nature of such services. The high cost of health care and poor quality-control of care for the terminally ill will awaken them to serious problems in the U.S. health-care system. Hefty payroll taxes will make them acutely aware of aging issues.

Estimates, for example, indicate that by the year 2040, when the average age of the baby boomer will be 85, Medicare spending for the population aged 65 and above could range from $147 to $212 billion (in 1987 dollars). The cost of nursing-home care could rise to between $84 and $139 billion (in 1985 dollars) by the year 2040. In 2040, there might be two to three times more individuals aged 85 and in nursing homes than there were individuals 65 and older in nursing homes in 1990 (Schneider & Guralnik 1990). These figures are subject to change between now and 2040, but they capture the inordinate stake baby boomers have in aging.

OLD-AGE ISSUES FOR SENIOR BOOMERS

Inexorably, baby boomers will become senior boomers. As members of the vanguard pass through their 40s, they will unilaterally redefine "old." Jones (1980) compares this population revolution to the opening of the frontier, the Industrial Revolution, the wave of immigration and migration of the last one hundred years. The aging of the baby-boom generation and, hence, the bulk of the population, will pilot longevity, diversity, and generational claims through the New Aging.

A Longer Life Span

In the area of longevity, planning for retirement will be the dominant issue as baby boomers approach 50 and realize the length of their lives will easily outdistance that of previous generations. When should they retire? Will they have sufficient savings to do so? As a group, baby boomers appear to be adequately accumulating assets and pensions. According to an analysis by Christine Macdonald, Richard Easterline, and Diane

Macunovich, baby boomers, on average, "are likely to enter old age in an even better economic position than pre-boom cohorts" (Macdonald et al. 1990, 2). Many baby boomers have adjusted to adverse labor market and economic conditions by remaining single, reducing childbearing, and boosting labor-force participation among females. These will have higher private and public employee pension coverage. In 1984, pension coverage for the oldest baby boomers was similar to that of their elders (approximately 70 percent) (Macdonald et al. 1990). With longer tenure in the labor force and more women enjoying occupational mobility, coverage and vesting rates are expected to increase further.

These pension and retirement coverage trends are good news, as is the high level of employment among boomers. However, dark clouds might be on the horizon. If private and public pension plans experience difficulties over the next two decades, this generation will be hit hardest. If the Pension Benefit Guaranty Corporation and Congress fail to guard pension and retirement funds diligently, we will witness their dissolution and bankruptcy, and baby boomers will pay a heavy price.

Baby boomers are also banking on their homes to be a financial retirement cushion as effective as their parents' homes have been. Houses have appreciated substantially since the 1960s, becoming lucrative investments for many older people during the 1980s. However, the baby-bust generation will provide retiring baby boomers with fewer buyers. In the future, owning a home might not pay off, and baby boomers will have to adjust accordingly.

Retired senior boomers must factor another variable into their retirement plans. With inflation, poor health, and the erosion of savings, their longer life span might only impoverish them. In addition, the eligibility age for receiving pensions and other benefits will undoubtedly increase well beyond age 67. Senior boomers might find themselves, in the last quarter of their lives, heavily dependent on the public benefits and services they worked so hard to avoid.

Social Security will remain significant, although the extent to which boomers acquire pensions and assets might make benefits less crucial for them in the third quarter of life than they are for many elderly today. Of more immediate concern to baby boomers is that Social Security continue to provide benefits to their parents. Baby boomers are as committed to the system's basic principles as their parents—perhaps more so (Light 1988). They know firsthand that Old-Age and Survivors Insurance gives them more freedom and mobility by allowing their parents a high degree of financial independence.

Baby boomers question, however, whether Social Security will be much of a deal for them. The 7.65 percent of their paycheck going for payroll tax can take out a bigger bite than income taxes, and the increase in the Hospital Insurance portion of that tax will add to the impact. They are discovering that they will have a lower rate of return compared to their parents and will pay higher taxes over a longer period. In 1980, for example, thirteen months of benefits equaled what the average retiree had paid into Social Security. According to Light (1988), by the 2020s it will take fifteen years for the average retiree to get back what was paid. Taking into consideration increased life expectancy and higher monthly benefits, of course, makes comparisons less dire, suggesting that Social Security will be a good deal for senior boomers. Assuming it maintains its basic function as social insurance, Social Security will be an even more crucial safety net for baby boomers as they retire. Hospital Insurance, Disability Insurance, survivor's benefits, Supplemental Security Income, and the relative weights of the system (proportioning benefits according to income) will protect many who have depleted their savings and assets.

The problem will be sustaining political support for the system during baby boomers' middle age and early retirement years when they feel less dependent on it. Baby boomers must be convinced that the system will be there when they need it. Problems with the surplus, for example, must be resolved to preserve the viability of Social Security in the long run. If baby boomers believe the surplus will be unavailable by their retirement and if taxes go up again early in the next century (to repay treasury notes), they will see no reason to continue paying payroll taxes today. Baby boomers will easily buy into the IRA syndrome (invest 2,000 a year and become a millionaire twenty years later), forgetting that Social Security provides many other important benefits. For this reason, the first crucial test of the political system in the 1990s regarding aging will be maintaining baby boomers' faith in the system.

Health care, of course, will also be a critical issue for baby boomers on the road to becoming seniors. Already they face the full brunt of a health-care system in disarray. Many of America's 37 million uninsured are baby boomers and their children. The three-tier health-care system (high-quality care for those with insurance, charity care for the medically indigent, and no care) is a fact of life. Long-term care, however, will be the primary health-care concern for aging baby boomers and their families. The immediate threat is nursing-home care—its high cost and low quality. The decision to institutionalize or move a parent will be just one of the emotional dilemmas baby boomers will face in middle age.

Chronic illness and diseases such as Alzheimer's and arthritis, accompanied by disability and dependence through a longer life span, will affect baby boomers. The book *Lifetrends* (Gerber et al. 1989) says baby boomers and other age groups that are physically, emotionally, and behaviorally handicapped will create an "intergenerational coalition based on disabilities." Eventually, baby boomers will also come face to face with the practices of their youth. The effects of drugs, drinking, and smoking will hit many in their 50s and 60s. For these and other reasons we can expect baby boomers to force the political system to provide comprehensive long-term and elder care and to be the political force behind development of a national health-care system. Baby boomers will recognize the tremendous return on investments in biomedical research aimed at curing senile dementia and other chronic problems. They will show little hesitation in supporting multiple increases in research funding.

A More Diverse Society

Lifestyles will vary tremendously. Ken Dychtwald, in his book *Age Wave* (1989), describes new concepts of leisure and recreation that will cause an explosion in country-club memberships, recreational-vehicle purchases, cruise taking, and senior-center development. New types of housing arrangements for singles will proliferate (mobile towns, congregate living facilities, shared housing). Many will go back to school for late-life education or retraining and will start new careers. Community volunteerism will increase among active, committed senior boomers (perhaps renewing their youthful idealism). Dychtwald forecasts the reinvention of family and social relationships as baby boomers mature and redefine aging. Romance without marriage for people in their 80s and 90s, and "share-a-man relationships," might be common. The "matrix family"—adult-centered, transgenerational, bound as much by friendship and choice as by blood and obligation—will evolve (Dychtwald 1989).

Four-generation households will increase, as will responsibility for care of the old and very old. The pressure on women to care for parents, husbands, grandparents, and children will be great. Many more baby boomers will be living alone and must learn to create informal support networks. The number of homeless elders might swell, absorbing those who were unable to save or who encountered unforeseen economic and social problems.

Older women will be an important part of the senior-boomer population. With their added life expectancy and greater numbers, they will be a powerful political force and can take their rightful place in the work force and the economy. Many will be living alone and adapting to life with fewer men.

During the aging of the baby-boom generation, the United States runs the danger of becoming a society stratified by age, race, and class. Minority groups—blacks, Hispanics, Asians, Pacific Islanders, Native Americans—will become the majority population. More importantly, they will be the mainstay of the labor force. As the dependency ratio for Social Security reaches two to one, the one person paying for Social Security benefits to every two retired baby boomers will be minority or immigrant. How the baby-boom generation responds to the needs and demands of minority and immigrant groups will influence their own welfare as well.

We are likely to see a growing division between the poor and higher-income groups unless major social and public changes are made during the 1990s. Retired senior boomers will be unable to ignore the demands and unmet needs of the have-nots. Many, unable to leave low-income areas and decaying inner cities, will be at the mercy of a hostile environment. Those able to move to secluded retirement communities or rural areas will discover that public assistance and an economy healthy enough to sustain their pension and retirement benefits depend on a work force comprised of the poor, minorities, and immigrants.

Diversity has the potential to create choice and opportunity, or a less secure old age for baby boomers. A diverse society can either foster competing demands for scarce public resources and pit senior boomers against other groups, or make for a more interesting and tolerant community.

Generational Politics

The politics of senior boomers may be divided among the oldest senior boomers, the baby busters, and the baby boomlet. Each of these has a generational identity and claim, making them a cohesive political block. Generational competition can also be intragenerational—between the poor and the affluent, liberals and conservatives, black and white, rural and urban, and among the mini-cohorts of the baby-boom generation. To the extent intragenerational competition and tensions develop, the influence of senior boomers as a whole will weaken. We might, however, see stratified politics where young and old minorities compete with young and old white individuals, and the poor of all ages and races ally against the affluent.

In either event, baby boomers are bound to display some generational identification and cohesion, at the very least to preserve whatever senior-citizen benefits and programs they require (e.g., long-term care, senior-citizen discounts, lower property taxes). This will certainly pit them against other age groups. Much of the competition will center around electoral strength and taxation. The political clout of 77 million senior citizens would certainly surpass anything we have yet seen. Much like the proverbial 100-ton gorilla, senior boomers will have the political muscle to get what they want, assuming they have common objectives. Old-age groups like the AARP will have a whole new constituency, and the art of pandering to special interests by politicians might reach new heights.

The baby boomers will be an inordinately large part of the electorate. In 1990, for example, voters aged 34–54 constituted 63.4 million votes, compared to 31.6 million voters 65 years and over. These numbers are projected to increase to 73.6 million middle-aged voters, compared to 33.8 million elderly voters, in 2000. The share of voters aged 30–44 has steadily increased from 32 percent of the electorate in 1986 to 35.5 percent in 1990 (Barnes 1991). These figures demonstrate that, as baby boomers reach middle age, their electoral strength could be tremendous if they share common agendas and vote as a bloc.

A distinction between "taxpayers" and "voters" will become evident during that time. Taxpayers will represent everyone paying taxes, while voters will be strictly those who register and vote. As a rule, senior citizens have the highest voting rates of any age group. The baby boomers will not only be the largest electoral segment of the population, but their aging will make them more likely to vote, meaning they will have a disproportionate effect on elections. As voters they can control taxes. In 1986, we saw this in California. White, non-Hispanics comprised 61 percent of the population; minorities made up 39 percent. Among those actually voting in the general election, 84 percent were white, non-Hispanics, while 16 percent were minorities (Field 1990). A further breakdown revealed that those 60 and older represented 30 percent of the voters, but only 13 percent of the nonvoters. In this case, *older*, white, non-Hispanics wielded tremendous electoral power over younger, minority voters.

Similarly, assuming diversity does not take a political toll, senior boomers can pretty much determine the outcome of school-bond measures, expansion of public programs, election of public officials, and ability of government to respond to social needs. The extent to which baby boomers will consolidate remains uncertain, however. Jim Castelli (1987) refers to the "myth of generational politics," arguing that the trend generation has no collective identity (only a small percentage actively engaged in protest activities), will not necessarily vote for someone their own age (a majority voted for Ronald Reagan), and has no inherent distrust of their parents and grandparents. Regardless, one thing remains certain: They will age collectively and become the largest group of older people ever in the United States. Sooner or, more probably, later, baby boomers will recognize their mortality and develop an interest in issues regarding the elderly. They will then profoundly affect the politics and policies of aging.

How will the baby boomers use this power? Will they support narrow, selfish, interest-group objectives (raising taxes to increase pension benefits, while opposing public education bond measures), or back a wide range of social causes? Will their political clout ensure social, health, and employment assistance for minority and immigrant groups, or will it be used to lower the property taxes of senior citizens? The real challenge to this aging, politically powerful generation will be to avoid becoming selfish.

Politically, many demands will be made on senior boomers. By the turn of the century, we will face the full brunt of things neglected during the 1980s and 1990s. Replacing a physical infrastructure in disrepair and improving America's ability to compete globally will require new taxes.

Bridges, water, sewers, and transportation will be heavy cost items. Capital for investment and new industry will require increased savings and government expenditures. The Savings and Loan debacle will carry over economically well into the next century. Developing a national health-care system for all age groups will require money. The moment of truth will come late in the 1990s when all these become obvious and unmanageable, and aging baby boomers will have to agree to raise taxes to pay for them. Upon whom will such taxes be imposed?

The aging baby boomers, as an age cohort, will also need to create common cause with minorities and immigrants. Their willingness and ability to live in a more racially and ethnically diverse America are critical. Multilingualism and multiculturalism are inevitable. Baby boomers will determine how smooth or difficult the transition will be. America's eurocentric orientation will give way to a Pacific Basin and Latin American world view, and baby boomers might be the first generation to vote for increased immigration.

Of crucial importance will be the attitude of senior boomers toward younger groups. Children will be fewer and more ethnically and racially diverse. They can be prized possessions or a disadvantaged constituency overshadowed by a huge older population. The plight of children in the 1980s and 1990s is a social tragedy of the first order. Homelessness, violence, illiteracy, poverty, and neglect have become the norm for an extraordinarily large proportion of America's kids. Senior boomers must accept social responsibility for the children, particularly minority and underclass, of the next two decades.

The watchword for aging baby boomers must be *intergenerational.* Baby boomers must support generational equity among all groups, avoiding media and political pigeonholing. Although the advent of baby boomers' midlife transition has set the stage for generational conflict among baby boomers, baby busters, and the baby boomlet, it can still be averted. Groups such as Generations United are actively organizing the elderly, baby boomers, and children's groups to unite and press for intergenerational legislation.

BABY BOOMERS IN THE NEW AGING

In the final analysis, baby boomers are the primary component of the New Aging. What they do and how their numbers and attitudes will affect an aging society remains to be seen. They will almost certainly make a dramatic impact, as they did in their younger years. But will their generation, as Samuelson has asked, "be grumpy, rigid and dull; a reflection of an increasingly security-conscious, stodgy and tired population? Or will it exhibit new vitality, as middle-aged Americans temper youthful energy with experience?" (1991). On the other hand, baby boomers can, as Strauss and Howe (1991) suggest, become the "elder-priests" who may lead America through the next century. Strauss and Howe view aging baby boomers as having great potential for realizing triumph or tragedy as a generational force in American history. Baby boomers have in their political hands the ability to determine America's future. Baby boomers must use their vast political clout to solve society's problems and to respond to the needs of all its citizens.

They will become important political players in the 1990s, revising entitlement programs and senior-citizen benefits. The changes made in this decade will later affect the baby boomers themselves. It is to their advantage to become self-styled gerontologists now, to understand why changes are necessary in the programs, benefits, and services for older persons, and make their voices heard in the debates and decisions surrounding those policies.

NOTE

1. One of the first serious attempts to understand the effect of baby boomers on an aging society occurred in 1990 at a forum convened by the Prudential Foundation and the Population Resource Center. The objective was to identify the crucial questions and issues shaping the baby boomers' retirement. The forum identified several key areas that require further investigation:

1. Will retirement be different, or exist at all, when Baby Boomers are ready to retire?
2. How will the United States ensure the economic growth needed to support boomers' retirement?
3. How will increased life expectancy, changing morbidity patterns, and rising health care costs affect the Baby Boom generation, their caretakers, and society as a whole?
4. What can we learn from other countries about supporting a large group of older citizens?
5. How are the baby boom generation's values and norms different from those of previous generations?
6. How will ethnic and racial heterogeneity within the baby boom and subsequent generations affect boomers' retirement?
7. What are the baby boomers' responsibilities as they age?
8. How will the changing role of women affect society and the retirement prospects of the baby boomers?

BIBLIOGRAPHY

"After the Boom." *Los Angeles Times*, April 26, 1990.
Barnes, James. "Age-Old Strife." *National Journal* 4 (Jan. 26, 1991): 216–19.

Butler, Katy. "The Great Boomer Bust: Competition with Our Parents Is Over, We Lost, What Now?" *Mother Jones*, June 1989, 32–37.

Castelli, Jim. "Baby Boom, Bang, Bust: The Myth of Generational Politics." *American Politics,* December 1987, 32–35.

Craeger, Ellen. "Baby Boomers Are Jealous of the Gold in Golden Years." *Detroit Free Press*, June 20, 1989.

Dychtwald, Ken. *Age Wave*. Los Angeles: Jeremy P. Tarcher, Inc., 1989.

Field, Mervin. "Falling Turnout—A Nonvoting Majority." *Public Affairs Report* (March 1990): 8–9.

Gerber, Jerry, Janet Wolff, Walter Klores, and Bene Brown. *Lifetrends*. New York: Macmillan Publishing Company, 1989.

Jones, Landon. *Great Expectations: America and the Baby Boom Generation*. New York: Coward, McCann & Geoghegan, 1980.

Light, Paul. *Baby Boomers*. New York: W.W. Norton & Company, 1988.

Longman, Phillip. "Taking America to the Cleaners." *The Washington Monthly*, Nov. 1982, 24–30.

Macdonald, Christine, Richard Easterline, and Diane Macunovich. "Retirement Prospects of the Baby Boom Generation." Unpublished paper, Jan. 1990.

Pifer, Alan, and Lydia Bronte. *Our Aging Society*. New York: W.W. Norton & Company, 1986.

Russell, Louise. *The Baby Boom Generation and the Economy*. Washington, D.C.: The Brookings Institution, 1982.

Samuelson, Robert. "As the Boomers Turn 50." *Washington Post*, March 20, 1991.

Schneider, Edward, and Jack Guralnik. "The Aging of America: Impact on Health Care Costs." *Journal of the American Medical Association* 263, 17 (May 2, 1990): 2335–40.

Scholz, Catherine. "A Profile of the Baby Boom Generation" Executive Summary, Population Resource Center, Washington, D.C., June 1990.

Strauss, William, and Neil Howe. *Generations: The History of America's Future, 1584 to 2069*. New York: William Morrow, 1991.

Torres-Gil, Fernando. "Aging for the Twenty-First Century: Process, Politics, and Policy." *Generations* (Spring 1988): 5–9.

6
PROGRAMS, BENEFITS, AND SERVICES: PREPARING FOR THE NEW AGING

The dogmas of the quiet past are inadequate to the stormy present.
... As our case is new, so we must think anew and act anew.

Abraham Lincoln

In the New Aging, programs and benefits now serving America's elderly population must be reorganized substantially. It is unwise to think we can continue using today's system of benefits and policies for a population in which one in five will be 65 years or over.

This chapter presents various solutions and recommendations for reorganizing the current system of benefits and policies. However, any change to present programs must involve larger political, economic, and societal changes likely to confront the United States as it enters the twenty-first century. These macro-level issues will be addressed in Chapter 7.

REDEFINING THE PREMISES OF AGING POLICIES

The three central forces described in this book—diversity, longevity, and generational tensions—illustrate why public policies of the Modern Aging require modification and reform. These forces have redefined aging in U.S. society and presage a new set of political and social roles for the elderly of the next century. Because this redefinition and these new roles have not been incorporated into existing policies, we must reconceptualize the premises underlying programs, benefits, and services originating over the last sixty years.

Simply stated, the United States in the 1990s and beyond will differ significantly from the United States of the 1930s–1960s, when our present approach to serving older people was developed. Earlier policy premises (for example, men work and women stay at home, few minorities, lower life expectancy) will make little sense in the next century.

Reorganizing our approach to providing benefits and services to older people, however, does not mean changing the underlying vision of those who created these policies. The architects of the Modern Aging period were responding to the poverty and political powerlessness faced by older people as a group when they developed programs such as Medicare and Social Security. This situation has changed. We can now alter the age-segregated nature of these categorical programs. We cannot, however, forsake the vision of their originators, a vision emphasizing community and civic responsibility, assistance for the less fortunate, and self-reliance in handling social problems independent of the impersonal forces of the marketplace. This vision implicitly acknowledged the interconnectedness of a capitalist economy to the need for a strong federal government.

Because the vision of the Modern Aging is as valid today as it was in earlier years, we must address the philosophical questions posed in Chapter 2—questions centering on how we view individual responsibility and the role of government in this highly individualistic, democratic, and free-market society. In the New Aging we must challenge our response to people dependent on others and our involvement with a growing older population in mainstream society. We must decide whether or not we can afford to view the elderly as entirely needy or greedy. During the early phase of the New Aging, we must find a balance between the public and private sectors while realigning federal intervention with state rights. Further, at the outset, we must determine how to prepare young people for a long life.

Solutions presented in this chapter and the next respond to these philosophical issues by introducing a series of premises elemental to political and legislative action in the 1990s. These are not new. They are, in part, comprised of the premises underlying the vision of the Modern Aging. However, coupled with the demographic realities facing the United States and much of the world, and addressing the effects of diversity, longevity, and generational claims, they can initiate a compassionate yet pragmatic restructuring of our current system of old-age benefits.

Reinvolving Family and Accepting Dependency

In the New Aging, the family will be more varied. The traditional extended family of the Young Aging period (prior to 1920), and even the nuclear family characteristic of the Modern Aging period, will no longer prevail. Single parents, housemates unrelated by blood, people in shared households, and family members separated geographically will be common. Families will be severely pressured economically and socially. More individuals will live alone, and more families will have four-generation households. Public and private sector policies must acknowledge these new relationships and provide options (e.g., through community-based, long-term care services and elder care in the work force) motivating family and nonfamily members to care for each other.

The notion of dependency will be a crucial aspect of public policy. The stereotype of a youthful, individualistic, and healthy society must no longer be assumed. With a longer life span, more frail and disabled people will create a greater level of dependency on others and the government. Dependency, however, does not imply helplessness. Dependent individuals can remain productive and active. The passage of the Americans with Disability Act in the early 1990s was a milestone in recognizing that the disabled might be somewhat less independent physically but are no less valued as members of the society.

"Dependency" implies that at some point we will all have to rely on others (due to physical limitation, emergency, chronic illness, loneliness). In most cases, the family will be our first recourse, but increasingly, extended social supports, such as friends or volunteers, and government-provided services will supplant the traditional family. Our goal should be to develop formal and informal services (community-based long-term care vs. nursing homes) that enable people to live independently while relying on others. Accepting dependency will focus our attention on eliminating physical and social barriers and recognizing that however healthy and physically strong we are now, programs assisting disabled and frail senior citizens benefit the entire society.

Relinquishing Age-Segregated and Interest-Group Politics

A central element in the New Aging is accepting what Thomas Cole (1988) calls "a new moral economy of the life course." The life course, in his view, has become homogenized by age: segregated schools for youth, careers for the middle-aged, and retirement for the elderly. We must relinquish age-based stereotypes of age-appropriate activities during life's course. We must move away from age-segregated policies that base eligibility on one's age, and from interest-group politics that pit old-age groups against other needy constituents. The 1990s must form a bridge from the age-based policies of the Modern Aging to life course programs entitling individuals to benefits and providing them opportunities based not on age but on need and ability (e.g., health care for all poor and disabled individuals, college education for the young and old).

Intergenerational must become the watchword of the New Aging period. Efforts in that direction are already occurring throughout the country.

Some communities, for example, are developing "intergenerational support systems," where older adults are recruited and matched with at-risk families to work together. Such families receive emotional support and assistance with specific self-selected tasks (e.g., locating appropriate housing) (Generations Together Exchange 1991). Other intergenerational programs assist at-risk youth through such activities as visits by high school students to nursing homes and retirees tutoring in elementary schools. Public policy can also incorporate intergenerational approaches. For example, Congressman Bill Hughes (D–N.J.) proposed a "Social Security Caregivers Act" that would allow any worker, male or female, to eliminate up to five years of either zero or very low earnings from their Social Security benefit calculation, if those years are devoted to caregiving responsibilities.

Viewing Older People as a Resource

During the Modern Aging, the elderly evolved into a vast, untapped national resource (through emphasis on retirement and leisure). In the New Aging, we must view them as a source of productivity, contribution, and opportunity, thereby lessening generational tensions. Harry Moody (1990) argues for a "Politics of Productivity," in which older people are offered retraining, good jobs, and flexible work opportunities. People in their 60s, 70s, and 80s can play a crucial role in overcoming labor shortages. Beyond productivity, they can reestablish their spiritual, social, and historical legacy, providing social leadership through activism and community support through volunteerism, rather than promoting narrow, self-serving interests.

In this vein, elders have a responsibility to give back to the society and to set an example of volunteerism. Whether it be environmental causes or supporting bond measures to rebuild highways, elders have a special role in affecting the quality of life in their communities. Notwithstanding the influence of certain cohort experiences and norms (e.g., expecting to retire into a life of leisure), persons in their later years can and should reconsider what it means to their life and others to reintegrate into the social fabric of their community. Too many difficult challenges and needs lie ahead for the elders of this and the next century not to be involved in addressing social needs.

Responding to a More Diverse Aging Society

Diversity will be the shadow under which issues of Social Security, long-term care, income security, and other policy debates fall. A more diverse older America means increasing complexity. Women, minorities, the poor, singles, and others will increase diversity within the older population. We must respond to their needs not by reacting to the group that lobbies most effectively, but by acting to meet the basic needs of all these groups. This means, for example, refusing to perpetuate the notion of age/race stratification where young minority populations are seen as battling white retirees for limited public resources (such as is the case when ballot initiatives compete for either funding public schools or creating long-term care programs). Rather, the emphasis should be on what these groups share and how they can help each other (e.g., white retirees teaching in inner-city schools, and scholarship programs for minority students who wish to become nursing-home administrators).

Avoiding Policies Forcing Competition

In the New Aging, economic resources will remain scarce. Groups will be pitted against each other easily. Political actions and policies fostering competition will undermine a highly diverse society in which people live longer and identify with a particular generation. Zero-sum budgeting, self-financing arrangements, and interest-group politics will cultivate divisiveness.

Ultimately, society must expand what most consider basic rights (such as health care) to prevent groups from fighting over limited benefits. Social insurance principles, in which everyone shares the cost and incurs the risks, must become a mainstay in financing such basic rights. In the interim, given fiscal realities, we must find ways to provide services to those in need. Means-testing benefits should be a last resort, but might be unavoidable if we do not expand economic resources, accept public responsibility, or adopt new policies such as raising the eligibility age for entitlement.

Preparing Younger Generations for Long Life

In the New Aging, an increased life span will be inevitable. Avoiding age-segregated approaches will require educating young people to manage a long life. New definitions of career development, education, preretirement planning, and leisure will force a reevaluation of social policies and private sector approaches to labor.

Young people must face the real possibility that they will live to be 100 years old and will be at least partially responsible for four- and five-generation families. We must use the 1990s to prepare our youth for the aging of the population in the next century.

Renewing Activist Government while Retaining Private Sector Responsibilities

The past thirty years have concentrated on whether the public or private sector can best respond to social concerns. This is no longer the issue;

both have responsibilities. In the New Aging we must not hamstring federal and state government leadership as it responds to social concerns. Clearly, the private sector—business, nonprofit organizations, religious, and volunteer groups—is unable to handle all the demands of a diverse aging society. Without federal and state leadership, we neglect problems until they become crises. Examples are decaying highways, growing numbers of homeless, and drug-related crimes.

Renewing activist government does not necessarily signal expanded public bureaucracies. It simply means that government officials will define social issues, apply pressure, offer encouragement in resolving problems, and step in if others fail to respond. The business community's primary mission is to provide economic productivity and prosperity. Its mandate should not include providing social benefits that government is better able to give (such as health-care coverage). On the other hand, we should reevaluate the role of the for-profit community in human services where profit-making takes precedence over social needs (such as is the case with nursing homes).

These premises must be the cornerstone of legislation, political action, and social policies as we head into the twenty-first century. Without consensus and commitment to such principles, we will continue arguing over what should be done while social needs go unaddressed.

A MODEL FOR ORGANIZATIONAL RESTRUCTURING

These premises set the stage for substantially altering the structure of public services and benefits. The politics of the last sixty years created a system where age was the primary criterion for receiving certain categorical benefits. Social Security provides partial benefits at age 62 and full benefits at 65. The Older Americans Act requires that beneficiaries be 60 years old. Housing programs use 62 as the eligibility age; Title V Senior Employment Programs use 55. Age criteria made sense when poverty and age discrimination among the elderly was endemic, life expectancy was lower, and older people comprised relatively less of the population.

Today, the situation has changed dramatically. People live longer; many more are over 55 years of age; greater absolute numbers will require health, income, and social services. Without dramatic economic expansion, these increasing numbers make continuing the current pace of expenditures for present programs implausible.

The overall success of programs such as the Older Americans Act, Supplemental Security Income, Disability Insurance, Medicare, and others in reducing poverty and improving income and social conditions among the elderly is indisputable. Several decades of expansion, however, have necessitated major organizational, legislative, and regulatory restructuring

Figure 6.1. Restructuring Social Policies

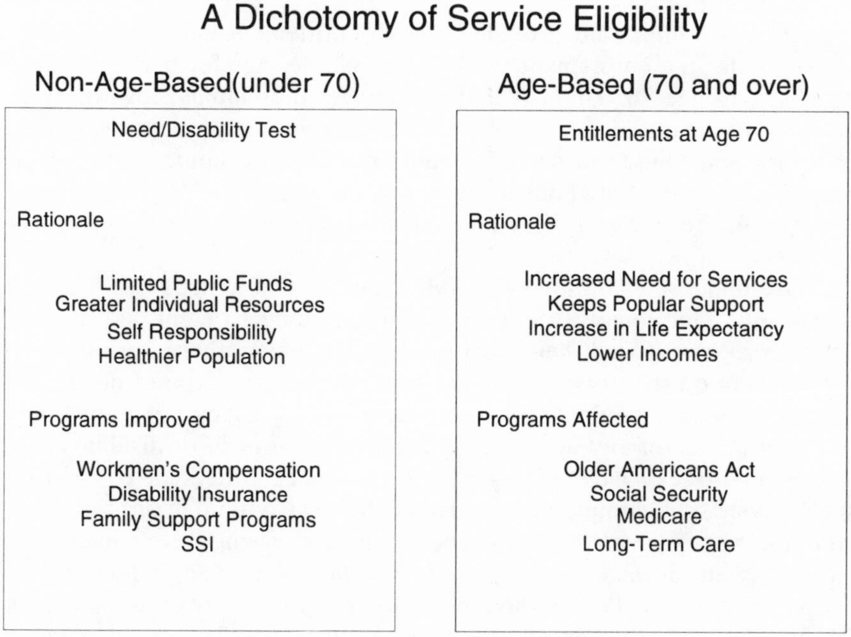

A Dichotomy of Service Eligibility

Non-Age-Based(under 70)	Age-Based (70 and over)
Need/Disability Test	Entitlements at Age 70
Rationale	Rationale
Limited Public Funds Greater Individual Resources Self Responsibility Healthier Population	Increased Need for Services Keeps Popular Support Increase in Life Expectancy Lower Incomes
Programs Improved	Programs Affected
Workmen's Compensation Disability Insurance Family Support Programs SSI	Older Americans Act Social Security Medicare Long-Term Care

Illustration prepared by Brian Louis Lipshy.

in order to accommodate the social, economic, and demographic realities of the New Aging. An overall change in our approach to social policies and programs for older people is first necessary in order to proceed with such restructuring.

Various proposals have been raised to meet the pressures and demands of the New Aging. Advocates for the elderly suggest a new cabinet agency be created to focus exclusively on senior citizens. Other ideas suggest merging Medicare and Medicaid and incorporating long-term care coverage. Still others propose privatizing entitlement programs, allowing individuals to use their Social Security contributions to purchase a private pension plan and providing tax incentives encouraging purchase of a private long-term care insurance program.

Notwithstanding the merits of these ideas, none address the fundamental gaps in and fragmentation of existing social policies, nor do they envision equity and access for all. Before approaching specific changes to programs and legislation, we must have a broad framework that applies across the board. Such a framework would lay out principles for examining changes for existing policies and programs. Figure 6.1 illustrates a dual-track system for determining eligibility for benefits and services, at least until we adopt more comprehensive social benefits, such as national health-care coverage.

Such a system would provide both an entitlement and a need-based track. Under the entitlement track, the eligibility age for benefits would be raised to age 70. Upon reaching this age, individuals, regardless of income and health status, would be entitled to a comprehensive system of health and long-term care (including nursing and home care), social services, employment, housing, and income benefits. They could then face the future knowing they and their families would retain basic necessities.

Those under age 70, however, *unless* economically needy or disabled (physically, emotionally, mentally), would no longer be entitled to categorical programs. Such benefits would target those otherwise unable to obtain them on their own and who demonstrate some type of need. The need track would eliminate age as a criterion for services and allow funds to target people of any age meeting the criteria of need or disability.

This dual-track system of eligibility is not novel. Others have proposed such a system, including the U.S. House Select Committee on Aging and gerontologists such as Andrew Achenbaum. Increasing the eligibility age has also been suggested, most notably by Alan Pifer (1986), who suggests age 75, Lee Smith (1987), who feels workers should stay on the job until 70, and Yung-Ping Chen (1987), who identifies age 73 as analogous to using age 65 in 1935. What is new about this idea is its explicit response to the demographic and economic realities of the New Aging. It also takes into account changes in dependency ratios—more older people to fewer young people—and the inevitable generational tensions that will arise when a smaller work force supports a large retiree population. The dual-track system is a middle-ground approach to either means-testing programs or adopting universal coverage for health, long-term care, and social services.

The dual-track system has disadvantages. It disregards individuals with lower life expectancies (i.e., black males and native Americans); it assumes some type of means testing for people under age 70; it departs radically from the current structure; and, many elderly groups will oppose it.

To deal with those disadvantages, benefits and coverage under such programs as Disability Insurance and Supplemental Security Income must be expanded in response to the issue of lower life expectancies and Workmen's Compensation must be strengthened. Ultimately, a national health-care system that provides universal coverage to all people (beyond the dual-track system) will help such groups. The issue of political opposition is crucial. Policies such as Social Security and the Older Americans Act retain broad support because so many older people are eligible. Increasing the age requirement might erode support. Requiring need and disability criteria imposes an income and disability assessment with attendant paperwork and eligibility requirements. In the absence, however, of fundamental reforms leading to broad-based and universal entitlement, however, we might have no choice.

Adopting fundamental reforms will take time, but we can view the dual-track system as a transitional step toward that end. In that regard, we might view types of change on a three-step continuum: incremental adjustments, transitional reorganizing, and fundamental reforms (see Figure 6.2).

Incremental adjustments to existing programs and policies would be short-term in nature, and would usually involve tinkering with an inefficient or ineffective program. Adding extra respite days to Medicare, eliminating the earnings limitation test, and developing an ombudsman program to nursing-home care are examples of good, albeit *incremental* steps. Transitional steps are longer-term and might include establishing home care as a basic feature of Medicare, instituting a long-term care program for old and younger disabled, requiring gerontology courses in primary and secondary grades, and instituting a dual-track system of eligibility. Fundamental reforms, such as creating a national health-care system, would dramatically change existing programs or offer new approaches to aging such as expecting greater productivity among elders.

The dual-track approach can be a transitional reorganizing of an existing set of programs or can, if we adopt no expansive social policies and do not have sufficient financial resources, serve as fundamental reform to existing programs. During the 1980s, we made incremental adjustments to existing policies while social problems worsened and needs increased. The 1990s should be a decade of transitional change, possibly becoming fundamental reform at the turn of the century. At the very least, we should adopt a dual eligibility system by 2010, before the baby boomers reach their 60s, or it might become politically impossible to impose it on them.

REFORMING SOCIAL POLICIES

As we consider a model for restructuring eligibility, we must reform social policies employing the continuum of incremental, transitional, and fundamental change. As described in Chapter 2, existing laws, regulations, and benefits at the federal and state level encompass several categories of policies. Each category requires some reform if it is to meet the exigencies of the New Aging.

Health Policy

Ideal fundamental reform would be creation of an American version of the Canadian national health-care system—a system allowing freedom of

Figure 6.2. Reforming the Benefits Structure

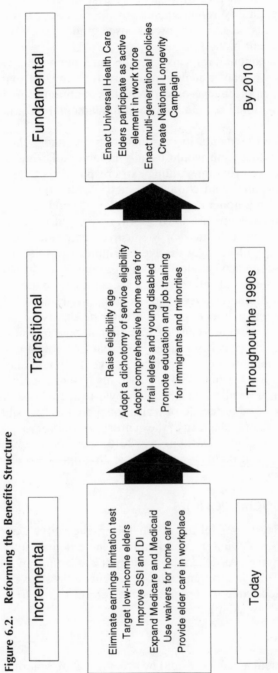

Incremental	Transitional	Fundamental
Eliminate earnings limitation test Target low-income elders Improve SSI and DI Expand Medicare and Medicaid Use waivers for home care Provide elder care in workplace	Raise eligibility age Adopt a dichotomy of service eligibility Adopt comprehensive home care for frail elders and young disabled Promote education and job training for immigrants and minorities	Enact Universal Health Care Elders participate as active element in work force Enact multi-generational policies Create National Longevity Campaign
Today	Throughout the 1990s	By 2010

Illustration prepared by Brian Louis Lipshy.

choice among providers and consumers but relying on a "single-payer" system and imposing national cost controls. Such a system would ease competition among generations and groups in need. Many disagree on if and when such a system could be created in the United States, given our peculiar political and philosophical characteristics (for example, individualism versus collective ideals).[1] By the early 1990s, however, most sectors of society—business, organized labor, the middle class, the elderly—had recognized the existing system of health care as unworkable, inequitable, and costly. An assortment of organizations and alliances, including the AFL-CIO, AARP, Consumers Union, National Association of Social Workers (NASW), American Nurses Association (ANA), the Washington Business Group on Health, and the National Leadership Coalition for Health Care Reform (an alliance of businesses, labor, senior-citizen, and consumer groups), had joined the fray, undertaking intense efforts to solve the health-care crisis. Even the American Medical Association, a staunch opponent of government involvement in health care, endorsed major reform and public intervention. A slew of legislative proposals aimed at establishing greater access to health and long-term coverage are under debate.

As escalating health-care costs, a large uninsured population, and an overburdened private sector create pressure for some system of comprehensive health- and long-term-care coverage, the arguments increasingly center around which model: Should it be a socialist/European system, a Canadian/public and private partnership, or a unique U.S. model based on the free market? The health-care systems of the Soviet Union and Great Britain are discredited in this country because of their inefficient centralized bureaucracies. The private sector approach, where insurance companies and businesses provide health-care coverage in collusion with labor unions, is increasingly seen as incapable of responding to inflation and the increasing number of uninsured. A public-private partnership (evident in the Canadian model) is still distrusted by legislators and the public.[2]

Medicare and Medicaid are in serious trouble. Medicare, according to the Social Security Board of Trustees, is expected to go bankrupt by 2005, and Medicaid is already a serious fiscal problem to states. Pressures will increase with the number of workers contributing to the Medicare trust fund per HI enrollee (whose numbers will decline from four to two by the middle of the next century) (Older Americans Report 1991). A transitional solution would be to recognize Medicare and Medicaid as part of the larger health-care crisis. While moving toward a national health-care system, we should combine dollars spent for Medicare and Medicaid and adopt a transitional system that is based on the dual system of eligibility and that:

- establishes a national cost-containment system built on the prospective payment system and relative value scales in the Medicare and Medicaid program;
- institutes a national home-care program with cost sharing among beneficiaries;
- shifts health-care expenditures from the current acute-care focus to chronic care and health prevention and promotion;
- establishes a system of community-based long-term care that includes a continuum of care—community, home, and institutional—and makes rehabilitation a primary objective;
- provides protection against catastrophic health-care costs;
- provides a public subsidy to purchase health insurance for the working poor and the unemployed (and avoids mandating that health insurance be provided by business).

Existing legislative proposals, especially those embracing the Pepper Commission Report's recommendation for a national health and long-term care system, embody many of these features. The Pepper Commission report and many state proposals, however, endorse mandated employee health-care coverage, which could seriously impact small businesses.

In the interim, incremental steps should move us toward transitional steps by adding home care to the Medicare program and by allowing states to include noninstitutional long-term care in their Medicaid programs (as was done in the Budget Reconciliation Act of 1990) and to experiment with incentives for individuals to purchase long-term-care coverage. The private sector should continue its efforts to promote private long-term-care insurance as well.

The 1990s will see great political interest in financing long-term care and increasing health-care coverage to the uninsured. The risk is that long-term care for the elderly will be seen as separate from health care to the medically indigent and the working uninsured. That schism must be avoided, and advocates for the elderly, the young or disabled, and the uninsured must seek a common cause and not pursue separate political health-care agendas.

Income Security

Income security will be both the goal and fear of future cohorts of elderly. Providing for income security today is crucial to realizing the retirement expectations of baby boomers and others. We must work toward a four-legged chair rather than a three-legged stool of retirement income. This chair would include the original three legs of the stool—savings/assets, private or public pensions, and Social Security—and a fourth, a system of public benefits safety-netting future generations. This fourth leg depends on our adopting the dual-track system of eligibility so we can afford a broad range of health, income, and social services for people over 70 years of age. Without it, today's youth face tremendous insecurity and vulnerability as they age and find their assets and pensions eroded by inflation and economic disruptions. Each of these legs, however, requires reinforcement.

Social Security must remain the bedrock in the New Aging, as it was in the Modern Aging. For much of the population, it will continue to be the primary source of retirement income. With increasing diversity, many more individuals will have no other secure source of income. We must maintain its basic principles—social insurance, universality, replacement rates, weighted formulas—while modifying its organizational structure. One popular suggestion for enhancing the status of the Social Security Administration is to make it an independent agency with a board of trustees that includes consumer representation. This would conceivably de-politicize it and give it greater autonomy from the huge Department of Health and Human Services. That would be a mistake, however. Organizationally, an independent Social Security Administration makes sense. For policy purposes and promoting intergenerational programs, though, it does not. Social Security is not just an old-age program. It covers younger disabled workers, widows, and the poor. Its categorical programs (e.g., Title XX Social Services Block Grant, Supplemental Security Income, Hospital Insurance) overlap with other programs in HHS, such as the Administration on Aging, National Institute on Health, Administration for Children, Youth and Families, and Health Care Financing Administration. If we are to integrate programs based on need and functional ability, reduce age segregation, and promote organizational efficiency, and accountability, SSA must remain within HHS. A more proper focus should be on reinstating the personnel cuts of the 1980s (at a time when caseloads and beneficiaries were expanding) and making the SSA more accessible to clients. During the 1980s major reductions occurred in SSA's staff that caused a deterioration in the agency's quality of public service. In 1990, SSA personnel totalled 63,000, down 17,000 from the staffing level of 1985. In addition, an 800 toll-free telephone system was instituted in the late 80s to bypass the agency's network of local Social Security field offices (U.S. Senate Special Committee on Aging 1991). That move further alienated those who were unable to get through busy lines, were provided wrong information, or preferred the personal service of district offices. Efforts by Commissioner Gwendolyn King and advocates such as Dr. Arthur Flemming to rectify those problems are moving SSA back toward its traditional role of providing well managed and personalized services to the public.

The Social Security system works. In fact, it's a good bargain. To today's generation of senior citizens, it represents an ingrained social contract, an implicit promise by government that anyone employed and contributing during his or her working life will have access to the system's myriad benefits: Old-Age and Survivors Insurance, Hospital Insurance, Disability Insurance, Supplemental Security Income, cost-of-living increases. No other pension can match its multifaceted approach at such a relatively low cost.

Nevertheless, Social Security requires some reforms. We must return to a pay-as-you-go approach, where contributions are used as outlays for current beneficiaries. As Senator Moynihan pointed out in 1990, we cannot trust the political system to wisely and efficiently preserve or administer a huge surplus. Pay-as-you-go also minimizes generational tension by keeping the payroll tax lower. To further avoid politicizing the administration of Social Security, it must be kept off-budget, where receipts and disbursements of the Social Security Trust Funds are removed from federal deficit estimates (as is planned in the 1990 Reconciliation Act). During the 1990s, we must avoid moves affecting the system's solvency or heightening fear by young people that Social Security will fail to pay benefits when they retire. Freezing the COLAs, pursuing "privatization," and paying off "notch babies" only disrupt the credibility of and public support for Social Security.[3]

During the 1990s, we must expand and improve programs serving the poor and disabled. With a dual approach to eligibility, SSI and DI will be crucial to such individuals, who will rely on them for their basic retirement income.

Pensions are potentially the most vulnerable part of retirement income. Bankruptcies of pension plans in the 1980s due to mergers, corruption, economic failures, and lack of federal oversight set the time bomb ticking in private pensions slated for the year 2000 and beyond. A lack of cost-of-living increases in private pensions guarantees that, with longevity, many retirees will outlive their pensions. The unfunded liability confronting local and state governments fuels generational claims emerging between taxpayers and retirees. To avoid another savings and loan debacle, a blue-ribbon presidential commission should be established to investigate and respond to the potential problems private and public pensions will face by the year 2010.

A final aspect of income security affects savings and assets. Longevity requires that we reduce incentives motivating early retirement, facilitate employment later in life, and encourage people to save. Early retirement policies will become outdated as companies face worker shortages ("Issues for Reauthorizing the OAA" 1990). Eliminating the earnings limitation test in Social Security would be a step in the right direction.[4] Adopting public and private initiatives to make working easier for retirees is also essential. This could be accomplished by adopting flextime or training programs, for example.

Along with strengthening the savings leg of the income-security chair comes establishing incentives and flexible plans for younger cohorts (those now in their 20s and 30s). The Individual Retirement Accounts (IRAs) of the 1980s remain a good idea. If we allow a Social Security surplus, we may want to consider Individual Social Security Retirement Accounts (ISSRAs), as proposed by Rep. John Porter (R–Ill.) in 1990 ("Let Workers Own Their Retirement Funds"). Porter suggested the portion of Social Security taxes not utilized for current beneficiaries be refunded in the form of ISSRAs. Although it has some major defects, such as implicitly assuming gradual privatization, this proposal points out the need to adopt creative ideas for today's youth, who must be more systematic in preparing for a long life span.

Housing Policy

The cost of shelter has escalated nationwide, creating a society of "equity haves" and "housing have-nots." The lack of affordable housing affects all ages and income groups including the elderly and first-time home buyers. Decimation of publicly funded housing during the 1980s, as well as drastic cuts to Section 202 and Section 8 housing subsidy programs, have contributed to the homeless problem and caused many to spend inordinately on housing.[5] On the other hand, many older people have reaped, through property appreciation, an incredible amount of home equity, allowing them a retirement income unimaginable decades earlier. This disparity will likely lead to generational tensions unless the housing crisis is alleviated during the 1990s.

This tension will extend to homebuyers unable to benefit from property-tax reductions established in the 1970s and 1980s and those enjoying housing appreciation and low property taxes. It will involve baby boomers hoping to similarly cash in, but finding in their later years that smaller age cohorts mean fewer homebuyers.

To avoid this tension, the 1990s must witness several incremental and fundamental reforms. The fundamental principle of housing as shelter rather than an investment or commodity must be reestablished. We must limit the mortgage tax deduction to the one home in which the taxpayer resides. The "once-in-a-lifetime" exclusion of gain for sale of homes by people 55 and over (where they can exempt up to $125,000 of profit) should be permitted only for those 70 years of age or older. (In 1986, the mortgage interest deduction on owner-occupied houses was $27 billion, while the exclusion of capital gains cost another $1.2 billion (Longman 1987). The savings from these measures should be used to assist first-time homebuyers, increase funding for publicly subsidized housing for low-income people of all ages, and develop congregate housing services for the disabled and elderly who require them.

Social-Service Policy

The current set of disparate social-service programs must be combined to create a single intergenerational human-service policy. Programs such as the Social Services Block Grant, the Older Americans Act, SSI, Food Stamps and others should be part of a Policy for Intergenerational Network (PIN), fostering interaction among generations by coordinating programs for child and elder care, home care for disabled young people and frail elderly, and recreation and educational programs for teenagers and elders. This PIN approach serves to link programs and projects throughout cabinet agencies. For example, the Low-Income Energy Assistance Program (DOE), congregate housing (HUD), Senior and Youth employment (DOL), and subsidized transportation (DOT), would be brought together to serve intergenerational needs.

Rather than harm agencies such as the Administration on Aging (AoA) and the Administration for Children, Youth and Families (ACYF), PIN would provide the administrative and legislative flexibility to allow services for children and teenagers in senior-citizen centers, provide information and referral services to both grandparents and grandchildren by area agencies on aging, and otherwise reduce age segregation.

PIN would work best if SSA remains part of HHS. In this way, coordination of services would be best accomplished. PIN could be housed in the White House, or the secretary of Health and Human Services could be directed to convene an interdepartmental PIN task force.

Civil Rights and Legal Protection

An important aspect of minimizing generational claims and responding to diversity will be renewed commitment to civil rights and affirmative action legislation. A highly diverse society can lead to divisiveness if constituent groups believe that only "survival of the fittest" insures equal opportunity. In the New Aging, all forms of discrimination—ageism, racism, sexism, nativism, and religious—must be fought. The Civil Rights and Equal Employment Opportunity Commissions must regain the leadership role they lost during the 1980s.

Volunteer Policy

Volunteerism is alive and well in the United States. Its revitalization is a positive legacy of the Reagan and Bush years. Programs such as ACTION, with its Peace Corps, Foster Grandparents, Retired Senior Volunteers, and other programs, should be expanded. The idea of a National Elder Care Corps, through which retirees could volunteer their talents and energies and, in exchange, receive credit toward social and health services, should be explored. A National Volunteer Care Bank, as proposed by the California legislature, would allow individuals to volunteer to provide nursing-home and long-term care services to the disabled and elderly, receiving in exchange a corresponding number of state-funded hours of care for their own parents and grandparents.

The concept of a National Service Corps is worthwhile for the 1990s and beyond. Such a proposal would require all young people to volunteer two years of military or civil service. In lieu of military service, youngsters could volunteer to work in one of many civic and social-service programs including senior-citizen programs.

MAKING PROGRAMS USER-FRIENDLY

Along with these policy reforms and adoption of a dual-track system of eligibility, another series of steps will be required to make the system user-friendly. Notwithstanding our limiting of age-segregated programs, increasing the eligibility age, and promoting intergenerational models, more senior-citizen programs will be needed in the coming years. The number of senior citizens 75 and over will increase most significantly and will require a vast array of services including nutritional, health, transportation, and housing. As we enter the 1990s, a set of incremental and transitional steps can ease utilization of such services by the aged and their families.

Excessive paperwork and complex forms frustrate families and service providers seeking federal and state assistance. An SSI application, for example, to be completed by the blind, disabled, destitute, or sick, involves up to fifteen pages of forms (Rich 1990). Medicare reimbursement claims can become a maze of forms, phone calls, denials, and long waiting periods. A *U.S. and World Report* review of the nation's top professional schools pointed out vividly why some young people are discouraged from entering medical school and working with the elderly ("America's Best Graduate and Professional Schools" 1990). The Medicare forms have about fifty boxes, and the manual explaining the form is more than three hundred pages long. A flu shot takes two minutes to administer but requires twenty minutes of staff time to answer the questions for Medicare reimbursement. No wonder some physicians, social workers, and other providers don't want to participate in Medicare or Medicaid programs. An expansion of public services must include streamlining eligibility and reimbursement criteria and paperwork or will flounder for lack of public support.

Making it easier for families and individuals to locate services is also key to building public support. Today, families and elders must approach Social Security district offices, area agencies on aging, health clinics, adult day-care centers, housing offices, and welfare departments to find the services they need to care for a disabled or frail older member. Figure 6.3 gives a graphic display of the myriad services and public policies that form a maze of community services for the elderly.[6]

Robert Binstock suggests establishing Aging Resource Centers (ARCs)—uniform and visible community sites for one-stop information, referral, and follow-up ("Issues for Reauthorizing the OAA" 1990). Another idea proposes co-locating Social Security field offices and the benefits counseling efforts of Medicare programs with local information and referral offices operated through area agencies on aging ("NAAA Urges Co-Location of AAA's With Social Security Field Offices" 1989). The National Association of Area Agencies on Aging (NAAAA) has gone so far as to advocate that community-based, long-term care service systems should integrate Medicare and Medicaid with existing area agencies on aging (AAAs), thereby avoiding duplication and waste. Others, such as the National Council on Aging, argue that this would further burden and diminish the Older Americans Act, which funds AAAs. In 1989, Rep. Henry Waxman suggested creating CARE agencies to establish eligibility, develop a plan, and monitor service provision, thereby making it easier for families and the elderly to obtain long-term care services. Besides organizational and jurisdictional debates on how best to streamline and coordinate the fragmented system, the question of how to coordinate programs and services to create accessible, client-centered systems serving the elderly and their families is also difficult. Many services are administered at the local level. City, county, and municipal governments must be taught how best to serve older persons. Toward this end, in 1990, the National Association of Area Agencies on Aging joined with the National Association of Counties (through an Administration on Aging grant) to educate county officials about national and local trends in aging.

Should a separate cabinet agency for elder affairs be created within the federal government? As discussed in Chapter 2, the organizational standing of senior-citizen services is not the issue. The goal should be to develop an organizational structure that lends itself to a dual-track system of eligibility and intergenerational programs, and facilitates utilization of public benefits for families and elders. Establishment of a cabinet-level agency will not guarantee these goals will be met. Relying on the existing arrangement within the Department of Health and Human Services and using interagency agreements with other cabinet agencies can work, given commitment and leadership by political appointees and civil servants.

Another important step is involving the nonprofit sector—charitable organizations, religious groups, community-based agencies—in the delivery and administration of programs for the elderly. The excessive role of the for-profit industry in managing nursing-home care must be reduced. Experience shows an incompatibility between making a profit or return on an investment and caring for a largely sick and dependent population.

Figure 6.3. Major Federal Programs Funding Community Services for the Elderly

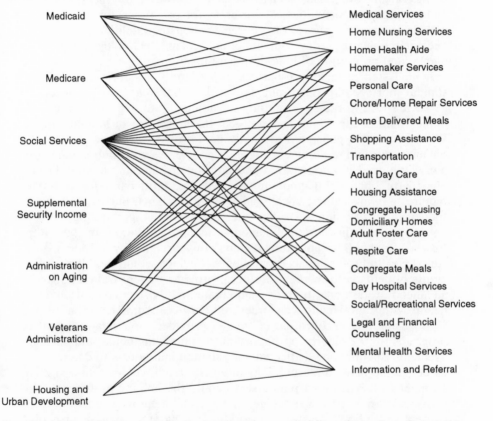

Illustration prepared by Brian Louis Lipshy, based on Katzper, *Modelling of Long-Term Care*, p. 16.

It also demonstrates that where for-profit dominates a social service, the public sector bears the more expensive burden of caring for those who cannot afford for-profit and fee-for-service programs.

The private sector, however, will play an important role in the New Aging, a role centering on workplace. Corporations and small businesses must make the well-being of their workers and retirees a priority. Promoting elder care as an employee benefit, creating flextime work opportunities, training the work force in new skills, and protecting pension plans will be the responsibility of the business community. Responding to the consumer demands of an aging society allows for myriad investment and for-profit opportunities. Major areas for private sector involvement include leisure and recreation, retirement housing facilities, information and communications, development of medical and technological advancements, and promotion of long-term-care insurance.

A final step in making programs user-friendly is addressing the substantial shortage of people trained to work with the elderly. Geriatricians, geriatric social workers, gerontologists, administrators of aging programs, nurses, and occupational and physical therapists are in limited supply. Without major expansion of decently paid providers trained to meet the unique needs and requirements of older people, we will continue to warehouse the aged in understaffed and poor-quality nursing homes. Development of home- and community-based long-term care, for example, requires administrators, vocational aides, physicians, nurses, and others trained in areas unique to aging, such as preventive gerontology, osteoporosis, osteoarthritis, senile dementia, and rehabilitation. In 1991, Rep. Edward Roybal (D–Calif.) took a step in this direction by introducing the Allied Health Professionals Promotion Act, which would establish project grants in fields with worker shortages, provide student traineeships and advanced professional training, and create an advisory council on allied health within the Health Resources and Services Administration.

Licensing and certification of trained providers and establishment of programs for the elderly are important to minimizing abuse and mismanagement. Encouraging dedicated and talented individuals to commit to a career in the fields of gerontology and geriatrics involves renewed commitment to the ideals of public service and the helping professions. Increased salaries, greater prestige, and societal acknowledgment of such careers will follow. At present, working in a nursing home or providing mental-health services to the elderly is seen as employment of last resort usually reserved for low-income and unskilled people.

PAYING FOR EVERYTHING

The bottom line in policy and politics is cost. Ultimately, responding to longevity, diversity, and generational claims concerns financing public benefits and services and imposing added costs on the private sector.

Paying for programs in the New Aging will be both obvious and difficult. Because we have various options for raising revenue, it will be easy to identify sources. Revenues can be obtained through new or expanded taxes, user fees, or self-financing arrangements (an increased tax on that group most likely to use the service). Selected excise taxes on cigarettes or alcohol, premiums and co-payments, and a lien on estates are other sources of revenue. The government can shift costs by requiring businesses to subsidize health and retirement benefits.

One of the more often mentioned sources of financing home care and long-term care has been to lift the wage cap ($51,300 as of 1990) on which the Medicare and Social Security payroll taxes are levied (lifting the Medicare Part A payroll contribution rate of 1.45 percent and the wage cap to $125,000 will raise $26.9 billion over five years). Doing so raises several billion dollars each year and affects the tax rate of a very small proportion of the population. On the other hand, the concern raised is that in an era of limited public dollars, those funds are better used to help AIDS victims, fund prenatal programs, and assist other more needy groups. Ideally, that tradeoff would not exist with a national health- and long-term-care coverage. Given fiscal realities, however, those funds should first go to the medically indigent and to fund prenatal, maternal, and child health, and social services to drug-addicted babies—the very groups without politically powerful groups to represent their interests. The die may already have been cast. The 1991 Omnibus Budget Reconciliation Act lifted the maximum level subject to Medicare payroll tax from $51,300 to $125,000, largely to reduce the federal deficit rather than strengthen the Hospital Insurance trust fund. This may encourage lifting the wage base for Social Security payroll tax as well, again for budgetary reasons rather than to promote social programs for needy groups.

The difficulty will be convincing taxpayers of the need for increased revenues and the value of services rendered. The fiscal controversies of the 1990s will not necessarily revolve around source of revenues. Rather, they will reflect the public's confidence (or lack thereof) that their tax dollars will be used as stated and efficiently expended. Surveys and the passage of bond measures and excise taxes on cigarettes and alcohol demonstrate individuals are willing to be taxed for the purpose of housing the homeless, improving schools, securing roads and bridges, fighting crime, and caring for the sick (Bailey, "The Reagan Era's Over, Isn't It Time We Got On with It?" 1990).

The challenge of elected and public officials is to restore the public's faith that government programs can be managed effectively and efficiently and that their tax dollars are earmarked for a clearly defined problem or social need. Responding to this challenge involves several broad administrative goals: ending government bashing and restoring respect for public servants; pursuing aggressive audits and investigations; minimizing the growth of large bureaucracies; relying on local agencies, nonprofit community-based organizations, and, where appropriate, private-sector agencies to deliver benefits; and requiring cost sharing among beneficiaries.

The public will support increased expenditures. The recognition that we must tackle social and economic problems unattended to during the 1970s and 1980s will force an increase in revenues. The baby-boom generation will use its vast electoral clout to demand more services for their parents and themselves. The question is not, "Will we spend more?" but, "Can we spend our dollars wisely and retain the public confidence?"

Preserving confidence in the midst of change depends on accurately predicting and efficiently responding to crises. If we can anticipate and prepare for hurricanes and earthquakes, we can identify and prepare for social change as well. We can build firm foundations; we can make shelter readily available; we can make certain everyone is insured. The New Aging need not be viewed as threatening and destructive, but as invigorating and productive.

NOTES

1. Elizabeth Kutza argues that service providers and advocates for the elderly must know America's political and economic culture well to understand the constraints and opportunities presented (Kutza 1990). Incrementalism (as opposed to drastic social reforms) is ingrained in our legislative and public system. The Constitution intends for Congress to work slowly and limit legislative initiatives. Individuals inherently distrust central government and large bureaucracies. The free market is expected to tackle social problems before government intervenes, and state and local governments are to provide leadership on public matters. Given these norms and expectations, it has often been said that the wonders of the American political system is not that it doesn't work, but that it works as well as it does.

2. The Canadian system of health care provides basic health and long-term care to its entire population. While we spend close to 12 percent of our GNP on health-care costs, Canada spends approximately 9 percent, yet it covers all, while 37 million Americans remain uninsured. The Canadian system has been in place since the mid-1960s. It consists of a sole payer for health care (the government) and imposes national cost containment on health-care expenditures. The provinces decide on allocation of health-care resources and contract to doctors, hospitals, and medical suppliers. In turn, individual consumers are free to select medical care. The Canadian system, although enjoying popularity in the United States, is not without fault. Elective surgery can require long waits; health-care providers earn less than in the United States; rationing of exotic and expensive technology occurs; health care costs are rising; and the system serves a much smaller population (25 million).

3. The Social Security notch refers to the difference in monthly Social Security benefits among some born before 1916 and others born from 1917 to 1921. Benefit levels were changed in 1972 and 1977 to correct an error giving recipients born

between 1917 and 1921 extraordinarily high replacement rates. Had this over-indexing of benefits stood, benefits would have exceeded recipients' preretirement income, and Social Security tax rates would have doubled. The correction created a political mess, with the "notch babies" feeling their benefits had been reduced unnecessarily. The Government Accounting Office (GAO) estimates the cost of compensating notch beneficiaries at $20 to $300 billion (U.S. Senate Special Committee on Aging 1991).

4. Some groups, including the Families USA advocacy group, argue against eliminating the Social Security earnings test. Doing so, they claim, would benefit higher-income beneficiaries (who are better able to find part-time work) and cost the federal government up to $28.1 billion over five years (Older Americans Report 1991). Other groups, such as the American Association of Retired Persons and the National Committee to Preserve Social Security and Medicare, favor liberalizing or eliminating the test.

5. By the early 1990s, there were signs that the housing crisis was gaining attention. The Cranston-Gonzalez National Affordable Housing Act of 1990, which attempts to establish housing policy within federal funding budget constraints, was the first major housing bill adopted since the Reagan administration. Around the same time, Congress attempted to include funding for the HOPE program (for elderly independence demonstration projects), and increased funding for additional housing units for the elderly and disabled, and for congregate services for frail older persons.

6. The Social Security Administration (SSA) under Commissioner Gwendolyn King recognizes the need to coordinate its programs and social services. In the early 1990s, for example, the agency began a service experiment, joining the Administration on Aging (AoA) in placing AoA employees in 12 SSA field offices. These employees provided information and referrals to clients over age 60.

BIBLIOGRAPHY

"America's Best Graduate and Professional Schools." *U.S. News and World Report*, March 19, 1990, p. 65.
Bailey, Douglas. "The Reagan Era's Over, Isn't It Time We Got On with It?" *The Washington Post National Weekly Edition*, April 16–22, 1990, 24.
Chen, Yung-Ping. "Making Assets out of Tomorrow's Elderly." *The Gerontologist* 27, 4 (1987): 410–16.
Cole, Thomas. "The Specter of Old Age: History, Politics, and Culture in an Aging America." *Tikkun* 3, 5 (Sept./Oct. 1988): 14–95.
"Early Retirement Policies Will Become a Thing of the Past." *Older Americans Report* (Jan. 26, 1990): 36.
Generations Together Exchange. A Newsletter Exchanging Information on Intergenerational Programs. Issue 6, Winter 1991.
"Issues for Reauthorizing the OAA." *Older Americans Report* (Feb. 16, 1990): 62.
Kutza, Elizabeth. "Responding to Diversity: Is American Society Capable?" In *Diversity in Aging*, edited by S. Bass, E. Kutza, and F. Torres-Gil. Glenview, Ill.: Scott, Foresman & Company, 1990: 101–28.

"Let Workers Own Their Retirement Funds." *The Wall Street Journal*, Feb. 1, 1990.

Longman, Phillip. *Born to Pay: The New Politics of Aging in America*. Boston: Houghton Mifflin Company, 1987.

Moody, Harry. "The Politics of Entitlement and the Politics of Productivity." In *Diversity in Aging*, edited by S. Bass, E. Kutza, and F. Torres-Gil Glenview, Ill.: Scott, Foresman & Company, 1990.

"NAAA Urges Co-Location of AAA's with Social Security Field Offices." *Older Americans Report* (Oct. 27, 1989): 414.

Older Americans Report. Silver Spring, Md., May 24, 1991, p. 204.

Older Americans Report. Silver Spring, Md., May 31, 1991, p. 219.

Pifer, Alan, and Lydia Bronte. *Our Aging Society*. New York: W.W. Norton & Company, 1986.

Rich, Spencer. "Hearing Told U.S. Stymies the Helpless." *The Washington Post*, April 6, 1990, p. A18.

Smith, Lee. "The War between the Generations." *Fortune*, July 20, 1987, pp. 78–82.

U.S. House Select Committee on Aging. "Long-Term Care and Personal Impoverishment: Seven in Ten Elderly Living Alone Are at Risk." Comm. Pub. No. 100–631. Washington, D.C.: U.S. Government Printing Office, 1987.

U.S. Senate Special Committee on Aging. "Developments in Aging: 1990." Vol. 1. Washington, D.C.: U.S. Government Printing Office, 1991.

7
AMERICA IN THE TWENTY-FIRST CENTURY

Tomorrow will give us something to think about.

Cicero, *Ad Atticum*

The New Aging embodies what the United States will become and what trends will affect it in the twenty-first century. America will look very different in the early part of the twenty-first century than it did during most of the twentieth. The Population Reference Bureau has predicted the following seven demographic trends will shape the social and economic fabric of the United States in the century ahead (Population Reference Bureau 1989):

1. the aging of the population
2. changes in household and family structures
3. changes in racial and ethnic composition
4. changes in residential patterns
5. changes in the distribution of income and wealth
6. changes in labor force needs
7. changes in the global demographic picture

These trends are affected by the three forces described in this book: diversity, longevity, and political and social generational claims.

We are not alone; other nations face similar pressures. America's chief economic competitors of the late twentieth century—Germany and Japan—are aging rapidly and also face social problems resulting from fewer

young workers. The developing Third World—Africa, Asia, the Pacific
Basin, and Latin America—will experience a larger boom of older people
through increased life expectancy and improved public health than Northern Hemispheric nations, including North America, Europe, and the Soviet Union. They must confront the additional problems of urbanization,
economic underdevelopment, Westernization, and the breakdown of traditional extended families who provide care to elders (American Society
on Aging 1989).

Chapter 6 presented possible solutions to the problems of demographic
and social change in the United States. What we do in this country might
be useful to other developed and developing nations. We might, in turn,
learn from their experiences. Our preparations for the next century cannot
be divorced from the broader political and societal changes affecting the
United States. Aging is but one of several transformations affecting our
country and much of the world.

GLOBAL PRESSURES

It is a cliché, albeit true, that we live in a global society, where what
happens elsewhere affects the United States, and actions here influence
the world. In the twenty-first century, demographics and aging will be
just two of several forces shaping our lives and influencing our adjustment
to the New Aging. Events occurring overseas or across borders affect
demographic and social trends in the United States. Geopolitical and
military actions will help or hinder our response to domestic matters. U.S.
leadership regarding other nations will determine the influence our successes and failures have on other countries facing similar challenges.

For example, our present international status as an economic power
will change. In the next century, the United States will be one of many
economic powers. Germany, France, Canada, and the economic pow-
erhouses of the Pacific Basin—Japan, Singapore, Taiwan, and Korea—
are now eclipsing America's economic dominance. The loss of economic
preeminence is not necessarily negative. It signals new opportunities
worldwide for other nations to share in an expanding global economy. It
means, however, that the United States must pay greater attention to
improving its social and economic productivity. How we compete and to
what extent we meet new global challenges in technology, trade, foreign
industry, new markets, and domestic productivity will directly influence
our ability to pay for expanded public benefits and social services. History
shows that in times of economic recession and depression, populations
are less willing to assist others through the public sector. Advocates for
the poor and disadvantaged have as much at stake in international trade
and economics as do business and labor.

Protecting the environment will be critical in the New Aging. It does little good to prepare for a long life span or ensure that older people receive long-term care, if people become ill or die earlier because of pollution and toxins. We know conclusively that cigarette smoking, alcohol, and illegal drugs shorten lives and create severe health problems. Unsafe drinking water, lead-poisoned fish, air pollution, and acid rain and radioactivity will shorten the life expectancy and debilitate the population. Better to protect the environment today than wait until suspected offenders (e.g., ozone-damaging aerosols) are proven beyond a doubt to cause environmental damage. Senior-citizen lobbies would do well to join the environmental movement to protect their children and grandchildren.

The nations most affecting the United States in the twenty-first century will not be Europe or the Soviet Union, but our next-door neighbors. Developments in Canada and Mexico will have immediate and long-lasting repercussions here. What happens or fails in the countries along our borders profoundly affects the United States. Canada, for example, is looked upon as a model for restructuring our health and social-welfare programs. However, any economic or political dislocation (such as independence for French Quebec) could affect our northern border and their social programs. Mexico, on the other hand, is our primary source of immigrants. Immigrants provide us not only with cheap and productive labor but keep our median age lower than it otherwise might be and provide tax revenues for entitlement programs.[1] Yet, immigration raises fundamental questions about social cohesion and national identity. Immigration and a high birthrate will make the Spanish-speaking, Latino population the largest minority group in the United States. A major development of the early 1990s might well be creation of a common economic market between Mexico, Canada, and the United States, as envisioned in the free-trade initiatives between Canada and the U.S. and the U.S. and Mexico. Such an event will result in dramatic and unpredictable economic and social consequences.

Another global issue concerns the ever-changing geo-political world in which the United States must be prepared to exercise leadership. The dissolution of the Soviet empire, democracy and unrest in Eastern Europe, the aftermath of the Persian Gulf war, and continuing problems in Central America require a strong U.S. presence worldwide. We cannot afford to return to the isolationism of the 1930s and 1950s, even when experiencing economic and social pressures ourselves.

The United States remains the only global power able to exert cultural, economic, and military influence on a fast-changing world. When oil supplies are disrupted, the international banking system experiences problems, or terrorists threaten, the United States must be prepared to respond. We must retain a strong military capable of defending the United States and assisting other nations. In the New Aging, however, U.S. armed forces will depend on a smaller, more racially diverse, youth population. The elders of the next century must concern themselves with the social needs of those groups if we are to maintain a well-educated and prepared military.

DOMESTIC CONCERNS

Diversity, longevity, and generational claims add complexity to domestic concerns facing the United States. These concerns go beyond aging, yet directly affect the lives of senior citizens. Economic disparity, disenfranchised youth, the changing work force, ethnic diversity, and the need to rebuild America will be improved or worsened by our response to diversity, longevity, and generational claims. Diversity might, for example, cause us to recognize the basic needs of all, or might simply create more interest-group competition for scarce public resources. Longevity might give us a productive older population or create a drag on the national economy. Generational claims can lead to alliances or conflict between age cohorts.

In the New Aging, the United States faces domestic problems unattended to during the 1980s and early 1990s. At the same time, it must respond to the needs of an aging society. Social welfare policy will be high on the political agenda, because the needs of middle class and the poor, minorities, young, women, disabled, and the work force must be addressed if we want a stable and prosperous society. The challenge will be to address domestic concerns without creating conflict between generations or scapegoating the elderly for our own lack of political will in solving domestic problems.

The Common Good gives us one framework for avoiding generational problems while responding to domestic issues. This report argues that all Americans "at one time or another have to rely upon our system of social welfare protections," and, therefore, social policies should reflect a life-cycle approach (Ford Foundation 1989). Such an approach would acknowledge the interconnectedness of life, from infancy through old age. Viewing social policies from this angle allows us to respond to domestic needs as an integral part of the New Aging.

One pressing domestic issue is the widening gap between the rich and the poor. Throughout the 1980s and into the 1990s, the poorest segment became poorer, while the earning power of the more affluent increased. Growth of "the truly disadvantaged" sector, mired in intractable poverty, increased. Expansion of this so-called "underclass," including blacks, Hispanics, and whites, was exacerbated by the drug epidemic. The only good news to come out of the late 1980s and early 1990s is that the public—from the corporate sector to academics—recognized increasingly that a growing underclass damages America's economic and international competitiveness. Political resolution remains snagged, however, in ideological and philosophical differences.

In the New Aging, a resolution to this problem is crucial. It is widely agreed that a poor young person is likely to become a poor old person. A functionally illiterate child or teenager lacking basic health care will invariably be highly dependent on public benefits and assistance through old age. The plight of the poor also affects the security of the elderly. Crime, drugs, and violence in urban areas as well as small towns force older people who can afford it to move to isolated retirement communities or walled residential compounds. The poor elderly left behind become vulnerable prey. History might show that the social and economic problems of the underclass in the latter part of the twentieth century (and the attendant drug crisis) were the Achilles' heel of the United States.

Relying on law and order alone to handle crime and social unrest must give way in the 1990s to a dualistic approach: a determined campaign against crime and drugs with a social welfare component. Partly as a result of the 1980s war on drugs, the U.S. prison population grew from 329,821 to 703,687 in just one decade. Of every 100,000 Americans, a record 271 were in prison (Pogatchnik 1990). A disproportionate number of these were members of the minority groups that will be our labor force in the next century: blacks and Hispanics. When released, what chance will prisoners have for good jobs, given their criminal records? If they are to be the workers among an older population, they must be educated and trained while in prison, and we must consider "amnesty." Perhaps we should, as the Japanese do, require that criminals be able to read and write as a condition of release. Amnesty (clearing a criminal record) could be provided to nonviolent criminals who perform volunteer service and improve their education.

As a domestic priority and a matter of national security, we must reinvest in America's young, particularly its minority youth. With one in five children living in poverty, we have the recipe for national disaster. Education is often suggested as a solution. It remains the single best vehicle for combating illiteracy, high drop-out rates, and the inability to compete in the work force. We must increase educational standards, providing teachers with greater prestige and salaries; invest more in public schools, establishing special-education programs for immigrants and the disadvantaged; and encourage local control and involvement. The elderly will play a special role. With their electoral clout, they can defeat or pass any school bond measure. Their volunteerism can assist young people requiring tutors or teachers with special skills. Senior-citizen groups must ally themselves with education advocates and public-school constituents in a political arena where generational politics can be a win-win situation for both young and old.

Reinvesting in America's youth includes expanding health care, particularly prenatal, maternal, and pediatric. Expanding Headstart and day-care facilities for working mothers provides job opportunities and minimizes the latch-key problem. In this regard, we must make it possible for mothers to stay at home with their children if they choose. Like other industrialized nations, we must adopt a family-allowance policy (i.e., tax credit, income supplement, expansion of the personal tax exemption) so mothers and fathers can elect to stay home and raise their children. Jonathan Rauch aptly noted, "When we grow old, we do not depend directly on our own children. Instead, we depend on other people's children" (Rauch 1989, 56). In an aging nation, with more elderly and fewer youth, kids are capital. We can't afford to have our population ravaged by drug addition of infants to teenagers, single heads of households unable to care for their young, and gang violence.

A changing work force bolsters the life-cycle approach to social welfare. An older population is, simply, highly dependent on the capabilities and productivity of the work force. If we have too few workers, or if a large segment of labor is unqualified to work in the new industries of the next century, we will be unable to provide benefits to the elderly, much less other groups. The work force in the New Aging will differ significantly in composition. Between 1985 and 2000, for example, the primary growth of the U.S. labor force will be among minorities (20 percent), immigrants (22 percent), and white females (42 percent). Only 16 percent of this growth will consist of white males (Population Reference Bureau 1989).

Therefore, in the New Aging, we must also invest in the education and training of labor. The private sector's primary political role must be to continue the push for educational reform and publicly and privately funded job training and retraining programs. The changing work force has a positive side—it serves as an incentive for employers to hire workers previously unskilled or difficult to reach, such as inner-city youth and the handicapped, and to better utilize minorities, women, and senior citizens. The risk, however, is that employers might opt to export their plants and jobs to countries offering a compliant and low-wage labor force or rely mainly on experienced white retirees. If we are to avoid the tensions a more diverse labor force can create, government and the private sector must join to prevent these easy outs.

America's changing ethnic profile might exacerbate the effects of the three central forces of the New Aging. The United States has always been a nation of immigrants. Throughout history we have painfully incorporated them into mainstream society. Eastern Europeans, Irish, Italians, Germans, Scandinavians, and other European, Balkan, Slavic, and Mediterranean groups met discrimination, then acceptance. By the twentieth century, Asian and Pacific Islanders and Hispanics were the new immigrants. The unique difference is that, early in the next century, they, along with blacks and Native Americans, will comprise the new majority. By

2056, whites are expected to become a minority group ("Beyond the Melting Pot" 1990).

In the New Aging, multiculturalism, alongside aging and domestic concerns, will challenge our social and political systems. If we fear ethnic diversity and allow racism and nativism to increase, political and social conflicts will arise between the new majority and a diminishing white population. If we continue to allow immigrants to become part of American society (with equal educational, political, and civil rights), the United States will benefit from this largely young, energetic, and loyal population.

Our aging society will need more immigrants to keep the median age low and bolster the work force. We must welcome, not fear them. Much of the greatness of the United States can be attributed to the talents and energy of its immigrants: Scandinavians promoting American agriculture; Japanese creating the citrus industry; Jews lending technological expertise; Mexicans and Puerto Ricans serving in the U.S. armed forces; blacks infusing American culture; Asians contributing to the U.S. economy. In the expected takeover of Hong Kong by China the United States might do well to allow all three-and-a-half million of its industrious citizens to immigrate.

In an aging and multicultural society, however, acculturation must be the cornerstone of social policy. Acculturation includes functioning as a member of U.S. society, speaking English, participating in the political process, and integrating oneself into social and civic life. It differs from assimilation, which implies surrendering one's ethnic identity and pride. Maintaining one's native language and culture are fine as long as one acculturates. Minority and immigrant advocacy groups must promote acculturation as the immigrant's primary goal. Such groups must also recognize our porous national borders. Until we can regulate and control the flow of undocumented immigrants, we will achieve neither social stability, nor the breathing space necessary to respond to demographic and social pressures, and it will be more difficult to acculturate recently arrived immigrants. We must take control of our northern and southern borders or we will see virulent forms of domestic nationalism.

A final issue concerns America's deteriorating physical infrastructure. Rebuilding roads, bridges, highways, as well as rail, bus, and sewer systems is an important element of the New Aging. If workers and retirees are to enjoy mobility, safety, and comfort, we must invest vast sums of public and private funds into rebuilding America. Building standards must be upgraded to include earthquake safety and accessibility to the physically handicapped. Rebuilding America will provide employment opportunities, reduce congestion and pollution, improve America's competitiveness, and prepare the United States for the large numbers likely to be physically disabled in later years.

Responding to these domestic concerns invariably involves budget deficits and fiscal pressures. The nation pleads poverty, and the public fears tax increases. As Haas says, we have fostered a "myth of American bankruptcy," and our political leaders blame budget deficits when they avoid resolving unarguable needs and problems (1990). We have the financial resources and can afford to pay more, but we lack the leadership, public consensus, and political courage to respond. In the past, when presented with a clear and compelling need, whether it was reconstruction after the Civil War, responding to the Depression and World War II, or educating the baby boomers, the public willingly provided the necessary public funds. Ironically, conservative and liberal parties today agree that major problems face the United States—the escalating number of poor children, deteriorating public education and health care, and family strife. We have only to agree upon who will pay to resolve them and how.

THE CONSEQUENCES OF INACTION

How we handle domestic issues will directly affect aging in the early twenty-first century. We can either recreate a strong, prosperous, livable America or accept a decline in quality of life. Diversity, longevity, and generational tensions can create problems or opportunities.

The consequences of inaction, however, will severely affect both the old and young. David Hayes-Bautista et al. (1988) using California as a worst-case scenario, provide a glimpse into how age, economic disparity, race, immigration, and a lack of investment in the physical and social infrastructure can create conflict in the New Aging:

By the late 1990s, California has become an age-race stratified society comprised of a largely white retiree population and a young Hispanic population. White retirees (including the aging baby boomers) use their political clout to expand services to the elderly by increasing payroll and state income taxes, while refusing to pay for other domestic needs. They leave the urban areas, now populated by Hispanics, minorities, and the poor, and settle in "safe" suburbs or rural areas— retirement havens—straining the state's limited transportation and water resources. The deteriorating public education system and physical infrastructure, as well as repressive laws designed to limit "non-American" languages and cultures, create resentment among Hispanics. A growing Third World economy (low wages, unskilled workers) undermines California's economic preeminence. By the year 2000, bitter Hispanic and poor populations launch a state ballot initiative to reduce senior-citizen public pensions and programs, generating racial and generational conflict which, in turn, creates civic discord.

Admittedly, this scenario is overly dramatic and not necessarily a portent of things to come. However, elements of it can already be seen in demographic changes facing California and the United States, the gap between the rich and poor (largely predicated on race and ethnicity), and the inattention being given the social and physical problems of the 1980s. Nevertheless, Hayes-Bautista et al. (1989) also present us with a best-case scenario:

By the late 1990s, aging baby boomers and young Hispanics form a political alliance. Recognizing that both groups require expanded health and educational programs and depend on the physical infrastructure, and that retirees need the talent and productivity of young Hispanics, they increase taxes and expand programs. Aging baby boomers, drawing on their youthful idealism, support bilingual education and promotion of a Latino intellectual tradition, encouraging a positive self-image among young Hispanics. A working alliance leads to an intergenerational and interethnic compact by which each group supports the political and social interests of the other. California, as part of the new common market along with Canada and Mexico, becomes an excellent place to invest. The state prospers. Its stable society becomes a model of multi-generational, multi-racial achievement.

A DECADE OF PREPARATION

Much remains to be done. We must respond to aging and other domestic concerns before the political demands of older baby boomers further complicate matters. We cannot assume baby boomers will be entirely unselfish and idealistic, as Chapter 5 indicates. The 1990s can be both a decade of opportunity and renewal, and a time to address social needs and revitalize America's leadership.

Our decisions in the 1990s will affect the elderly both of tomorrow and today. Those now in their 60s and 70s, including the financially secure, shielded from the nation's domestic problems, will see an increase in life expectancy. Someone 60 years of age in 1990 can reasonably expect to live to see 80 in the year 2010, and even reach 90 in the year 2020.

Figure 7.1 shows the direct stake today's elderly have in the decisions made or avoided during the next decade by illustrating worst- and best-case scenarios through the year 2020. It shows how the various generations discussed in this book will continue to be affected by the political and social events of the next 30 to 40 years. By 2020, for example, today's elders will require extensive health and long-term care, and will be unable to live in areas with poor public transportation or high crime rates. They will be dependent on an elaborate and expensive social welfare system. Their children and grandchildren will depend on a strong economy to lessen the financial burden of caring for their elders. If young minority members are unable or unwilling to be productive and pay higher taxes, they might use their enhanced political power (since they will be the majority population) to countermand age benefits. To prevent this, we must use the next decade to address domestic concerns. Foresight, compassion, even self-interest can be powerful motivators in preparing for the New Aging.

Figure 7.1. People and Events, 1990–2040

	1990	2000	2010	2020	2030	2040
Major Legislation Related to Aging: Worse-case vs. Best-case Scenarios		Current age and benefit structure retained / or / Age requirements raised and dichotomy of service eligibility established	Intolerable cost for old-age programs emerges / or / National health and long-term care system negate need for a dichotomy of service eligibility		Baby Busters and Baby Boomlet lose Social Security and old-age Benefits / or / Baby Busters and Baby Boomlet enjoy expanded services and quality of life in their old age	
Major Events: Worse-case vs. Best-case Scenarios		Insufficient revenues continue neglect of needs and infrastructure / or / Expanded revenues increase investment and resolution of neglected problems	Social turmoil: Baby Boomers force high taxes on young minority work force and expand senior benefits / or / Universal health and long-term care for all age groups is established; educational reform upgrades skills of work force		Minorities and immigrants become majority and dominate politics to force and countermand age benefits / or / A Multicultural and multigenerational society is recreated	
Age of:						
Baby Boomlet	10	20	30	40	50	60
Baby Busters	20	30	40	50	60	70
Baby Boomers	40	50	60	70	80	90
Silent Generation	60	70	80	90	100	110
Swing Generation	70	80	90	100	110	120

Illustration prepared by Brian Louis Lipshy.

In the 1990s, middle-aged baby boomers will be at the peak of productivity. They can use their higher earning power to increase the Social Security surplus (if we don't return to pay-as-you-go) or their personal savings. Unemployment rates should be relatively low, and increased productivity might reduce the federal deficit. The relative increase of older people will decline due to the low birthrate of the 1930s and early 1940s. The baby buster generation—those relatively few born during the 1970s—will reduce expenditures on public education.

In many respects, we are in the midst of a slow-motion crisis. If we don't act soon though, the economic and social problems of the 1980s will explode by the year 2000. As a nation, we have traditionally done our best work during moments of immediate crisis. The Civil War ended slavery and united a nation; good government and progressive legislation remedied the exploitative practices of the oligarchies of the latter nineteenth century; two world wars created a new world order; dissent during the 1960s brought civil rights and ended an unpopular war. Today, we are in a good position to act because we know what awaits us. Acting on that knowledge, however, is difficult.

Making health and long-term care a basic right for all U.S. citizens alongside public education, services for veterans, and a strong national defense, is a necessary ideal and practical goal. A national health-care system, in whatever guise, will alleviate potential conflict among diverse groups for limited health-care resources. With the support of the business community, labor, senior citizens, and other constituencies, we must use the 1990s to make access to universal health care a national right.

Establishing a national longevity campaign is crucial as well. Health-care promotion (antismoking and physical fitness campaigns), funded by public and private sources, are already in vogue. A national longevity campaign would include these efforts and would target the young in educating about longevity. Gerontology courses in primary and secondary schools will not only reduce ageism but prepare our children for lives that could easily stretch to 100 years.

Such a campaign should include greater commitment to research: biomedical, social, and behavioral. Basic and applied research is indispensable in improving quality of life among an aging population and reducing expenditures over the long term. In the New Aging, where age 70 will be required for receipt of entitlement and people will live longer, research can reduce the risks of debilitating illnesses. Alzheimer's and senile dementia, arthritis, and incontinence are the leading causes for nursing-home use. Finding solutions to these chronic problems will go far in reducing dependency in old age.

Generational claims will be inevitable in the New Aging. We must invest in the needs of younger groups and the disadvantaged, and promote intergenerational policies to minimize tensions. It is ironic that support for public expenditures benefiting the baby boomers' youth—money spent on education, for example—far exceeded that offered today's more ethnically and racially diverse youth population. Spending money on our young is nonideological and nonpartisan. It is good business, and good public policy to help people throughout their life cycle in order to reduce resentment toward older people who might have benefited as youngsters from programs no longer available.

CAN OUR POLITICAL SYSTEM RESPOND?

Will our political system be capable, during the next decade and beyond, of responding to the challenges of a more diverse and older America? American politics are frequently criticized for the influence of money on elected officials, the power of incumbency, the selfishness of narrow-interest groups and the politicians beholden to them, the fragmented nature of Congress, and the reliance of presidential administrations on polling data to dictate their actions. The American system of government, however, is no better or worse today than it was during the last century or earlier. Similar criticisms were voiced during the late 1920s and 1950s when government was perceived as unresponsive to social and economic change.

Nevertheless, the system could use some incremental reforms. Adopting multiyear budgets, providing the president with a line-item veto (as many governors enjoy), providing higher salaries to elected officials while restricting honorariums and speaking fees, enacting term limits, and limiting lobbying among appointed and elected officials would make the political process more honest and efficient.

The key component, however, is leadership. Responding to problems and opportunities in the United States during the twenty-first century will require enlightened leaders. What constitutes effective leadership during hard times is difficult to ascertain. Thomas Jefferson, Abraham Lincoln, Franklin Roosevelt, Dwight Eisenhower, and Martin Luther King, Jr., were dissimilar though able leaders with vision and commitment. Will the 1990s produce leaders of like caliber to safely guide us into the future?

The advent of the baby-boom generation as a political force in the 1990s makes this a pressing issue. The period of the Modern Aging enjoyed sterling leadership from individuals like Wilbur Cohen and Robert Ball, architects of Medicare and Medicaid, Arthur Flemming, champion of national health care, Maggie Kuhn, advocate for young and old, and many others. These individuals were committed to public service and leadership and to resolving societal problems, not meeting the needs of specific interest groups. How will we fashion such leadership throughout the next several decades, especially among a generation unusually individualistic and disdainful of impersonal bureaucracies, whether they be big government, business, or labor?

Promoting such leadership can be accomplished in various ways. The White House Fellowship program, developed by Lyndon Johnson, is one. Establishing a council of elders to work with budding new leaders and to share ideas is another. The fact is, among today's younger groups, providing public and political leadership is viewed as a risky, messy, unsavory affair. That view cynically reflects the adage: The beauty of the American political system is that we get what we deserve. If we scorn politicians we will get unsavory elected officials. If we reward and respect political leadership, we will get the best and brightest, as we did from the 1930s to the 1970s.

What must this leadership encompass? John Gardner (1988a; 1988b) cautions us not to confuse it with status, power, or authority. Leadership defines and articulates ideas. It promotes a view of life that serves the greatest number. Leadership is vision articulated pragmatically, calling for involvement, community participation, collective values, and, where necessary, public sacrifice. Leadership avoids nihilism and narcissism and offers optimism alongside tough-minded realism. Leadership in the 1990s must promote an affordable domestic agenda that is, at the same time, expansive enough to alleviate social problems. It must decry predictions of failure and decline, while educating the public about the consequences of passivity. It must excite the public imagination to renew national greatness by meeting social challenges and resolving social problems. In this context, leaders must eschew opinion polls catering to the public's transitory whims or pitting one group against another.

Leadership in the 1990s must involve all sectors of society. Traditionally, political and policy elites have come from East Coast universities, businesses, and law firms. They share a similar profile—white, male, highly educated. The maintenance of our political system in the face of dramatic demographic and economic changes depends on the inclusion of members from diverse populations—minorities, immigrants, the poor, women, the disabled, those from rural areas—as fully active participants and leaders. Their continued exclusion through discrimination, lack of education, or gerrymandering only weakens the ability of the political system to respond.

Our political system is capable of handling the challenges of the 1990s and responding to the exigencies of the New Aging. People, not processes, shape political actions. U.S. history demonstrates that Americans want compassionate and effective government. They will not long tolerate an economically and socially divided country in which many lead hopeless lives. In time, the people will force government to act. By the latter 1990s, we can expect that our own (successful) version of *perestroika*—a reor-

dering of national priorities—and leadership will be the key to retaining
the public's faith that its political system can and will respond.

THE FUTURE OF AN AGING AMERICA

This book has sought to describe the future of America by examining
the effects that diversity, longevity, and generational claims will have on
an aging society. Its central premise is that maintaining the existing structure of benefits and services for the elderly will not adequately serve a
rapidly changing nation. In the New Aging, where we will view old age
and the elderly much differently, we must keep the vision of the Modern
Aging period while restructuring its programs, benefits, and eligibility
criteria. If we fail to do so, we can expect not only intolerable public and
private expenditures, but competition and conflict among diverse groups
for limited funds and services.

During the New Aging, we must also concern ourselves with our ability
to compete with other nations and to maintain a prosperous and stable
society. The United States has been the world's laboratory for handling
diversity and change, and, by and large, it has done so successfully. Our
economic and military successes have made the twentieth century the
"American Century." The decline of the United States as a world power
is of continuing concern, however. A focus on the nation's economic and
social ills and the seeming inability of our political system to resolve them
has led some to believe we are destined to become a second-rate power
early in the next century.

Such talk is misplaced and counterproductive. It negatively affects aging
in the twenty-first century. If we decline as a nation and are unable to
maintain a strong economic and social system relative to others, the effects
of aging, ethnic diversity, and change will be divisive. Senior boomers
will face an insecure retirement. We must adopt a tough-minded yet op-
timistic realism about our future or create self-fulfilling prophecies.

Joel Kotkin and Yoriko Kishimoto, in their classic book, *The Third
Century* (1988), predict that the United States will retain its status as a
world power. They say that, unlike other nations, the United States has
an enviable *sokojikara*, or self-renewing power, which includes a tradition
of unparalleled entrepreneurship, innovation, creativity, risk-taking, and
productivity. Our natural resources are assets unmatched by Japan, Germany, or the Soviet Union. Further, these nations have no tradition of
immigration, and "immigrants may help to save the United States from
the demographic decline now threatening Japan and Europe" (Kotkin and
Kishimoto 1988). These strengths are reinforced by our "empire of the
mind," an openness to ideas and peoples that has made American culture
a phenomenon worldwide.

We must include aging and adaptability among what Kotkin and Kishimoto view as our latent strengths. The elderly are a vast natural resource whose talent, activism, and energy can contribute mightily to the nation's economy, as well as its spiritual and social fiber. Adaptability is our proven capacity to change and embrace new ideas, peoples, and technology.

If in the 1990s we apply our inherent strengths to resolving domestic concerns, the twenty-first century can be the "Second American Century" (Buchanan 1990). The New Aging is about the politics and change facing America and how all generations can contribute to a new society. The future that lies ahead may appear difficult and challenging, but it promises to be exciting and rewarding if we act boldly and with foresight.

NOTE

1. Analysis of social-welfare expenditures consistently shows that immigrants contribute more to the tax and economic base of the country than they use in social and health-care services. Immigrants to the United States tend to be young, in good health, and hard-working. To the extent they use human services, they draw heavily on prenatal and maternal health programs and emergency rooms. Otherwise, their use of social services is lower than that of the general population.

BIBLIOGRAPHY

American Society on Aging. "Scholars Say Third World Unprepared for Responsibilities of Age Boom." *Aging Connection* (Feb/March, 1989): 5.

"Beyond the Melting Pot." *Time*, April 9, 1990, 28–35.

Buchanan, Patrick. "Manifest Destiny, Northern Version." *The Los Angeles Times*, April 15, 1990.

Ford Foundation. *The Common Good: Social Welfare and the American Future*. Detroit, Mich.: Ford Foundation, May 1989.

Gardner, John. *The Changing Nature of Leadership*. Washington, D.C.: Independent Sector, July 1988a.

———. "The Task of Motivating." Leadership Papers no. 9. Washington, D.C.: Independent Sector, February 1988b.

Haas, Lawrence. "Pleading Poverty." *National Journal*, September 15, 1990, pp. 2192–96.

Hayes-Bautista, David, Werner Schink, and Joge Chapa. *The Burden of Support: Young Latinos in an Aging Society*. Stanford, Calif. Stanford University Press, 1988.

Kotkin, Joel, and Yoriko Kishimoto. "If Our Economy Is So Weak, Why Is Everyone Investing in It?" *Washington Post National Weekly Edition*, Jan. 25–31, 1988, 23.

———. *The Third Century: America's Resurgence in the Asian Era*. New York: Crown Publishers Inc., 1988.

Pogatchnik, Shawn. "California Leads U.S. in Inmate Increase." *Los Angeles Times*, May 21, 1990, A3.

Population Reference Bureau. "America in the 21st Century: A Demographic

Overview." Washington, D.C.: Population Reference Bureau and the Population Resource Center, May 1989.

Rauch, Jonathan. "Growing Old." *National Journal* (December 31, 1988): 3234–43.

Schulz, J., A. Borowski, and W. H. Crown. *Economics of Population Aging: The "Graying of Australia, Japan, and the United States."* New York: Auburn House, 1991.

BIBLIOGRAPHY

Aaron, Henry, ed. *Social Security and the Budget*. Washington, D.C.: The National Academy of Social Insurance, University Press of America, 1990.

Aaron, Henry. "When Is a Burden Not a Burden? The Elderly in America." *The Brookings Review* (Summer, 1986): 17–24.

Aaron, Henry, Barry Bosworth, and Gary Burtless. *Can America Afford to Grow Old?* Washington, D.C.: The Brookings Institution, 1989.

AARP. "A Portrait of Older Minorities" Washington, D.C.: American Association of Retired Persons, 1986.

———. "A Profile of Older Americans: 1987." Washington, D.C.: American Association of Retired Persons, 1987.

———. "A Profile of Older Americans: 1990." Washington, D.C.: American Association of Retired Persons, 1990.

Achenbaum, Andrew. *Old Age in the New Land: The American Experience since 1790*. Baltimore: The Johns Hopkins University Press, 1978.

———. *Shades of Gray: Old Age, American Values, and Federal Policies since 1920*. Boston: Little, Brown and Company, 1983.

"After the Boom." *Los Angeles Times*, April 26, 1990.

American Society on Aging. "Scholars Say Third World Unprepared for Responsibilities of Age Boom." *Aging Connection* (Feb./March 1989): 5.

"America's Best Graduate and Professional Schools." *U.S. News and World Report*, March 19, 1990, 65.

"America's Income Gap: The Closer You Look, The Worse It Gets." *Business Week*, April 17, 1989, 78.

ASAP. *Advocates Senior Alert Process* 7, no. 6 (March 1991).

"Baby Boomers to Continue Fast Pace of Start-Ups in the 90's." *The Wall Street Journal*. June 19, 1989.

Bailey, Douglas. "The Reagan Era's Over, Isn't It Time We Got On with It?" *The Washington Post National Weekly Edition*, April 16–22, 1990, 24.

Barnes, James. "Age-Old Strife." *National Journal* 4 (Jan. 26, 1991): 216–19.

Bengston, Vern. "Generations and Aging: Continuities, Conflicts, and Reciprocities." Presidential Address to the 43rd Annual Meeting of the Gerontological Society of America, Nov. 17, 1990, Boston, Mass.

Bengston, Vern, Neal Cutler, David Mangen, and Victor Marshall. "Generations, Cohorts, and Relations between Age Groups." In *Handbook of Aging and the Social Sciences*, edited by Robert Binstock and Ethel Shanas. New York: Van Nostrand Reinhold Company, 1985: 304–38.

"Beyond the Melting Pot." *Time*, April 9, 1990, 28–35.

Binstock, Robert. "The Politics and Economics of Aging and Diversity." In *Diversity in Aging*, edited by S. Bass, E. Kutza, and F. Torres-Gil. Glenview, Ill.: Scott, Foresman & Company, 1990.

Binstock, Robert. "The Aged as a Scapegoat." *The Gerontologist* 23, 2 (1983): 136–43.

Blumenthal, David, Mark Schlesinger and Pamela Brown Drumheller, eds. *Renewing the Promise: Medicare and Its Reform*. New York: Oxford University Press, 1988.

Buchanan, Patrick. "Manifest Destiny, Northern Version." *Los Angeles Times*, April 15, 1990.

Butler, Katy. "The Great Boomer Bust: Competition with Our Parents Is Over, We Lost, What Now?" *Mother Jones*, June 1989, 32–37.

Callahan, Daniel. *Setting Limits: Medical Goals in an Aging Society*. New York: Simon & Schuster, 1987.

"Can L.B.J.'s Great Society Ever Exist?" *Los Angeles Times*, July 14, 1989.

Carlson, Allan. "Depopulation Bomb: The Withering of the Western World." *Washington Post*, April 13, 1986.

Castelli, Jim. "Baby Boom, Bang, Bust: The Myth of Generational Politics." *American Politics*, December 1987, 32–35.

Chakravarty, Subrata, and Katherine Wesman. "Consuming Our Children?" *Forbes*, Nov. 14, 1988, 222–32.

"The Challenge of a Four-Generation Society in America." *Chicago Tribune*, June 15, 1988.

Chen, Yung-Ping. "Making Assets out of Tomorrow's Elderly." *The Gerontologist* 27, 4 (1987): 410–16.

Cole, Thomas. "The Specter of Old Age: History, Politics, and Culture in an Aging America." *Tikkun* 3, 5 (Sept./Oct. 1988): 14–95.

"The Coming Conflict as We Soak the Young to Enrich the Old." *The Washington Post*, Jan. 5, 1986.

Commonwealth Fund Commission. "Aging Alone: Profiles and Projections." A report of the Commonwealth Fund Commission of Elderly People Living Alone, Baltimore, Md. Prepared by Judith D. Kasper, 1988.

"Company-Financed Pensions Are Failing to Fulfill Promise." *New York Times*, May 29, 1990, A1.

Coughlin, Ellen. "Worsening Plight of the 'Underclass' Catches Attention of Researchers." *The Chronicle of Higher Education*, March 30, 1988: A4-A8.

"The Cost of Growing Old." *The Economist*, June 3, 1989.

Craeger, Ellen. "Baby Boomers Are Jealous of the Gold in Golden Years." *Detroit Free Press*, June 20, 1989.
Crystal, Stephen. *America's Old Age Crisis*. New York: Basic Books, Inc., 1982.
————. "Measuring Income and Inequality among the Elderly." *The Gerontologist* 26, 1 (1986): 56–59.
Day, Christine. *What Older Americans Think: Interest Groups and Aging Policy*. Princeton, N.J.: Princeton University Press, 1990.
Detlefs, Dale, and Robert Myers. *1989 Guide to Social Security*. Louisville, Ky.: William M. Mercer-Meidinger-Hansen, November 1988.
Durkheim, E. (1893). *The Division of Labor in Society*. New York: The Free Press, 1964.
Dychtwald, Ken. *Age Wave*. Los Angeles: Jeremy P. Tarcher, 1989.
"Early Retirement Policies Will Become a Thing of the Past." *Older Americans Report* (Jan. 26, 1990): 36.
EBRI News. "U.S. Pension Funds Attract Policymakers' Attention." Washington, D.C.: Employee Benefit Research Institute, May 9, 1990.
Eribes, R. A., and Rawls, M. B. "The Underutilization of Nursing Home Facilities by Mexican American Elderly in the Southwest." *The Gerontologist* 18, 1 (1978): 371.
Estes, Carroll, Robert J. Newcomer and Associates. *Fiscal Austerity and Aging*. Beverly Hills, Calif.: Sage Publications, 1983.
Fairlie, Henry. "Talkin' bout My Generation." *The New Republic*, March 28, 1988, 19–22.
Ficke, Susan, ed. "An Orientation to the Older Americans Act." Washington, D.C.: National Association of State Units on Aging, July 1985.
Field, Mervin. "Falling Turnout—A Nonvoting Majority." *Public Affairs Report* (March 1990): 8–9.
"For Most Employers, Seeing Is Ignoring." *Washington Post National Weekly Edition*, April 9–15, 1990, 22.
Ford Foundation. *The Common Good: Social Welfare and the American Future*. Detroit, Mich.: Ford Foundation, May 1989.
Garcia, Kenneth. "Law May Force Loss of Low-Income Apartments." *Los Angeles Times*, June 4, 1991.
Gardner, John. *The Changing Nature of Leadership*. Washington, D.C.: Independent Sector, July 1988a.
————. "The Task of Motivating." Leadership Papers, no. 9. Washington, D.C.: Independent Sector, February 1988b.
Gelfand, Donald. *The Aging Network*. 3d ed. New York: Springer Publishing Company, 1988.
Generations Together Exchange. A Newsletter Exchanging Information on Intergenerational Programs. Issue 6, Winter 1991.
Gerber, Jerry, Janet Wolff, Walter Klores, and Bene Brown. *Lifetrends*. New York: Macmillan Publishing Company, 1989.
Gerth, Jeff. "Panel Is Told of Lax Monitoring of Pension Plans." *The New York Times*, August 3, 1989.
Gibson, Rose. "Defining Retirement for Black Americans." In *Ethnic Dimensions of Aging*, edited by Donald Gelfand and Charles Barresi. New York: Springer Publishing Company, 1987, pp. 224–38.

Gould, Stephanie, and John Palmer. "Outcomes, Interpretations, and Policy Im-
    plications." In *The Vulnerable* edited by John Palmer, Timothy Smeeding,
    and Barbara Boyle Torrey. Washington, D.C.: The Urban Institute Press,
    1988, pp. 413–42.
Gray, Robert, and Joan Szabo. "Social Security: Hard Choices Ahead." *Nation's
    Business,* April 1990, 18–25.
"Grays on the Go." *Time,* February 22, 1988.
Haas, Lawrence. "Pleading Poverty." *National Journal,* September 15, 1990,
    pp. 2192–96.
Harrington, Michael. "Inequality Haunts America as Taxes Favor the Rich, Pen-
    alize the Middle Class." *Los Angeles Times,* Jan. 24, 1988.
Hayes-Bautista, David. "Hispanics in an Age-Stratified Society." In *Hispanics
    in an Aging Society,* edited by Fernando Torres-Gil. New York: Carnegie
    Corporation, 1986, 21–28.
Hayes-Bautista, David, Werner Schink, and Joge Chapa. *The Burden of Support:
    Young Latinos in an Aging Society.* Stanford, Calif.: Stanford University
    Press, 1988.
Hayflick, Leonard. "Origins of Longevity." In *Modern Biological Theories of
    Aging,* edited by Huber R. Warner, Richard L. Sprott, Robert N. Butler,
    and Edward L. Schneider. New York: Raven Press, 1987.
Heclo, Hugh. "Generational Politics." In *The Vulnerable,* edited by John Palmer,
    Timothy Smeeding, and Barbara Boyle Torrey. Washington, D.C.: The
    Urban Institute Press, 1988, pp. 381–412.
"Here's the Latest Criticism of Social Security: It Works." *The Washington Post,*
    Jan. 20, 1986.
Herz, Diane. Bureau of Labor Statistics. "Employment Characteristics of Older
    Women, 1987." *Monthly Labor Review* (September 1988): 3.
Hewitt, Paul, and Neil Howe. "Generational Equity and the Future of Genera-
    tional Politics." *Generations* 12, 3 (Spring 1988): 10–13.
Hudson, Robert, and John Strate. "Aging and Political Systems." In *Handbook
    of Aging and the Social Sciences,* 2d ed., edited by Robert Binstock and
    Ethel Shanas. New York: Van Nostrand Reinhold Company, 1985, pp. 554–
    88.
Hughes, William. "Private Pension Coverage Declining." *Aging Today* (February/
    March 1991): 9.
"Issues for Reauthorizing the OAA." *Older Americans Report* (Feb. 16, 1990):
    62.
Janeway, Elizabeth. "Who Says Old?" *World Monitor* (June 1989): 42–47.
Jones, Landon. *Great Expectations: America and the Baby Boom Generation.*
    New York: Coward, McCann & Geoghegan, 1980.
Katzper, Meyer. *Modelling of Long-Term Care.* Washington, D.C.: U.S. De-
    partment of Health and Human Services, 1981.
Kennedy, Paul. *The Rise and Fall of the Great Powers.* New York: Random
    House, 1987.
Knight, Jerry. "Protesting All the Way to the Bank." *The Washington Post,*
    National Weekly Edition, March 25–31, 1991.
Koitz, David. "Social Security: Its Impact on the Deficit." *CRS Review* 9, 5
    (May, 1988): 24–26.

Kosterlitz, Julie. "Gray Power." *National Journal* (July 29, 1989): 1957.
———. "Measuring Misery." *National Journal* (August 4, 1990): 1892–96.
———. "Who Will Pay?" *National Journal* (March 8, 1986): 570–74.
———. "Young vs. Old." *National Journal* (December 10, 1988): 3160.
Kotkin, Joel, and Yoriko Kishimoto. "If Our Economy Is So Weak, Why Is Everyone Investing in It?" *Washington Post* National Weekly Edition, Jan. 25–31, 1988, 23.
———. *The Third Century: America's Resurgence in the Asian Era.* New York: Crown Publishers, 1988.
Kutza, Elizabeth. "Responding to Diversity: Is American Society Capable?" In *Diversity in Aging,* edited by S. Bass, E. Kutza, and F. Torres-Gil. Glenview, Ill.: Scott, Foresman and Company, 1990, pp. 101–28.
Lammers, William, and David Klingman. *State Policies and the Aging.* Lexington, Mass.: Lexington Books, 1984.
Leavitt, Thomas, and James Schulz. "Time to Reform the SSI Asset Test?" Washington, D.C.: Public Policy Institute, American Association of Retired Persons, June 1988.
Lee, Philip, and A. E. Benjamin. "Intergovernmental Relations: Historical and Contemporary Perspectives." In *Fiscal Austerity and Aging: Shifting Government Responsibility for the Elderly,* edited by Carroll Estes, Robert Newcomer, and Associates. Beverly Hills, Calif.: Sage Publications, 1983, pp. 59–81.
"Let Workers Own Their Retirement Funds." *The Wall Street Journal,* Feb. 1, 1990.
Levy, Frank. *Dollars and Dreams: The Changing American Income Distribution.* New York: Russell Sage Foundation, 1987.
Light, Paul. *Baby Boomers.* New York: W.W. Norton & Company, 1988.
Longman, Phillip. "Age Wars." *The Futurist,* January-February 1986, 8–10.
———. *Born to Pay: The New Politics of Aging in America.* Boston: Houghton Mifflin Company, 1987.
———. "Justice between Generations." *The Atlantic Monthly,* June 1985, 73–81.
———. "Taking America to the Cleaners." *The Washington Monthly,* Nov. 1982, 24–30.
Lowy, Louis. *Social Policies and Programs on Aging.* Lexington, Mass.: D.C. Heath and Company, 1980.
Macdonald, Christine, Richard Easterline, and Diane Macunovich. "Retirement Prospects of the Baby Boom Generation." An unpublished paper, Jan. 1990.
McKenzie, Richard. "The Retreat of the Elderly Welfare State." *Wall Street Journal,* March 12, 1991.
"Many Americans Are Losing Economic Ground." *National Journal* (December 10, 1988): 3156.
Margolis, Richard. *Risking Old Age in America.* Boulder, Colo.: Westview Press, 1990.
Marshall, Victor. "Tendencies in Generational Research: From the Generation to the Cohort and Back to the Generation." In *Intergenerational Rela-*

tionships, edited by Vjenka Garms-Homolova, Erika Hoerning, and Doris Schaeffer. Lewiston, N.Y.: C. J. Hogrefe, 1984, pp. 207–18.

Martz, Larry, and Rich Thomas. "Fixing Social Security." *Newsweek*, May 7, 1990, 54–58.

Minkler, Meredith. "Generational Equity and the New Victim Blaming: An Emerging Public Policy Issue." *International Journal of Health Services* 16, 4 (1986): 539–51.

Moody, Harry R. *The Abundance of Life: Human Development Policies for an Aging Society*. New York: Columbia University Press, 1988.

——. "The Politics of Entitlement and the Politics of Productivity." In *Diversity in Aging*, edited by S. Bass, E. Kutza, and F. Torres-Gil. Glenview, Ill. Scott, Foresman & Company, 1990.

Morrison, Malcolm. "Work and Retirement in an Older Society." In *Our Aging Society*, edited by Alan Pifer and Lydia Bronte. New York: W.W. Norton & Company, 1986, pp. 341–66.

"Moynihan Urges Social Security Tax Cut, Return to Pay-as-You-Go Benefits System," *The Los Angeles Times*, Dec. 20, 1989.

"NAAA Urges Co-Location of AAA's with Social Security Field Offices." *Older Americans Report* (Oct. 27, 1989): 414.

National Council of La Raza. *The Hispanic Elderly: A Demographic Profile*. Washington, D.C.: National Council of La Raza, October 1987.

"Nation's Elderly Are Mobilized for the Election Year." *The Philadelphia Inquirer*, 1988.

Nelson, Gary. "Social Class and Public Policy for the Elderly." In *Age or Need?: Public Policies for Older People*, edited by Bernice Neugarten. Beverly Hills, Calif.: Sage Publications, 1982, pp. 101–30.

Neugarten, Bernice. "Policy for the 1980's: Age or Need Entitlement?" In *Aging: Agenda for the Eighties*, National Journal Issues Book. Washington, D.C.: The Government Research Corporation, 1979, pp. 48–52.

O'Hare, William, Taynia Mann, Kathryn Porter, and Robert Greenstein. "Real Life Poverty in America." A report of the Center on Budget and Policy Priorities and the Families USA Foundation, Washington, D.C., July 1990.

"Older, Slower-Growing America Predicted." *The Washington Post*, Feb. 1, 1989.

Older Womens League. "The Picture of Health for Midlife and Older Women in America." Washington, D.C.: Older Womens League, 1987.

——. "The Road to Poverty: A Report on the Economic Status of Midlife and Older Women in America." Washington, D.C.: Older Womens League, 1988.

——. "Selected Data on Persons Age 65 and Over." Washington, D.C.: Older Womens League, 1988.

Orloff, Ann Shola, and Theda Skocpol. "Why Not Equal Protection? Explaining the Politics of Public Social Spending in Britain, 1900–1911, and the United States, 1800s–1920." *American Sociological Review* 49 (1984): 726–50.

Palmer, John, and Stephanie Gould. "Economic Consequences of Population Aging." In *Our Aging Society*, edited by Alan Pifer and Lydia Bronte. New York: W.W. Norton & Company, 1986, pp. 367–90.

Palmer, John, Timothy Smeeding, and Barbara Boyle Torrey, eds. *The Vulnerable*. Washington, D.C.: The Urban Institute Press, 1988.

Peterson, Peter. "The Morning After." *The Atlantic Monthly*, October 1987, 43–69.

Pifer, Alan, and Lydia Bronte. *Our Aging Society*. New York: W.W. Norton & Company, 1986.

Pogatchnik, Shawn. "California Leads U.S. in Inmate Increase." *Los Angeles Times*, May 21, 1990, A3.

Population Reference Bureau. "America in the 21st Century: A Demographic Overview." Washington, D.C.: Population Reference Bureau and the Population Resource Center, May 1989.

———. "America in the 21st Century: Social and Economic Support Systems." Washington, D.C.: Population Reference Bureau and the Population Resource Center, December 1990.

———. "Death and Taxes: The Public Policy Impact of Living Longer." Washington, D.C.: Population Reference Bureau and the Population Resource Center, September 1984.

"The Power of the Pension Funds." *Business Week*, Nov. 6, 1989.

Pratt, Henry. "National Interest Groups among the Elderly: Consolidation and Constraint." In *Aging and Public Policy: The Politics of Growing Old in America*, edited by William P. Browne and Laura Katz Olson. Westport, Conn.: Greenwood Press, 1983, pp. 145–80.

Preston, Samuel. "Children and the Elderly in the United States." *Scientific American* 251, 6 (1984): 44–49.

"Profile of Tomorrow's New U.S." *U.S. News and World Report*, Nov. 24, 1986, 32.

R L Associates. "The American Public Views of Long-Term Care." Princeton, N.J.: R L Associates, October 1987.

Rapson, Richard, ed. *The Cult of Youth in Middle-Class America*. Lexington, Mass.: D.C. Heath and Company, 1971.

Rauch, Jonathan. "Growing Old." *National Journal* (December 31, 1988): 3234–43.

———. "Kids as Capital." *The Atlantic Monthly*, August 1989, 56–61.

Rich, Spencer. "Hearing Told U.S. Stymies the Helpless." *The Washington Post*, April 6, 1990, A18.

———. "Look Again: The Anti-Poverty Programs Do Work." *The Washington Post* National Weekly Edition, May 21, 1984, 23.

———. "Lower Benefits Backed for Well-to-Do." *Washington Post*, Feb. 27, 1991.

Riley, Matilda White, and John W. Riley, Jr. "Longevity and Social Structure: The Potential of the Added Years." In *Our Aging Society*, edited by Alan Pifer and Lydia Bronte. New York: W.W. Norton & Company, 1986, pp. 53–78.

Rivlin, Alice, and Joshua Wiener, with Raymond Hanley and Denise Spence. *Caring for the Disabled Elderly: Who Will Pay?* Washington, D.C.: The Brookings Institution, 1988.

Rosenblatt, Robert. "Bankruptcy of Part of Medicare Feared." *Los Angeles Times*, May 18, 1991.

Rowen, Hobart. "The Hidden Deficit." *The Washington Post* National Weekly Edition, Dec. 12–18, 1988, 5.

Russell, Louise. *The Baby Boom Generation and the Economy*. Washington, D.C.: The Brookings Institution, 1982.

Samuelson, Robert. "As the Boomers Turn 50." *Washington Post*, March 20, 1991.

Sanchez, Jesus. "Tension over Pension Reform." *Los Angeles Times*, May 23, 1991, p. B1.

Schmitt, Ray, and Carmen Solomon. "Meeting the Pension Obligation: Underfunding and Overfunding Issues." Washington, D.C.: Congressional Research Service, the Library of Congress, May 8, 1987.

Schneider, Edward, and Jack Guralnik. "The Aging of America: Impact on Health Care Costs." *Journal of the American Medical Association* 263, 17 (May 2, 1990): 2335–40.

Scholz, Catherine. "A Profile of the Baby Boom Generation." Executive Summary, Population Resource Center, Washington, D.C., June 1990.

Schulz, J., A. Borowski, and W. H. Crown. *Economics of Population Aging: The "Graying of Australia, Japan, and the United States."* New York: Auburn House, 1991.

Schulz, James. *The Economics of Aging*. 4th ed. Dover, Mass.: Auburn House Publishing Company, 1988.

Shipp, R. "Paying for the Baby Boom's Retirement." Washington, D.C.: Congressional Research Service, Library of Congress, 1988.

Siegel, Jacob, and Cynthia Taeuber. "Demographic Dimensions of an Aging Population." In *Our Aging Society*, edited by Alan Pifer and Lydia Bronte. New York: W.W. Norton & Company, 1986.

Smith, Lee. "The War between the Generations." *Fortune*, July 20, 1987, 78–82.

Smolensky, Eugene, Sheldon Danziger, and Peter Gottschalk. "The Declining Significance of Age in the United States: Trends in the Well-Being of Children and the Elderly since 1939." In *The Vulnerable*, edited by John Palmer, Timothy Smeeding, and Barbara Boyle Torrey. Washington, D.C.: The Urban Institute Press, 1988, pp. 29–54.

"Social Security at 50 Faces New Crossroads." *U.S. News and World Report*, Aug. 12, 1985.

"Social Security Drain Worries Under-45 Set." *Chicago Sun-Times*, January 1990.

"Social Security Should Benefit Only the Elderly Poor." *Business Week*, Jan. 16, 1989, 20.

Socrates. *The Republic*. Book I/327c–330a.

Sowell, Thomas. *Ethnic America*. New York: Basic Books, 1981.

Spencer, Gregory. U.S. Bureau of the Census. "Projection of the Hispanic Population: 1983–2080." *Current Population Reports*, ser. P-25, no. 995. Washington, D.C.: Government Printing Office, November 1986.

Starobin, Paul. "Who Comes Out Ahead?" *National Journal* (Sept. 22, 1990): 2255–58.

Stone, Robyn. "The Feminization of Poverty and Older Women: An Update." Washington, D.C.: National Center for Health Services Research, February 1986.

Strauss, William, and Neil Howe. *Generations: The History of America's Future,
1584 to 2069.* New York: William Morrow, 1991.

Taeuber, Cynthia. "Diversity: The Dramatic Reality." In *Diversity in Aging:
Challenges Facing Planners and Policymakers in the 1990s,* edited by S.
Bass, E. Kutza, and F. Torres-Gil. Glenview, Ill.: Scott, Foresman &
Company, 1990, pp. 1–46.

"Tax Hike Needed to Fund Infrastructure, Economists Tell JEC." *Tax Notes*
(July 24, 1989).

Teltsch, Kathleen. "In Sea of Studies, an Anatomy of One." *The New York
Times,* May 30, 1989.

"300 Billion Whopper." *U.S. News and World Report,* Feb. 11 1991, 51–53.

Torres-Gil, Fernando. "Aging for the Twenty-First Century: Process, Politics,
and Policy." *Generations* (Spring 1988): 5–9.

———. "An Examination of Factors Affecting Future Cohorts of Elderly Hispanics." *The Gerontologist* 5, 2 (1986): 140–46.

———, ed. *Hispanics in an Aging Society.* New York: Carnegie Corporation,
1986.

———. "Interest Group Politics: Empowerment of the Ancianos." In *Hispanic
Elderly in Transition,* edited by S. Applewhite. Westport, Conn.: Greenwood Press, 1988, pp. 75–94.

———. "The Latinization of a Multigenerational Population: Hispanics in an
Aging Society." *Daedalus* 115, 1 (Winter 1986): 325–48.

———. "The Politics of Catastrophic and Long-Term Care Coverage." *Journal
of Aging and Social Policy* 1, no. 1/2 (1989): 61–86.

———. "White House Conferences on Aging." In *The Encyclopedia of Aging,*
edited by George Maddox. New York: Springer Publishing Company, 1987,
pp. 692–93.

Uchitelle, Louis. "Company-Financed Pensions Are Failing to Fulfill Promise."
The New York Times, May 29, 1991.

U.S. Bureau of the Census. "Projections of the Hispanic Population: 1983–2080."
Current Population Reports, ser. P–25, no. 995. Washington, D.C.: U.S.
Government Printing Office, 1986.

———. *Statistical Abstract of the United States: 1989.* 109th ed. Washington
D.C.: U.S. Government Printing Office, 1989.

———. "Voting and Registration in the Election of November, 1988 (Advance
Report)." *Current Population Reports,* ser. P–20, No. 435. Washington,
D.C.: U.S. Government Printing Office, 1989.

U.S. Department of Health and Human Services. "America's Centenarians: Data
from the 1980 Census." Washington, D.C.: U.S. Government Printing
Office, 1987, p. 12.

———. "Fast Facts and Figures about Social Security." Washington, D.C.: Social
Security Administration, 1988.

U.S. Department of Health and Human Services. Social Security Administration.
Social Security Bulletin: Annual Statistical Supplement. Washington, D.C.:
U.S. Government Printing Office, 1990.

U.S. Department of Justice. *1987 Statistical Yearbook of the Immigration and
Naturalization Service.* Washington, D.C.: U.S. Government Printing Office, 1987, table 2, p. 3.

U.S. General Accounting Office. "Retirement before Age 65: Trends, Costs, and National Issues." GAO/HRD 86–86. Washington, D.C.: U.S. Government Printing Office, July 1986.

U.S. House of Representatives Select Committee on Aging. "Long-Term Care and Personal Impoverishment: Seven in Ten Elderly Living Alone Are at Risk." Comm. Pub. No. 100–631. Washington, D.C.: U.S. Government Printing Office, 1987.

———. Subcommittee on Retirement Income and Employment. "Supplemental Security Income (SSI): Current Program Characteristics and Alternatives for Future Reform." August 1988 Comm. Pub. No. 100–669. Washington, D.C.: U.S. Government Printing Office, 1988.

———. Working Documents, 1991.

"U.S. Payment of Disability Claims Faulted." *Los Angeles Times*, May 20, 1991.

U.S. Senate Special Committee on Aging. "America in Transition: An Aging Society." Information Paper serial no. 99-B. Washington, D.C.: U.S. Government Printing Office, June 1985.

———. "Developments in Aging: 1989." Vol. 1. Washington, D.C.: U.S. Government Printing Office, 1990.

———. "Developments in Aging: 1990." Vol. 1. Washington, D.C.: U.S. Government Printing Office, 1991.

———. "How Older Americans Live: An Analysis of Census Data." Serial no. 99-D. Washington, D.C.: U.S. Government Printing Office, October 1985.

U.S. Senate. *Aging America: Trends and Projections*. Washington, D.C.: U.S. Government Printing Office, 1986.

———. *Aging America: Trends and Projections*. Washington, D.C.: U.S. Government Printing Office, 1988.

———. *Aging America: Trends and Projections*. Washington, D.C.: U.S. Government Printing Office, 1989.

Villers Foundation. *On the Other Side of Easy Street: Myths and Facts about the Economics of Old Age*. Washington, D.C.: The Villers Foundation, 1987.

Vobejda, Barbara. "Average Household Shrinks as More in U.S. Live Alone." *The Washington Post*, May 1, 1991.

Waymack, Mark, and George Taler. *Medical Ethics and the Elderly: A Case Book*. Chicago: Pluribus Press, 1988.

Welniak, Edward. U.S. Bureau of the Census. "Money, Income for Households, Families, and Persons in the United States: 1987." *Current Population Reports*, ser. P–60, no. 162. Washington, D.C.: U.S. Government Printing Office, 1989.

"What's Wrong—and Right—with the Porter Plan." *The Wall Street Journal*, Feb. 8, 1990.

Williamson, J. B., L. Evans, and L. A. Powell. *Politics of Aging*. Springfield, Ill.: Charles C. Thomas, 1982.

Wilson, William Julius. *The Truly Disadvantaged*. Chicago: The University of Chicago Press, 1987.

The Wyatt Company. "Population Aging: A Misunderstood Phenomenon." *Wyatt Newsletter* 6, 4 (April 1990): 1–2.

INDEX

AAB (American Association of Boomers), 4

AALL (American Association for Labor Legislation), 62

AAOAS (American Association for Old Age Security), 62

AARP, *see* American Association of Retired Persons

ABB (Association of Baby Boomers), 85, 87, 130

Acculturation, 171

Achenbaum, Andrew, 61, 67, 148

ACTION, 38, 156

ACYF (Administration for Children, Youth, and Families), 153, 156

ADEA (Age Discrimination in Employment Act of 1967), 38, 50–51, 117

Administration for Children, Youth, and Families (ACYF), 153, 156

Administration on Aging (AoA), 48, 49, 55, 59, 153, 156

Adult day care, 37, 55

Adult Day Care program, 55

AFDC (Aid to Families with Dependent Children), 45, 101

AGE, *see* Americans for Generational Equity

Age: definitions of, 10–12; *see also* Generational claims

Age-based organizations: description of, 52–58; politics and, 75, 77, 78–80, 90

Age discrimination, 21, 36, 90, 97

Age Discrimination and Employment Act of 1967 (ADEA), 38, 50–51, 117

Ageism, 36, 51, 90, 156, 175

Age-segregated programs, 1, 2, 68, 143–144

Age Wave (Dychtwald), 135

Aging; history of, 1–2; policies, 141–142

Aging Resources Center, 158

Aid to Families with Dependent Children (AFDC), 45, 101

Allied Health Professionals Promotion Act, 160

Alzheimer's disease, 46, 134, 175

American Association for Labor Legislation (AALL), 62

American Association for Old Age Security (AAOAS), 62

American Association of Boomers (AAB), 4

American Association of Retired Persons (AARP), 63, 107, 136, 151; politics and, 75, 78, 81, 83, 87, 91

American Medical Association, 151
Americans for Generational Equity
    (AGE), 4, 75–76, 85, 130
Americans with Disability Act, 51,
    143
America's Old Age Crisis (Crystal),
    100
AoA, *see* Administration on Aging
Arkansas, 22
Arthritis, 134, 175
Asians: baby boomers and, 135; de-
    mographics and, 34; diversity and,
    18, 19, 23, 83, 135; in 21st century,
    170
Asset income, 95, 112, 132
Assimilation, 171
Association of Baby Boomers (ABB),
    85, 87, 130

Baby boomers, xii, 2, 13, 28, 66, 89,
    127–139; demographics and, 34; di-
    versity and, 18, 135–136; economics
    and, 101, 102, 106, 109–110, 119,
    120; education of, 128, 129, 132,
    135, 172; generational claims of, 15–
    16, 89, 109–110, 136–138; housing
    policy and, 128, 155; longevity and,
    27, 128, 131, 132–135; myths and
    facts about, 127–130; program re-
    structuring and, 149; reforms and,
    155; in 21st century, 173, 175, 176
Baby boomlet, 13, 128
Baby busters, 13, 16, 18, 109, 133,
    175
Ball, Robert, 7, 15, 176
Berry, Joyce, 49
Binstock, Robert, 5, 100, 158
Blacks, 22, 23, 62, 99, 114; baby
    boomers and, 135; demographics
    and, 34; diversity and, 19, 22, 23,
    83, 114, 135; income security and,
    95–96; longevity of, 25, 27, 43; poli-
    tics and, 77, 83; program restructur-
    ing and, 148; in 21st century, 168,
    169, 170, 171
Board-and-care facilities, 52, 58
*Born to Pay: The New Politics of Ag-
    ing in America* (Longman), 113

Borowski, A., 102
Budget Enforcement Act of 1990,
    106–107
Budget Reconciliation Act of 1990,
    152, 154
Bush, George, 15, 106, 156
Butler, Katy, 130

Cabinet agency for elder affairs, 59,
    147, 158
California, 23, 50, 55–58, 137, 172,
    173
California Pension Movement, 78
Callahan, Daniel, 4
Canada, 149, 151
Capital gains taxes, 37, 98, 155
Carnegie, Andrew, 62
Carter, Jimmy, 64
Case management, 37, 39, 52, 120
Castelli, Jim, 137
Catastrophic Drug Insurance (CDI),
    44
Central America, 167
Chen, Yung-Ping, 117, 148
Child care programs, 20, 170
Children, 24, 76, 144, 156, 170; baby
    boomers and, 130, 131, 133, 138
Civil liberties, 50–51
Civil rights, 38, 64, 76, 128, 129, 156
Civil Rights Act of 1964, 51
Civil Rights Commission, 38, 156
Civil service, 157
Civil Service Retirement System
    (CSRS), 111
Cohen, Wilbur, 7, 15, 176
Colorado, 22
The Common Good, 168
Commonwealth Commission on El-
    derly People Living Alone, 114
Congregate housing, 155, 156
Congress, 3, 76, 85, 176; DI and, 43;
    federal deficit and, 121; MCCA and,
    80; pension plans and, 133; Social
    Security and, 106, 107
Crown, W. H., 102
Crystal, Stephen, 5, 100
CSRS (Civil Service Retirement Sys-
    tem), 111

Day, Christine, 76
Demographics, 33–36, 61
Department of Energy (DOE), 50, 156
Department of Health and Human
 Services (HHS), 48, 49, 50, 52–53,
 153, 156, 158
Department of Labor (DOL), 110, 156
Department of Social Services (DSS),
 55–58
Department of Transportation (DOT),
 156
Department of Veterans Affairs, 59
Departments of Mental Health, 58
Departments of Rehabilitation, 58
Dependency, 68–69, 142–143
DI, *see* Disability Insurance
Disability Insurance (DI), 37, 39, 40,
 154; baby boomers and, 134; description of, 43; diversity and, 21,
 23, 115; economics and, 94, 115,
 119; generational claims and, 113;
 longevity and, 117; restrictions on,
 64; restructuring of, 146, 148
Disabled, 47, 50, 55, 58, 68, 105, 177;
 baby boomers and, 134; diversity
 and, 84; generational claims and,
 113; income security and, 97; legislation benefitting, 51; longevity and,
 27, 134; politics and, 76, 84, 89, 91
Diversity, xii-xiii, 3, 9, 12, 17–25, 27,
 28, 71; aging policies and, 141; baby
 boomers and, 18, 135–136; civil
 rights and, 156; demographics and,
 34; economics and, 20–22, 93, 104,
 105, 108, 114–116; family changes
 and, 19–20, 23; generational claims
 and, 85; geographic distribution
 and, 22–23; longevity and, 82; politics and, 76, 82, 83–84, 90; racial/
 ethnic, 19, 83, 171, 178, *see also*
 Minorities, diversity and; reform
 and, 153; responding to, 144–145; in
 21st century, 165, 168, 172, 178
DOE (Department of Energy), 50, 156
DOL (Department of Labor), 110, 156
Dollars and Dreams (Levy), 119
Domestic issues, in 21st century, 168–
 172

DOT (Department of Transportation),
 156
Drug abuse, 146, 168, 169
DSS (Department of Social Services),
 55–58
Dual-track eligibility system, 147–149,
 151–152, 153, 154, 157, 158
Dual-value systems, 67
Durkheim, Emile, 10
Dychtwald, Ken, 135

Eagles, Fraternal Order of the, 62
Easterline, Richard, 132
Economics, 20–22, 93–121; fact vs.
 fiction in, 98–108; of income secu-
 rity, 94–98
Education, 10, 67, 121; of baby boom-
 ers, 128, 129, 132, 135, 172; eco-
 nomics and, 103, 116; generational
 claims and, 16–17; late-life, 97, 117,
 135; in 21st century, 169, 172, 175,
 176
EEOC (Equal Employment Opportu-
 nity Commission), 38, 51, 156
Elizabethan Poor Law of 1601, 60
Energy assistance programs, 11, 50
Environmental protection, 166–167
Equal Employment Opportunity Commission (EEOC), 38, 51, 156
ERISA, 118
Europe, 1, 18, 19, 60, 151, 166, 167,
 179
Euthanasia, 26
Executive Life Insurance Company,
 111

Families USA, 99
Family: diversity and, 19–20, 23; gov-
 ernment policies and, 170; rein-
 volvement of, 142–143
Federal budget deficit, 3, 66, 104, 121,
 171–172, 175
Federal Council on Aging, 38, 59
Federal vs. state control, 69–70
Flemming, Arthur, 15, 48, 153, 176
Florida, 22, 23
Food stamps, 48, 99, 103, 156

Foster Grandparent Program, 38, 79, 96, 156
Four-legged chair model, 94, 110, 152–153

Gardner, John, 177
General Accounting Office (GAO), 110
Generational claims, xii–xiii, 9, 12–17, 27, 28, 49, 64, 66; aging policies and, 141; of baby boomers, 15–16, 89, 109–110, 136–138; civil rights and, 156; demographics and, 35; diversity and, 85; economics and, 93, 97, 98, 102, 103, 104, 105, 108–114; housing policy and, 155; identification issues in, 16–17; longevity and, 85; politics and, 76, 84–89, 90; pressures caused by, 3; program restructuring and, 148; reforms and, 154, 155, 156; in 21st century, 165, 168, 172, 175–176, 178
Generations United, 86, 138
Geographic distribution, 22–23
Geriatrics, 65, 160
Germany, 1, 10, 116, 165, 178
Gerontology, 65, 87, 160, 175
GI bill, 130
Gould, Stephanie, 102–103
Gramm-Rudman-Hollings legislation, 106
Gray, Robert, 104
Gray Panthers, 15
Great Britain, 18, 151
Great Depression, 13, 34, 62, 63, 78, 88, 108–109, 115, 131, 172
Group identity, 77–78

Haas, Lawrence, 172
Handicapped, *see* Disabled
Hayes-Bautista, David, 172, 173
Hayflick, Leonard, 25
HCFA, *see* Health Care Financing Administration
Headstart program, 170
Health Care Financing Administration (HCFA), 45, 49, 55, 120, 153
Health-care policy, xiii, 28; baby boomers and, 134; description of, 37; economics of, 100; generational claims and, 15; reforming of, 149–152; in 21st century, 169–170, 173, 175
Health insurance, 3, 116, 117, 134, 152
Health Maintenance Organizations, 452
Health Resources and Services Administration, 160
Heclo, Hugh, 5, 97
Hewitt, Paul, 13, 15
HHS, *see* Department of Health and Human Services
HI (Hospital Insurance), *see* Medicare, Part A of
Hispanics: baby boomers and, 135; demographics and, 34; diversity and, 18, 19, 20, 22, 23, 83, 114, 135; economics and, 95, 96, 99, 114; politics and, 77, 83; in 21st century, 168, 169, 170, 172, 173
History of aging, 1–2
Home care services, 37, 55, 68; expanded benefits in, 65; Medicaid and, 52; Medicare and, 44, 45; private sector in, 69, 120; restructuring of, 148
Home equity, 21, 133, 155; generational claims and, 15, 109–110; income security and, 94, 95; longevity and, 116
Homelessness, 4, 66, 138, 146, 161
Hospice care, 37, 44
Hospital Insurance (HI), *see* Medicare, Part A of
Hospitalization, 26, 44
House Select Committee on Aging, xi, 148
Housing Act of 1959, 50
Housing and Community Development Act of 1974, 49, 50
Housing and Urban Development (HUD), 49, 50, 156
Housing policy: baby boomers and, 128, 155; programs in, 37–38, 49–50;

reform of, 155; restructuring of, 146, 148
Housing subsidies, 11, 99–100, 130
Howe, Neil, 13, 15, 139
HUD (Housing and Urban Development), 49, 50, 156
Hughes, Bill, 108, 144

Illinois, 23
Illiteracy, 115, 116, 138, 169
Immigrants, 16, 62; baby boomers and, 135, 138; diversity and, 17–18, 19, 24, 135; economics and, 101, 112, 119; in 21st century, 167, 169, 170, 171, 177, 178
Income, 20–22, 129
Income security: diversity and, 144; economics of, 94–98; reform and, 152–155
Income tax, 51
Individual Retirement Accounts (IRAs), 16, 116, 134, 155
Individual Social Security Retirement Accounts (ISSRAs), 155
Inflation, 21, 22, 82, 103, 114, 151; baby boomers and, 133; generational claims and, 15, 111; income security and, 96–97; longevity and, 133
Infrastructure decay, 171, 172, 173
Insurance companies, 37, 39, 151
Interest groups, 1, 3, 62, 65, 143–144; representing the elderly, 78–80
Intergenerational Earnings Test Elimination Act, 108
IRAs (Individual Retirement Accounts), 16, 116, 134, 155
ISSRAs (Individual Social Security Retirement Accounts), 155

Japan, 24, 165, 169, 178, 179
Johnson, Lyndon, 44, 177
Jones, Landon, 132

Kennedy, John F., 75, 129
King, Gwendolyn, 48, 153
Kishimoto, Yoriko, 178–179

Kotkin, Joel, 178–179
Kuhn, Maggie, 7, 15, 176

Labor force: baby boomers in, 133; diversity and, 21; generational claims and, 16; in 21st century, 170
Labor unions, 75, 101, 111, 129, 151
Lamm, Richard, 4
Leadership, 176–178
Legal policies, 38, 156
Levy, Frank, 119
Life expectancy, 25, 26, 60, 61, 63, 71, 146, *see also* Longevity; age definitions and, 10; anticipated increase in, 128; DI and, 43; diversity and, 19, 20, 22; economics and, 93, 94, 102, 103, 105; politics and, 81, 90; program restructuring and, 148; in 21st century, 166, 173
Lifetrends, 134
Light, Paul, 134
LIHEAP (Low-Income Home Energy Assistance Program), 50, 156
Lobbies, *see* Interest groups
Longevity, xii-xiii, 9, 12, 16, 25–28, 43, 154, *see also* Life expectancy; aging policies and, 141, 142; baby boomers and, 27, 128, 131, 132–135; dependency and, 143; diversity and, 82; economics and, 104, 105, 107, 108, 114, 116–118; generational claims and, 85; politics and, 76, 81–83, 90; preparing for, 145; in 21st century, 165, 168, 172, 178
Longman, Phillip, 113, 130
Long-term care, xiii, 37, 55, 160; baby boomers and, 134, 135, 136; diversity and, 144; economics and, 120, 121; expanded benefits in, 65; generational claims and, 113; restructuring of, 147; state-level services for, 51, 52; in 21st century, 173, 175; volunteerism and, 157
Low-Income Home Energy Assistance Program (LIHEAP), 50, 156
LTV Corporation, 96

Macdonald, Christine, 132
Macunovich, Diane, 132–133

Mandatory retirement, 51, 63, 94, 107, 117
Margolis, Richard, 99
Marriage, 20, 131
Maturational hypothesis, 17
MCCA, see Medicare Catstrophic Coverage Act of 1988
McLain, George, 78
Means-testing, 103, 107, 112, 120, 145, 148
Medicaid, 27, 38, 39, 40, 48, 55, 64, 176; cost of, 45, 58, 66; description of, 37, 45–46; diversity and, 22, 115; economics and, 96, 100, 101, 103, 104, 115, 120; expansion of, 65; ideological dilemmas in, 68; passage of, 63; politics and, 75, 79; pressures on, 3, 4; reforming of, 151–152; restructuring of, 147; state contributions to, 51, 52; user-friendly model of, 157, 158
Medi-Cal, 55
Medicare, xi, 7, 10, 11, 38, 39, 40, 55, 64, 109, 176; baby boomers and, 132; cost of, 40, 44, 58, 66; description of, 37, 44–45; economics and, 96, 100, 103, 105, 113, 120; expansion of, 65; generational claims and, 15, 85, 86, 87, 88, 113; ideological dilemmas in, 68; income security and, 96; longevity and, 118; Part A of, 37, 40, 42, 44–45, 46, 105, 133, 134, 151, 153, 154, 161; Part B of, 40, 44, 45, 80; passage of, 63; politics and, 75, 78, 79, 85, 86, 87, 88; pressures on, 3; redefining of, 142; reforming of, 151–152; restructuring of, 146, 147, 149; user-friendly model of, 157, 158
Medicare Catstrophic Coverage Act (MCCA) of 1988, 3, 44, 65, 98; politics and, 76, 80–81, 82, 83–85, 87
Medi-gap insurance, 80
Men, longevity of, 25, 26
Mentally ill, 4
Mexico, 167
Middle age, 11, 16
Migration, 22–23, see also Immigrants

Military Retirement System, 111
Military service, 157
Minorities, 3, 62, 64, see also specific minority groups; aging policies and, 142; baby boomers and, 135, 137, 138; demographics and, 34; diversity and, 18, 83, 84, 114, 115, 135, 145, see also Diversity, racial/ethnic; economics and, 95–96, 99, 100, 101, 112, 114, 115, 119; generational claims and, 16, 87, 89, 112; longevity and, 117; politics and, 76, 77, 83, 84, 87, 89, 91; program restructuring and, 148; in 21st century, 165, 168, 169, 170–171, 172, 173, 177
Modern Aging period, 9, 36, 62, 64, 65, 71, 113, 127, 143, 144, 153; age definitions in, 11; economics of, 97; family in, 142; historical perspective on, 1–2; leadership in, 176; politics in, 76, 81, 82, 89, 90
Montana, 22
Moody, Harry, 5, 118, 144
Morbidity rates, 25, 26
Morrison, Malcolm, 117
Mortality rates, 19, 25, 26
Mortgage tax deduction, 155
Moynihan, Daniel, 4, 86, 106, 107, 112, 154

NAAAA (National Association of Area Agencies on Aging), 158
National Affordable Housing Act, 50
National Association of Area Agencies on Aging (NAAAA), 158
National Association of Counties, 158
National Council of Senior Citizens (NCSC), 63
National Council on Aging (NCOA), 63, 75, 158
National Elder Care Corps, 156–157
National health-care coverage, 5, 70, 116, 148, 149–151, 176
National Institute on Aging (NIA), 49, 55
National Institutes of Health (NIH), 55, 153

National Leadership Coalition for Health Care Reform, 151

National Retired Teachers Association, 63

National Taxpayers Union Foundation, 4, 105

National Volunteer Care Bank, 157

Native Americans, 48; baby boomers and, 135; demographics and, 34; diversity and, 19, 83, 135; politics and, 83; program restructuring and, 148; in 21st century, 170

NCOA, *see* National Council on Aging

NCSC (National Council of Senior Citizens), 63

Need vs. greed argument, 69, 97–98

Neugarten, Bernice, 5, 15

New Deal, xi, 6, 13, 15, 78

New York, 23, 50

NIA (National Institute on Aging), 49, 55

NIH (National Institutes of Health), 55, 153

Nixon, Richard, 63

North America, 166

Nursing-home care, 55; baby boomers and, 132; longevity and, 26; Medicaid and, 37, 45, 100, 104; private sector in, 69, 120, 146, 158; program restructuring and, 148, 149; state role in, 52; in 21st century, 175; volunteerism and, 157

Nutrition programs, 38, 68, 96

OAA, *See* Older Americans Act

OASI, *see* Old-Age and Survivors Insurance

OBRA 90 (Omnibus Budget Reconciliation Act of 1990), 42, 46, 103

Office of Human Development Services (OHDS), 49, 55

Ohio, 23

Oklahoma, 22

Old-Age and Survivors Insurance (OASI), 37, 38, 39, 40, 45, 46, 55, 154; baby boomers and, 133; de-scription of, 42–43; economics and, 113, 115

Older Americans Act (OAA), xi, 11, 38, 39, 47–48, 55, 58–59, 70, 158; age entitlement in, 146; description of, 38, 48–49; economics and, 94, 96, 100, 120; expanded benefits under, 65; passage of, 63; politics and, 78; reforming of, 156; restrictions on, 64; restructuring of, 148; state contributions to, 51; Title IV of, 48; Title V of, 48, 96, 117, 146

Older Workers Protection Act, 51

Old-old, 11, 15, 16, 20

Omnibus Budget Reconciliation Acts: of 1989, 45; of 1990 (OBRA 90), 42, 46, 103; of 1991, 161

Oregon, 4

Organizational restructuring model, 146–149

Pacific Basin, 18

Pacific Islanders, 19, 23, 34, 83, 135, 170

Palmer, John, 102–103

Parental and Family Leave bill, 86

PBGC, *see* Pension Benefit Guaranty Corporation

Peace Corps, 38, 156

Pennsylvania, 23

Pension Benefit Guaranty Corporation (PBGC), 21, 96, 110, 118, 133

Pension plans, 160; age eligibility for, 82; baby boomers and, 132, 133; diversity and, 21, 83, 114; economics and, 100, 101, 102–103, 110–112, 113, 114, 119, 120; generational claims and, 15, 88, 89, 110–112, 113; income security and, 94–95, 96, 97, 152; introduction of, 62; longevity and, 82, 118; politics and, 83, 88, 89; pressures on, 3; reforms and, 152, 154; restructuring of, 147

Pepper, Claude, 7, 15

Pepper Commission, 152

Peterson, Peter, 101

PHS (Public Health Service), 55

Pifer, Alan, 128, 148

PIN (Policy for Intergenerational Network), 156
Policy for Intergenerational Network (PIN), 156
Politics, 75–91; current issues in, 80–89; participation in, 77–80; in social policy development, 60–66
Poor, 3, 4, 64, 66; baby boomers and, 136; decrease in, 64; diversity and, 21, 22, 23, 24, 114, 115, 136; economics and, 99–101, 103, 104, 105, 114, 115; generational claims and, 85, 87; politics and, 85, 87, 91; programs targeted for, 39; in 21st century, 168–169
Porter, John, 155
Preston, Samuel, 85
Private sector, 2, 36, 158, 160; demographics and, 34; economic issues and, 119–120; health-care policy and, 152; housing policy in, 38; longevity effect on, 82; responsibilities of, 69, 145–146
Privatization, 64, 101, 154
Property taxes, 37, 51, 82, 136, 155
Public Health Service (PHS), 55
Public housing, 37, 50

Railroad Retirement System, 42
Rauch, Jonathan, 170
Reagan, Ronald, 15, 17, 43, 64, 70, 129, 137, 156
Recessions, 22, 64
Rehabilitation Act of 1973, 51
Respite care, 37, 45
Retired Senior Volunteer Program (RSVP), 38, 156
Retirement, 3, 10, 43, 161; age eligibility and, 82, 105, 116–117, 118, 119, 154; for baby boomers, 132, 133; diversity and, 20–21, 83, 114; economics and, 98, 100, 101, 103, 105, 107, 110, 111, 116, 119, 120; generational claims and, 15, 89, 110, 111; income security and, 94, 95, 96; longevity and, 26, 82, 116–117, 118; mandatory 51, 63, 94, 107,

117; as new concept, 61; politics and, 83, 89
Rivlin, Alice, 4–5
Rockefeller, John D., 62
Roosevelt, Franklin, 62, 75
Roybal, Edward, 160
RSVP (Retired Senior Volunteer Program), 38, 156
Rural areas, 22, 49, 87, 89, 115, 177

Samuelson, Robert, 138
Savings, 110, 112, 116; income security and, 94, 95, 96, 152, 155
Savings-and-loan industry, 64, 98, 110, 138
Schulz, J., 102
SCORE (Service Corps of Retired Executives), 38
Seattle, 22
Section 8, 37, 49–50, 1552
Section 202, 37, 49, 50, 155
Section 2176 Home and Community-Based Waivers, 51, 52
Senate Special Committee on Aging, 106
Senior and Youth Employment, 156
Senior boomers, 34, 132–138, 178
Senior-citizen discounts, 82, 136
Senior Companion Program, 38
Senior Executives program, 117
Service Corps of Retired Executives (SCORE), 38
Setting Limits (Callahan), 4
SHMOs (Social/health maintenance organizations), 37, 39
Silent generation, 13, 15, 16
Skilled nursing care, 44, 46
SMI (Supplementary Medical Insurance), *see* Medicare, Part B of
Smith, Lee, 148
Social changes, 19–20
Social Day Care program, 58
Social/health maintenance organizations (SHMOs), 37, 39
Social policies: description of, 36–52; political development of, 60–66; reforming of, 149–157
Social Security, xi, 7, 11, 28, 55, 64,

109, 111, 144; age eligibility and, 10, 16, 146; baby boomers and, 106, 132, 133–134, 135; cost of, 40, 66; diversity and, 21, 22, 23, 104, 105, 114, 144; economics and, 94, 95–96, 97, 98, 100, 101, 103, 104–108, 112, 113, 114, 119, 120; generational claims and, 15, 16, 85, 86, 87, 88, 104, 105, 112, 113; ideological dilemmas in, 67; income security and, 94, 95–96, 97, 152–154, 155; longevity and, 104, 105, 107, 116, 117, 118; pay-as-you-go financing of, 4, 106, 112, 118, 119, 154; payroll taxes and, xiii, 3, 79, 86, 97, 104–105, 106, 112, 119, 133, 154, 161; politics and, 75, 78, 79, 85, 86, 87, 88, 90; pressures on, 3; privatization of, 101; redefining of, 142; reforming of, 152–154, 155; restructuring of, 146, 147, 148; surplus revenue in, 106–107, 119, 134, 155, 175; taxation of, 39, 106, 118; in 21st century, 175; user-friendly model of, 157, 158

Social Security Act, 38, 40–42, 62, 94; Title XVI of, *see* Supplemental Security Income; Title XVIII of, *see* Medicare; Title XIX of, *see* Medicaid; Title XX of, *see* Social Services Block Grant

Social Security Administration (SSA), 26, 47, 49, 55, 59, 105, 153, 156

Social Security Board of Trustees, 151

Social Security Caregivers Act, 144

Social Security SSI Modernization Task Force, xi, 48

Social-service policy, 38, 156

Social Services Block Grant (SSBG), 38, 39, 40, 55, 153; appropriations of, 47; description of, 46–47; economics and, 96, 101; enactment of, 63; reforming of, 156

Soviet Union, 151, 166, 167, 178, 179

SSA, *see* Social Security Administration

SSBG, *see* Social Services Block Grant

SSI, *see* Supplemental Security Income

State-level services, 51, 69–70

State units on aging (SUAs), 55

Strauss, William, 139

SUAs (State units on aging), 55

Sullivan, Louis, 49

Summers, Tish, 7

Supplemental Security Income (SSI), xi, 10, 37, 39, 40, 45, 46, 55, 66, 153, 154; baby boomers and, 134; description of, 47–48; diversity and, 21, 22, 23, 115; economics and, 94, 96, 100, 101, 113, 115, 119; enactment of, 63; generational claims and, 113; reforming of, 156; restructuring of, 146, 148; user-friendly model of, 157

Supplementary Medical Insurance (SMI), *see* Medicare, Part B of

Swing generation, 18, 42, 63, 88, 131; generational claims of, 13–15, 16

Szabo, Joan, 104

Tax benefits, 37, 98

Tax credits, 98, 116, 170

Tax deductions, 105

Taxes, 42, 44, 103, 116; baby boomers and, 134, 137–138; capital gains, 37, 98, 155; income, 51; increases needed in, 121, 161, 172, 173; for Social Security, *see* Social Security, payroll taxes and; on Social Security benefits, 39, 106, 118

Tax exemptions, 37, 170

Tax incentives, 147

Texas, 23

The Third Century, 178–179

Third-party reimbursements, 39, *see also* specific programs

Third World countries, 166

Three-legged stool model, 94, 152

Title V Senior Employment Program, 48, 96, 117, 146

Townsend, Francis, 62, 78

Townsend Movement, 62, 75, 78, 81, 89, 97
Transportation programs, 11, 50, 68, 121, 156
Truman, Harry, 63
Twenty-first century, 165–179; domestic issues in, 168–172; global pressures in, 166–168

UMTA (Urban Mass Transportation Act), 50
Unemployment, 21, 175
Universal entitlement programs, 38–39, 48, 67, 118, 149
Urban Mass Transportation Act (UMTA), 50

Veterans' benefits, 60, 61, 67, 175
Volunteer programs, 36, 144; baby boomers and, 135; description of, 38, 50; economics and, 96, 100; reforming of, 156–157; in 21st century, 169
Voting, 3, 16, 75, 77; baby boomers and, 136–137; demographics in, 35

Washington Business Group on Health, 151

Watergate scandal, 13, 64
Waxman, Henry, 158
Weatherization Assistance Program, 50
White House Conferences on Aging: 1961, 63, 98; 1971, xi, 63, 98; 1981, xi, 64, 98
White House Fellowship program, 177
Whites: baby boomers and, 137; diversity and, 19, 20, 22, 83, 115, 145; economics and, 95, 115; longevity and, 25, 26; politics and, 77, 83; in 21st century, 168, 171, 172
Wiener, Joshua, 4–5
Women, 3, 22, 61, 64; as baby boomers, 133, 135; diversity and, 18, 19, 20, 21, 22, 23, 83, 84, 114, 115; economics and, 95, 99, 100, 101, 114, 115; longevity of, 25, 26; politics and, 76, 83, 84, 87, 89, 91; in 21st century, 170, 177
Workmen's Compensation, 117, 148

Young Aging period, 1, 9, 60, 142
Young-old, 10, 15, 16, 26
Yuppies, 13, 130–131

ABOUT THE AUTHOR

FERNANDO M. TORRES-GIL is President of the American Society on Aging. He is currently Professor of Social Welfare at the University of California, Los Angeles. Prior to that he was Professor of Gerontology and Public Administration at the Andrus Gerontology Center of the University of Southern California. Dr. Torres-Gil has served as Special Assistant to two Secretaries of the Department of Health and Human Services. He was a delegate to two White House Conferences on Aging and was Staff Director of the U.S. House of Representatives Select Committee on Aging.